Sir Francis Chichester has managed to reawaken the world to one man's capacity to seek and to endure. He has served men by living their dreams of acting with tenacity and courage under pressure."

—*Time*

We get the day-to-day story of the planning, the decisions, his own lively reports of what the days and nights were like, the good and bad adventures . . . This is not a log that one can sum up. It is a report by a great adventurer, who also happens to be a writer, of one of man's greatest of lonely enterprises."

—*Harper's*

Chichester's extraordinary feat was the result of constant unremitting attention to detail. . . . Above all [his] narrative reminds us how men can transcend their apparent physical limitations when they are doing something that they very much want to do. He admits to being frightened. . . . He would indeed be superhuman had he never wavered. But it is the Chichester who puts on a green velvet smoking jacket to celebrate his 65th birthday that one comes back to, the Chichester who sheds a tear while enjoying a bottle of Montrachet on his wedding anniversary, Chichester the happy man."

—*Economist*

At an age when most of us are staying in armchairs, the 65-year-old Sir Francis Chichester accomplished the fastest circumnavigation of the globe in a small sailing vessel . . . and wrote the story of his adventure in a book that will be read for as long as its great predecessors, such as Joshua Slocum's accounts."

—*Library Journal*

GIPSY MOTH

CIRCLES THE WORLD

BOOKS BY

SIR FRANCIS CHICHESTER

Flight Narratives: *Solo to Sydney*, 1931

   Alone Over the Tasman Sea, 1933: republished 1945,
      republished in the Aviation Classics Series of the Temple
      Press, 1966

Sailing Narratives: *Alone Across the Atlantic*, 1961

   Atlantic Adventure, 1962

Autobiography: *The Lonely Sea and the Sky*, 1964

Navigation: *Astro-Navigation* (Four Volumes), 1940–42

   Pinpoint the Bomber (a game for teaching navigation), 1942

   also a Planosphere, a Sun Compass and a Star Compass,
      1942–44

   The Pocket Map and Guide of London

Anthology with Commentary: *Along the Clipper Way*, 1966

GIPSY MOTH

CIRCLES THE WORLD

Sir Francis Chichester

with an Introduction by Jonathan Raban

INTERNATIONAL MARINE / McGRAW-HILL

Camden, Maine • New York • San Francisco • Washington, D.C. •
Auckland • Bogotá • Caracas • Lisbon • London • Madrid • Mexico City •
Milan • Montreal • New Delhi • San Juan • Singapore • Sydney •
Tokyo • Toronto

International Marine
A Division of The McGraw-Hill Companies

10 9 8 7 6 5 4 3 2 1
Copyright © 1967 Sir Francis Chichester
Line illustrations and maps © 1967 by Hodder and Stoughton Ltd.
Introduction copyright © 2001 Jonathan Raban

Library of Congress Cataloging-in-Publication Data

Chichester, Francis, Sir, 1901–1972.
 Gipsy Moth circles the world / Sir Francis Chichester ; introduction by
Jonathan Raban.
   p.   cm.
 Originally published: 1st American ed. New York : Coward-McCann, 1968.
 ISBN 0-07-136449-8 (alk. paper)
 1. Chichester, Francis, Sir, 1901–1972—Journeys. 2. Gipsy Moth IV (Yacht).
 3. Voyages around the world.   I. Title.
 G420.C47A3 2000
 910.4'1—dc21   00-044992

Printed on 55# Sebago by R. R. Donnelley, Crawfordsville, IN
Design by Dennis Anderson
Page layout by Publishers Design and Production Services

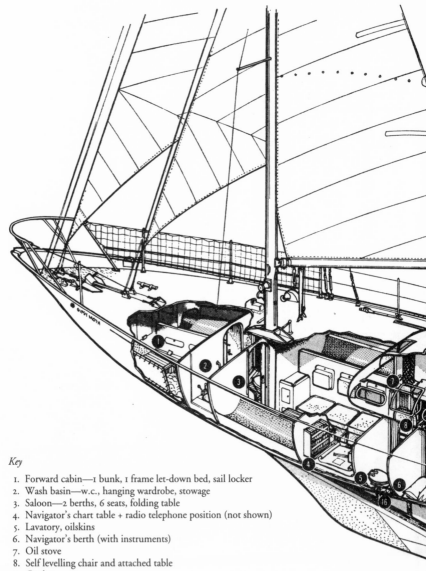

Key

1. Forward cabin—1 bunk, 1 frame let-down bed, sail locker
2. Wash basin—w.c., hanging wardrobe, stowage
3. Saloon—2 berths, 6 seats, folding table
4. Navigator's chart table + radio telephone position (not shown)
5. Lavatory, oilskins
6. Navigator's berth (with instruments)
7. Oil stove
8. Self levelling chair and attached table
9. Cooker
10. Sink and crockery stowage
11. Heater outlet
12. Cockpit with instruments, steering and engine controls and winch handle stowage
13. Engine with generator
14. Dinghy
15. Hasler self-steering gear
16. Tanks (fresh water, fuel for stove and engine)

Section of Gipsy Moth IV

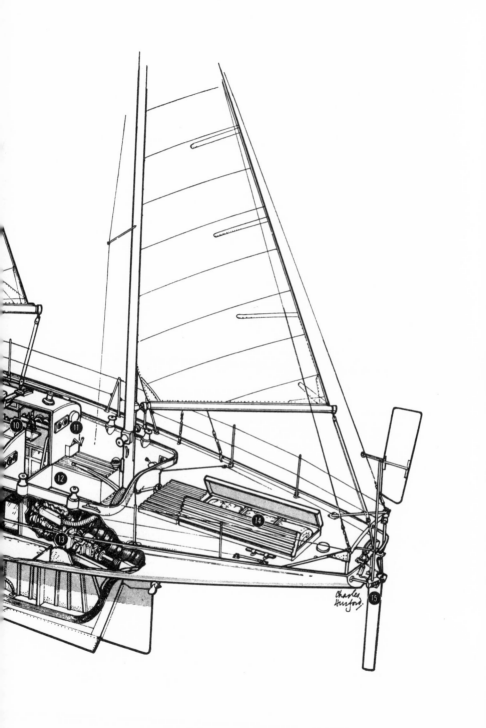

CONTENTS

LINE DRAWINGS, MAPS, AND PHOTOGRAPHS

Line Drawings and Maps
by Charles Hurford, Colin Mudie and A. Spark

Photographs

INTRODUCTION

By JONATHAN RABAN

ON THE morning of July 7th 1967, an extraordinary scene took place on the south bank of the Thames at Greenwich, where an elderly man, wearing thick spectacles, and looking like a frail bag of bones inside his clothes, kneeled bareheaded before the Queen, and was dubbed a knight of the realm with, it is said, the same sword that the first Queen Elizabeth had knighted Sir Francis Drake on his return, in 1580, from his round-the-world voyage in *The Golden Hind*.

For Britain in the mid-1960's, the occasion was richly laden with meaning. Sir Francis Chichester's solo circumnavigation of the world, greeted with all the pomp and circumstance that Buckingham Palace could command, was seen as a precious symbol of national regeneration. This was a period in which the pound was falling, inflation rising, the last of the colonies were shaking off their bonds, and there was mounting industrial unrest. The one area in which Britain could be seen to shine was viewed by the Establishment with something close to horror. Bishops, Conservative politicians, and home-grown moralists of every hue deplored the rise of Carnaby Street, the Beatles, the Rolling Stones, and all the rest of the triumphant youth-culture of psychedelia and short skirts.

So the second Sir Francis became an iconic figure to hold up against the decadence of Swinging Liverpool and Swinging London. He was old enough to be Mick Jagger's grandfather. He came from one of the ancient "county" families of England, and spoke in the crisp accent of a true-blue gentleman. Despite lifelong myopia, and a diagnosis of terminal lung cancer, Chichester had achieved something to astound the world with; a solitary, heroic feat of manly fortitude and daring. To a Britain robbed (as many Britons then believed) of its overseas possessions, Sir Francis restored the glorious illusion of British mastery of the seven seas. As the great anthem of English jingoism has it, "Rule Britannia! Britannia rules the waves! / Britons never, never, never shall be slaves!" That morning in Greenwich, with live TV coverage of the ceremony (*Gipsy Moth IV* looking impossibly tiny in the background), people found something to celebrate in themselves as they watched their screens in pubs and clubs across the country. Their new, stooped, short-sighted knight reminded them of the salt in their veins, their brave historic past, their English mettle. Sir Francis stood as a living refutation to the seedy claims of sex, drugs, and rock-and-roll.

More than thirty years on, the meaning of Chichester's circumnavigation has undergone a radical change. Yet it means hardly less in the twenty-first century than it did in 1967, for Chichester (as we see only now) decisively altered the terms on which lone sailors would put to sea. He has turned out not to be a sentimental throwback to the past (as I confess I saw him that morning), but a harbinger of the future.

He was by no means the first person to sail alone around the globe. Nearly all his predecessors though, like Joshua Slocum, Harry Pidgeon, Alain Gerbault and many others, treated their voyages as extended cruises, and were as interested in the earthy parts of the world as in its watery ones. They took their time. The palm for leisurely circumnavigation must surely go to the redoubtable British yachtsman, Edward Allcard, who took thirteen years to complete the circle, at an average speed of a little over one quarter of a knot. Chichester defined his "wonderful venture," as he calls it in *Gipsy Moth Circles the World*, as a race against time, a merciless test of personal endurance and boat speed. His wife Sheila spoke of his voyage as "a great spiritual adventure, a sort of pilgrimage," and one needs the language of religious austerity and ritual suffering to properly describe Chichester's peculiar achievement.

From the start, he was determined to pit *Gipsy Moth IV* against the Victorian clipper ships which traversed the world on the same course that he would take. It was a punitive and quixotic challenge. Since the speed of a sailing ship is a function of its wetted length,* and *Gipsy Moth*, at 53' overall, was only a fraction as long as, say, *Cutty Sark*, at 212', there could on the face of it be no competition. If both vessels were sailing at their optimum speeds, *Gipsy Moth* would be doing something over eight knots, while *Cutty Sark* would

---

*"Wetted length," not waterline length, is the key factor, though the usual equation for hull-speed is to take the square root of the length of the boat along the waterline, and multiply it by 1.3, 1.35, 1.4, or even 1.5, depending on which authority you consult. When the hull of almost any sailing boat is heeled 25° or 30°, its effective waterline length is substantially increased, which explains why most

romp past at around seventeen knots. It's true that the Bermuda-rigged racing yacht could sail far closer to the wind than the square-rigged clipper; but in the south-east trades or in the savage westerlies of the Southern Ocean, this would be a trifling advantage.

Small as *Gipsy Moth* was when set beside a clipper, she was a gigantic handful for a single man as old and slightly built as Chichester. To get her going at her best, he would often have to set a total of about 1,500 square feet of Dacron sails, distributed around the rig like so many pieces of washing. When a squall hit, the labor of taking down so much sail was both exhausting and dangerous. By contrast, one thinks of the small, tubby, sea-kindly ketch, *Suhaili*, in which Robin Knox-Johnston sailed nonstop around the world in 1968–69. Knox-Johnston, less than half of Chichester's age, carried barely half of Chichester's daunting sail area. He spent more days at sea (313, as against Chichester's total of 226), but as Knox-Johnston's book, *A World of My Own*, makes plain, his days were vastly more comfortable. Knox-Johnston could find serenity in his solitude on the ocean; to the hard-driven, hard-driving Chichester, serenity was alien to his nature.

It was Chichester who set the records and the times to beat, and in the years since his pioneering voyage, singlehanded sailing round the world has been done in Chichester's style, not Robin Knox-Johnston's. With successive leaps and bounds of marine and electronic technology, boats have grown longer, sails bigger, times (much) shorter. Global singlehanded races are organised on an industrial scale, as trials of stamina and feats of athletic survival. Nothing could be further from that idyllic world of the unhurried lone sailor, conjured so infectiously by Joshua Slocum in *Sailing Alone Around the World*:

> I learned to sit by the wheel, content to make ten miles beating against the tide, and when a month at that was all lost, I could find some old tune to hum while I worked the route all over again, beating as before. . . . The days passed happily with me wherever my ship sailed.

Tell that to Francis Chichester.

---

boats—even my own sedate cruising ketch—can make gratifying improvements on their theoretical hull-speed, given a wind strong enough to heel them over. Chichester on several occasions saw *Gipsy Moth IV* come within kissing distance of 10 knots, which suggests that the boat's wetted length may have been nearly ten feet longer than its specified length-along-the-waterline of 39½'.

HIS BIOGRAPHER, Anita Leslie,* records a childhood of classic English misery. Francis's father, the ninth son of a philoprogenitive baronet, was an Anglican clergyman of cold and steely demeanor, who took no pains to conceal the fact that he found his own second son by far the least lovable of his four unlovable children. The Georgian rectory, in the village of Shirwell, Devon, was an emotional ice-house. Francis Chichester became a goggle-eyed self-communing solitary, happiest outdoors, where he kept the company of birds and fish. Boarding school (he was sent away from home at age six) was no escape; thrashed and bullied, he learned to bully in his turn. At thirteen, he went to Marlborough College, a famously tough establishment. During World War I, when Chichester was a pupil there, the school's general atmosphere was that of a particularly brutal prisoner-of-war camp, in which the boys were flogged, usually by each other, and starved into severe malnourishment. Chichester showed no academic talent and his poor eyesight ensured his humiliating failure on the playing fields. This grim upbringing and education might be calculated to produce, with equal chances of success, either a sedated wreck in a psychiatric ward, or a phenomenally hardy and competitive loner.

He left school at 17 to work on a Leicestershire farm, where he fell for the farmer's daughter, and took a violent beating from the farmer. Chichester then embarked on a ship bound from Plymouth to New Zealand, where he found a job as a hand on a sheep station. In short order, he became a gold prospector, a door-to-door subscription salesman, a real-estate agent, and the co-founder of a successful timber company. By 1929, when he was 27, he had made a small fortune, at least on paper, and when he returned to England in the summer of that year he bought a single-engined Gipsy I Moth airplane, in which he planned to fly to Australia and, eventually, around the world.

That anyone so afflicted by myopia should set out to become expert at celestial navigation is a measure of Chichester's ferocious will-power. Within a few months he managed to transform himself into a magician with a sextant—a half-blind man who was at home with vast interstellar distances, and who could work out the notoriously difficult "lunars" (as Slocum did) without recourse to Green-

---

Francis Chichester: A Biography, by Anita Leslie. New York: Walker & Co., 1975.

wich Mean Time. Amy Johnson—no less—is reputed to have called Chichester "the greatest navigator in the world."

His flying exploits brought him the public attention that he craved. One acquaintance would later say of him that he was "clever at backing into the limelight." In the age of Lindbergh and Saint-Exupéry, the lone aviator was a popular hero, and Chichester was bent on securing himself a place in the pantheon and the record books. But his career as a flier came to an abrupt end in 1931, when he crashed into a span of unmapped overhead telephone wires in Katsuura, Japan. He was lucky to escape with his life.

He was turning 52, happily married (on his second try), and a London businessman (a publisher of maps and guides), when he bought his first boat, in September 1953. This was *Gipsy Moth II*, named in memory of his plane, an eight-ton cutter that Chichester converted for offshore racing. With the same impatient disregard for the usual learning-curve that he showed when becoming a flier, he turned himself into a sailor, more or less overnight. In April 1958, he was diagnosed as suffering from lung cancer (though David Lewis, a London doctor, and a fellow-competitor in the first solo Transatlantic race, evidently disagreed; in his book about the race, *The Ship Would Not Travel Due West*, Lewis calls Chichester's ailment a "lung abscess"). In any case, there was no surgery. Chichester took what amounts to a nature-cure in the south of France, and came away healed.

In the summer of 1960, Chichester was sailing a new boat, *Gipsy Moth III*, in the first singlehanded race across the Atlantic. At 39½' overall, the third *Gipsy Moth* was by far the longest and fastest boat (three were 25', one was 21'), and Chichester arrived in New York eight days ahead of his nearest rival. Dissatisfied with his 40-day passage, Chichester sailed the course again in 1962, and shaved nearly seven days from his 1960 record. But in the second transatlantic race of 1964, he was comfortably beaten to the finish by Eric Tabarly, sailing the longer and faster *Penduick II*.

Length equaled speed, and so the fourth *Gipsy Moth* came into being, even longer, even faster. Sailing the Atlantic alone was quickly losing its glamour and originality. Five men had sailed in the '60 race; fifteen left Plymouth in '64. Only a world circumnavigation could now provide the blaze of glory commensurate with Chichester's own compulsive need to shine.

Books about leisurely circumnavigations were themselves written at leisure, allowing the rose-tinted glow of comfortable retrospect to play on the experience they record. We shall never really know the truth of Slocum's seagoing; his book is an artistic recasting of his voyage, and if Slocum was ever in a state of panic or despair, he has taken pains to cover his tracks. The extraordinary—and sometimes unsettling—candour of *Gipsy Moth Circles the World* is in part a product of the speed at which it was written, sometime in the crowded period between May 28th, when *Gipsy Moth* crossed the line at Plymouth, and early September 1967, when the book went to press. Chichester came back to England with eight log books, filled with a total of 200,000 words. Writing *Gipsy Moth Circles the World*, he adhered closely to the language and narrative contained in the logs. There was little conscious retrospect. In his book, he relives the voyage, blow by blow, sail-change by sail-change, and in the process he allows the reader astonishingly intimate access to how it felt to be Francis Chichester. We are nakedly exposed to his explosive bursts of temper, his intimations of spiritual emptiness, his tenderest affections, his terrors—to the full force of Chichester's unpredictable and unstable internal weather.

We have the log books to thank for that. Enforced solitude is often the making of a writer, and so it was with Chichester. He used his logs as confidants, trusting them with his most painful thoughts because there was no-one else to listen. Much of what he told his logs must have been edited out when he wrote his book, yet enough has remained for the reader to feel that he is almost inside the skin of this complex, wounded, irascible and unexpectedly touching personality.

He was more thoroughly *alone* than any other singlehander on record. It is a convention of sailing narratives that a bond be established between the sailor and his boat, to the point where "We" (meaning man and boat together) are the twin heroes of the story. No such bond existed between Chichester and *Gipsy Moth IV*. Within a few days of leaving port, he had the bitter conviction that he had the wrong boat for the voyage. It (not *she*) was too tender, given to violent hobbyhorsing, and inclined to veer wildly off-course when heeled. It had the wrong winches, the wrong rig, the wrong windvane-pilot, the wrong keel-design, the wrong interior. Again and again, Chichester berates the boat's designer, John Illingworth, for having talked him into accepting this temperamental racing machine, when what he needed was another boat altogether. "Vicious" is his repeated word for the boat, and his voyage is as much lonely struggle against *Gipsy Moth IV* as it is against the combined forces of wind and sea.

Chasing the chimera of the clipper passages—the magic 100 days between England and Australia—Chichester tortured himself with calculations of distances-run and days-to-go. He used the clippers as a goad to punish himself and punish the boat, and one keenly feels his anguish as he sees *Gipsy Moth* slipping behind in its race against those phantoms from the Victorian past. It's hard to resist guessing at the phantoms from Chichester's own past whom he was trying to outrun as he tore down the latitudes, from the stony-faced, unforgiving Rector of Shirwell to the captains of games at Marlborough who kept him off the team because he couldn't see the ball. Whoever, whatever the phantoms may have been, they were clearly there. Something far more deeply personal than clipper ship statistics was driving Chichester on this purgatorial voyage.

Islanded among the frustrations, tribulations, and "shemozzles" is one of the most oddly memorable scenes in sailing literature. Somewhere above the Sierra Leone Rise, 600 miles off the African coast, and fast closing with the Equator, Chichester celebrates his 65th birthday (a British milestone, because it is the date on which men can begin to draw from the state their weekly old-age pension). The new pensioner, dressed in his old, green velvet smoking jacket, toasts himself with champagne-and-brandy cocktails, and cherishes the pair of silk pyjamas that his wife Sheila has given him for his birthday. His mood is uncharacteristically radiant. The miles are streaming by at a steady 7 knots; a tape is playing in the cabin. "This must be one of the greatest nights of my life," Chichester tells his log. Then, thinking of his wife and son, and imagining their deaths, he asks, "Is it a mistake to get too fond of people?" The question reveals more of the man than any other line in the book.

His birthday celebrations are rudely terminated by a squall, which lays *Gipsy Moth* over on its side, and has Chichester, naked and hungover, fighting down 950 square feet of sail to save his boat from foundering. This is always how it seems to be for Chichester: happiness is a fleeting moment, an illusion, in a world of unrelenting harshness and toil.

The heart of Chichester's purgatory lay in the Roaring Forties of the Southern Ocean, where his spirits reached their nadir but his writing flowered. As no other sailing author has done, he gives to the Southern Ocean a moral dimension that richly overshadows its great waves and incessant gales.

He was exhausted, "feeble as a half-dead mouse," by the time he rounded the Cape of Good Hope, and he confessed to his "intense depression" and "sense of spiritual loneliness":

> I felt weak, thin, and somehow wasted, and I had a sense of immense space empty of any spiritual—what? I didn't know. I knew only that it made for intense loneliness, and a feeling of hopelessness. . . .

And again:

> I find hard to describe, even to put into words at all . . . the spiritual loneliness of this empty quarter of the world. I had been used to the North Atlantic, fierce and sometimes awesome, yes, but the North Atlantic seems to have a spiritual atmosphere as if teeming with the spirits of the men who sailed and died there. Down here in the Southern Ocean it was a great void. I seemed planetary distances away from the rest of mankind.

After his pit-stop in Sydney, followed by his capsize in the Tasman Sea, Chichester confided to his log:

> I could not be more depressed. Everything seems wrong about this voyage. I hate it and am frightened.

If one takes Sheila Chichester's hint, and thinks of Chichester's voyage as a version of *Pilgrim's Progress*, here was the Castle of the Giant Despair.

Yet for all his loneliness, contact with other people appears to have been no balm for Chichester. When human beings—with the exception of his wife and his son—enter his narrative, they nearly always do so as nuisances and intruders. He is plagued by voices on the radio, inquisitive ships' captains, journalists, and he shoos them off for trespassing on his solitude. To a "girl reporter" from the London *Sunday Times*, who wanted to know what his first meal had been after his successful rounding of Cape Horn, Chichester tartly cabled: "Strongly urge you stop questioning and interviewing me which poisons the romantic attraction of this voyage."

As in his boyhood, he found solace not in people but in the creatures of the sea. It is another convention of sailing narratives (especially singlehanded ones) that, as the boat takes leave of the land and all it stands for, the sailor befriends a bird, or a fish, as a signal that he had forsaken civilisation and entered the community of nature. In Chichester's case, birds and fish were his best companions, and, unlike most sailors, he bestowed on them the keen attention of a lifelong amateur naturalist. In *Atlantic Adventure* (1962), he had "Pidge," a stray French racing pigeon, which flew on board *Gipsy Moth III*, and is a major character in the book. In *Gipsy Moth Circles the World* he dotes on storm petrels, or Mother Carey's chickens. Twice in the voyage these birds blundered aboard the yacht, and were enthusiastically mothered by Chichester.

> Something soft and warm, not cold like ropes and gear are, fluttered in my face, startling me. It was a Mother Carey's Chick, dazzled by the light. I picked it up and put it in a safe place in the cockpit, and after I had finished my job I put it on the after deck, from which it could hop into the air of sea as it might like best when I put the lights out. A Mother Carey's Chick is the most wild creature I know, yet it is both soft and delicate, and with most charming manners. It will not attack, and stays cosy and warm in one's hand. It is so small that one's hand easily closes round it.

But just as the squall spoiled his birthday party, the little bird is dead by the next morning. Back in the North Atlantic, Chichester fished two Portuguese men-of-war out of the floating sargasso weed, and kept them in a bucket as pets.

> Their mauve-and-blue-tinted air bladders nosed their way around the bucket, and I was surprised to see how they shot out their long dangling tendrils in a flash.

Chichester's tenderness for warm, soft birds and stinging jellyfish is in striking contrast to his instinctive hostility to the ships' captains and girl reporters; and in his descriptions of both animals one senses the ghostly lineaments of self-portraiture at work, as if Chichester was himself half-storm petrel, half-Portuguese man-of-war.

IN THE END, he had rivaled the times of the clipper ships (and beaten many of the slower ones). It was a magnificent—if desperate—voyage. Laden with celebrity and honors, Sir Francis might reasonably have taken to pottering around the coast with his wife and son. But he was unappeasable in his need to prove more to the world, and to himself. As his last book, *The Romantic Challenge* (1971), recounts, Chichester was to be found in 1970, aged 69, aboard an even longer boat, *Gipsy Moth V* (57' LOA), with an even bigger sail area, thrashing back and forth across the Atlantic in pursuit of a new chimera—the 200-mile day, 2,000 miles in ten days flat. It came as no surprise that he could not—quite—match these arbitrary and quixotic numbers, and perhaps it was just as well for him that he did not. Heroic failure (by his own exalted lights, though by no-one else's) perfectly suited his Stoic temperament. Such failure, or so I suspect, confirmed his instinctive view of the world as a hard and pitiless place, where there are no true successes, and the measure of a man lies in the mettle he displays in his inevitable defeat.

Gipsy Moth Circles the World, an international bestseller when it was first published in 1967–68, is now reissued as the first title in The Sailor's Classics series. Chichester's voyage was a classic of its kind. His book is a classic document of self-punishing endurance. Chichester was in his own way an explorer in the tradition of Scott and Shackleton. Unlike Scott and Shackleton, in these pages he bares himself and his mood-swings to the reader's gaze, and one is privileged to be his intimate on this loneliest and most harrowing of voyages.

GIPSY MOTH

CIRCLES THE WORLD

ONE

THE DREAM

THIS IS A fairy story for me. Long, long ago, as the best fairy stories begin, I wanted to fly round the world alone. At the end of 1929, I had flown from London to Sydney alone in my Gipsy Moth plane, rigged as a land plane. I wanted to circle the world alone and the only way I could see of doing it was by fitting out the Gipsy Moth as a seaplane, which would enable me to route my voyage through Japan and Northern Canada, where there were no airfields at suitable intervals. So I learnt how to fly a seaplane, converted the Gipsy Moth into one, and set off again from Sydney. How I flew into the half-mile span of steel telephone wires stretched across the harbour at Katsuura and was catapulted into the harbour is another story. That ended my solo attempt, and, indeed, it was only a miracle that I escaped alive. That was in 1931.

As the years passed, this urge to circle the world alone lay dormant in me, like a gorse seed which will lie in the earth for fifty years until the soil is stirred to admit some air, or light, and the seed suddenly burgeons. And so it was with me, only flying, meanwhile, gradually lost the attractions of pioneering to become a matter of technical training and piloting expertise, and all the places that I had hoped to go to, where an aeroplane had never been, had not only seen aeroplanes, but had grown used to them, and the usage of them.

I will not go into details about how in 1953 I changed over from flying to ocean racing in yachts. I have already described this in my book *The Lonely Sea and the Sky*. After the record-breaking attempt I made in 1962, in my solo voyage across the North Atlantic in my yacht *Gipsy Moth III*, I decided that there was a chance of circumnavigating the world solo in an interesting, attractive way. Hundreds of yachtsmen have sailed round the world, including many sailing alone. Nearly all these have followed the well-beaten trail along the Trade Wind belts. I think most of them have taken about three years over the voyage. But I knew only of eight yachts which had circumnavigated by way of Cape Horn. Actually, there was a ninth which I did not know about—Bernard Moitessier's *Joshua*, in which Bernard and his wife Françoise had rounded the Horn, though I do not think they had circumnavigated. The Horn was the big attraction in a voyage round the world. For years it had been in the back of my mind. It not only scared me, frightened me, but I think it would be fair to say that it terrified me. The accounts of the storms there are, quite simply, terrifying. The tale of ships lost in that region could never be completed because there have been so many.

I told myself for a long time that anyone who tried to round the Horn in a small yacht must be crazy. Of the eight yachts I knew to have attempted it, six had been capsized or somersaulted, before, during or after the passage. I hate being frightened, but, even more, I detest being prevented by fright. At the same time the Horn had a fearsome fascination, and it offered one of the greatest challenges left in the world.

I started reading up every interesting account I could find, and from every success or failure there was something to be learned. Finally, I began to cheer up; most of the yachts were, I considered, unsuitable for the task, yet only two had been lost with their crews. I thought that, with a suitable craft, and suitable tactics, I could make the voyage.

The second interest for me was that I saw a chance of making the fastest voyage round the world that had ever been made in a small boat. I planned a two-passage voyage, with Sydney the only port of call. This was the only way to make speed. I got the idea from 1929, when I tried to beat the time of Hinkler's wonderful solo flight from England to Australia. The chief reason for my failure then, in my opinion, was that I planned two flights a day and lost hours of valuable daylight dealing with all the authorities, passport, customs, etc., in two different countries each day, whereas Hinkler made one long flight per day. I certainly would have made one long flight if I had been able to get permission to carry more petrol—I was only allowed to fit two extra tanks—but I ought to have overcome this obstacle somehow.

To sail a yacht from Plymouth to Sydney in one stage was a most formidable proposition: could it be done? I measured it off somewhat hurriedly, and made it 13,750 miles. This was along the old clipper way, which the square-rigged ships followed, and reckoned the fastest route after they had experimented with every kind of diversion over a hundred years, and with ten thousand ships. (When, later, I measured it more carefully and slowly, it came out at 14,100 miles.) What was the best time that I could hope to do this in? In 1964, in the second solo race across the Atlantic, I was beaten by Lieutenant Eric Tabarly of the French Navy, who had a boat specially built for the race; his speed was 105½ miles per day for the east–west crossing of the Atlantic. On the west–east passage home after the race I had my son Giles with me, and we averaged 126 miles per day. I reckoned that the clipper way would be more like the west–east passage across the Atlantic than the east–west. On the other hand, a passage of 14,000 miles was a very different proposition from one of 3,200 miles. However, I reckoned that 126 miles per day was a fair target, at least one that I could aim for, and hope to hit.

I had known that there would be a boat or boats specially built for the 1964 Transatlantic race, and I dare say that I could have got myself a new boat, too, if I had really tried; but I did not want to try then, because by now I had set my heart on the round-the-world voyage, and already the Transatlantic race had become secondary in importance to me. I saw it as a chance to test my theories as to what would be the best kind of hull, gear and tactics for this round-the-world voyage. The 1964 race had fourteen starters, and it was a slice of good luck for me that I was beaten, coming second to the Frenchman, Eric Tabarly. My sporting cousin, Tony Dulverton, went along to see my wife Sheila during the race and said, "Why had I not got a suitable boat which would stand a chance against the Frenchman?" He added that he would provide me with a boat for the next race in 1968. When I got back to England I told him of my round-the-world-Cape-Horn ambitions, and he agreed to provide me with the boat that I wanted.

Now I must go back a bit in time. Before the 1964 race I had been to the naval architect, John Illingworth, and discussed a *Gipsy Moth IV* for trans-ocean solo racing. His firm of Illingworth and Primrose was to design it, and preliminary sketches were prepared. At or about the time of the race a place was booked in Souter's boatyard at Cowes for building this yacht in 1965. The price quoted me by John was within my range, provided that I sold *Gipsy Moth III* first. The construction was to be of a multiskinned hull; that is to say, a number of thin skins or plankings laid diagonally across each other and glued together, so that the hull would be, in effect, a moulded piece of plywood. I asked for a scow-shaped hull, that is to say of broad beam, shallow draught, and flattish bottom, with a deep keel. John said this would not do, because a scow-shaped hull would pound too heavily in the open sea. I was happy to leave the hull design entirely to him. I had a great admiration for his successes in ocean racing. While I was still in America after the 1964 Transatlantic solo race, a cable arrived from Illingworth and Primrose suggesting that I should share the cost of the mould for this boat with Lort Phillips, who was building a boat for my rival in the race, Valentine Howells. I was upset at the thought of sharing what I had always assumed was a design exclusive for myself, and so I abandoned this particular project.

Perhaps I should observe here that singlehanded racing is very different from racing with a full, and probably expert, crew. With a good crew, a boat can be expected to sail at its greatest possible speed the whole time. With a singlehander, it is a different case. He cannot man the helm, and keep the sails trimmed for their maximum efficiency, for twenty-four hours a day, as can be done with a crewed-up boat. Success for the singlehander depends largely on his judgement as to what will be the best rig, and tactics, while he is asleep. He also depends enormously on what kind of boat he has, what effort-saving gear he uses, and what fatigue he can spare himself by using cunning tactics. With a lot of crewed-up yachts, all sailed at their maximum speed, the race would go to the best boat, which might well mean that there was no true race at all, and for that reason handicapping is essential. In a singlehanded race across an ocean handicapping is nonsense.

After sailing back across the Atlantic from the 1964 race I was, as usual after a long voyage, in an optimistic, happy mood, and when Tony Dulverton said that he wanted to build a boat for me, I suggested again that Illingworth and Primrose should be the designers. Tony said that Camper and Nicholsons must build it, because they have the reputation of being the best yacht-builders in the world, and they had built his grandfather's yacht. Sheila also was keen to build at Camper and Nicholsons. She reckoned that we would get the best from them and believed in having it. At a meeting of the architects, the builders, Sheila and me, Tony announced that the boat must be built in the best possible way, regardless of expense. This ensured, of course, that it would be an expensive boat. I am a business man, and I was one of the few pioneer aviators, if not the only one, who made the money which was used to pay for the aeroplanes he flew. My yachts, *Gipsy Moth II* and *Gipsy Moth III*, were also paid for with money that I had saved in business, so I could never have entered into the deal that was made, whereby Camper and Nicholsons, unable to quote a definite price for the boat, were not restricted as to the amount it would cost. However, Tony said, generously, that I was to have no worry whatever about finance; I was to be free to get on with preparations for the voyage.

John Illingworth's original design was for a yacht of only 8 tons displacement, but after this meeting he increased the length of the boat from 48 to 54 feet. I said, facetiously, that it might as well have a few more feet and become a Twelve Metre! I then said that although my original wish as to size was 9 tons Thames Measurement, I would agree to increasing the size, so that the *displacement* was 9 tons; but that it must not be any bigger. Perhaps I should explain here that "Thames Measurement" is a conventional formula for expressing the tonnage of yachts, while "displacement" represents the actual weight of a boat. Accepting the Thames Measurement figure for the displacement would mean a substantially bigger boat. Illingworth said he wanted the size for speed, and that it would be a very light, easily driven hull. I said that the mainsail must not exceed 300 square feet; his plan had a mainsail of less than 300 square feet, a mizzen of about 140 square feet and the largest foresails were a working jib of 200 square feet and a genoa staysail, also of 200 square feet. This seemed a very small sail plan for a 54-foot boat, and I said so. He said that the hull would be of such light displacement that it would be easily driven by this sail area. I believed, however, that the boat would scarcely have moved in light airs with that sail plan, and it was fortunate that I asked for a jib 50 per cent larger; and I also asked for two big genoas, three times as big as his biggest foresail, that is, 600 square feet each. I objected to the long, pointed counter on the plan, which seemed to me to be a potential weakness, and the length was cut down to 53 feet 1 inch. I did not gain much, however, because the self-steering gear was then perched up beyond the counter. The design had a short, deep keel amidships, with a separate rudder and skeg aft. I thought this design would be unsafe running in big seas down south, and John agreed to extend the keel to the rudder. Building was to start at the end of 1964, and to be finished by September 1965.

Almost every week Sheila and I went down to Portsmouth to talk about the boat and to see how things were going, chiefly in the hope of getting things done. The summer dragged on; often there seemed to be no change whatever from one week to another. It became obvious that the boat could not possibly be finished by autumn. We then got another promise that it would be finished by January.

According to John Illingworth, *Gipsy Moth IV* was going to be a very fast boat indeed. I used to lie awake at night imagining her steering down the faces of the great Southern Ocean rollers and, with surfing, perhaps, going so fast that she would be able to challenge the great runs of the clippers. Her waterline length was 39½ feet so that her theoretical maximum speed should have been in any case close to 200 miles per day. (The theoretical maximum speed of an ordinary boat—that is, one that does not rise half out of the water and plane—is a function of the waterline length.)

One of the things that worried me was that John insisted on having a specially big, powerful and heavy self-steering gear designed for the boat. I could not understand this because Colonel Hasler's standard self-steering gear had brought about half the competing boats across the Atlantic safely in the 1963 singlehanded race without any problems, or breakdowns. But John argued that the heavier gear was essential for the bigger boat. If I had insisted on Hasler's standard gear, changing the design of the boat, if necessary, to accommodate it, I think now that I might have saved myself a great deal of worry and grim work.

After reading Lubbock's books on the clippers, I came to the conclusion that their average passage time from Plymouth to Sydney was 100 days.* I could try to equal this, an average speed of 137½ miles per day, or so I thought then, basing my calculations on my original rough measurement of the distance to Sydney. Actually, it entailed a daily speed of 141 miles, or nearly six knots, day and night, for over three months. I decided that when the time came I would give out that I was trying to equal 100 days, a good round number, which people could understand. What I was really after was a voyage round the world faster than any small boat had made before; but I did not want to say anything about this; I still had the feeling, inherited from the early flying days, that disclosing a particularly difficult objective was to invite failure.

---

* Captain Jagoe said later that 100 days was the average of the fastest clippers, that 127 days was the average of all the clippers.

What fast small boat circumnavigations was I competing against? Vito Dumas, the Argentinian, had circled the world in a year and ten days, and during his voyage he made the longest solo passage that had been made until now, 7,400 miles. But his circle was round the bottom of the globe, and while this does not diminish the fine achievement of his voyage, it gave him a route of some 20,000 miles only; a circumnavigation where the vessel passes through two points on the earth's surface which are diametrically opposite each other would be more like 30,000 miles. No other small boat seemed to have completed a circumnavigation in any time approaching that of Vito Dumas.

I begged Camper and Nicholsons to get the boat finished by the end of January 1966, so that I could see her in the water before I left for a month's get-fit visit to the South of France. However, she was not launched until March. There was a launching party—something I don't approve of, because I think that the time to celebrate is *after* a boat has done something, not before. Sheila launched the boat. Sheila has a sure, almost uncanny, instinct concerning ships and boats, and if she had been left alone on this occasion all would have gone well; unfortunately, she took advice from Charles Blake, the manager of Camper and Nicholsons. Now Charles is a most delightful person, amusing, friendly, kindly and knowledgeable, a man that any boy would give a term's pocket money to have as an uncle. But in this small matter he slipped up; he said to Sheila, "You don't need to *throw* the bottle of champagne—just let it drop down to the stem." Sheila did so, *and the bottle did not break*! I was horrified; my heart sank; I thought, What a terrible omen. At her next try, she did it her own way, and the bottle smashed against the stem perfectly. Then the hull stuck on the greased ways, and would not move towards the sea. I had a cold despair of premonition in me. I jumped down, and pushed with my shoulder against one of the launching cradles. I knew that this must seem odd to the people watching, but I was determined that if any slightest effort of mine could make that boat go, she should have it applied. Slowly, she began to move, and finally floated off on the water. There, the hull floated high on the surface; she didn't look right. Then, two or three tiny ripples from a ferry steamer made folds in the glassy surface, and *Gipsy Moth IV* rocked fore and aft. "My God," Sheila and I said to each other, "she's a rocker!"

TWO

FRUSTRATIONS

AT THE first trial in the Solent, the very first thing that we noticed was that the mainsail fouled the lower shroud while the yacht was still on the wind, so these shrouds had to be fitted with levers, and every time I wanted to sail slightly off the wind on a close fetch I had to move up to the mainmast, release the leeward lever, and tie back the shroud to the mainmast to prevent it from chafing the sail. One of my first demands for a singlehander's boat is that there should be *no* levers or runners—I had had the rig of *Gipsy Moth III* changed to get rid of the back stay levers. Yet here I was with this boat, which had to carry me round the world, with not only levers on the lower shrouds, but also *another* pair of levers on the back stays, which were clumsy to operate every time I wanted to set a mizzen staysail. The next thing that happened, far more serious, was that a puff of wind, only Force 6, heeled the boat right over, so that the masts were horizontal, parallel with the water surface. John Illingworth and Colonel "Blondie" Hasler were on board for this trial. We all had different views on how far over *Gipsy Moth* went. John said she was nowhere near horizontal. Blondie said, "I thought at the time she went over 80°, but afterwards I thought to myself one probably exaggerates, and that she probably did not go over so far." I was sitting on the edge of the cockpit, and I kept watching the mast and never took my eyes off it as I particularly wanted to see how far over she would go. Campers' men told me that she lay over with her toe rail under water when on her mooring in a moderate puff of wind. Here was a boat which would lay over on her beam ends on the flat surface of the Solent; the thought of what she would do in the huge Southern Ocean seas put ice into my blood.

John decided to slip her again as soon as the tides were favourable, to cut away chunks of deadwood in the keel, and to fill the holes thereby made until 2,400 pounds of lead had been added to the keel. But as she could not be slipped until April I had her to myself to do some preliminary solo sailing in her for two or three weeks. One day in the Solent I was furling the mainsail. With only the headsails and the mizzen up she would still heel 30–40°. On the deck which I had requested to be flush, so that big waves could sweep it, without meeting any superstructure to carry away, there were two skylights made of metal and armoured glass by a French firm. These were two items of equipment on the boat which always worked perfectly, but unfortunately I had not then got used to having glass in the middle of the deck; it was slippery, wet with spray, my feet shot from under me and, owing to the heel of the boat, I came down a most colossal crash on my thigh. The pain was intense for a while, but eased as I finished off the job and put the boat back to her mooring. I found a purple-black bruise about five inches in diameter on my thigh but the pain went off, and I went about my ordinary business, with no pain or trouble for four days. Then I noticed that this purple-black patch was spreading, and that it was down below my knee, and up into my buttock. Now the pain began, and I found my foot half-paralysed. This partial paralysis, or if that is not the right word, complete loss of feeling and power of movement, attacked one part of my foot at a time—at one time the small toes might be out of action, another time the big toe, another time the outside of the foot, and so on. Like a fool I did not go to my doctor: the truth was, I was frightened that he would try to stop my voyage. I worked hard with exercises, trying to get back the movement in my foot and leg. It was a bad handicap, not so much because I had lost all balancing control in that leg, for I knew that I could get along on the boat without it, using my hands, and by pressing some part of my body against the mast or a shroud to keep balance, but because I could not walk, or do my daily exercises which are essential to keep me fit. Indeed, it was to be fifteen months before I could begin to walk enough to get real exercise from it.

Well, the boat was slipped, which cost me a month's valuable sailing trials. The shipwrights made a fine job, sawing out huge chunks of wood from the keel deadwood, and pouring in molten lead in its place. When *Gipsy Moth* was relaunched she was better, but still horribly tender, lying over to a light breeze. The discomfort below was great. All along during the building, John had demanded that all the fittings and furnishings must be as light as possible to save weight. For example, he specified that the bunks should not have any lining between them and the hull. As the deck leaked all

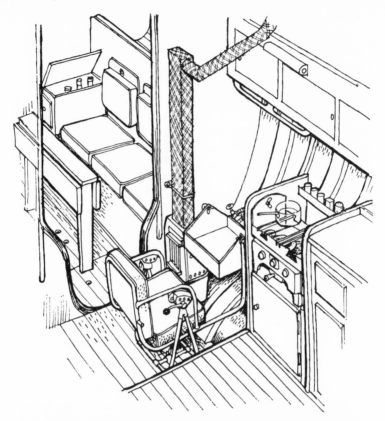

Galley Section showing the chair with attached table on a swinging balance next to the cooker. On the other side is the oil heater with guarded chimney which, with the flue-pipe, are used for drying clothes.

the way along where it joined the hull, when I got into the open sea, this would have meant that, lying in a bunk, I would have had the water streaming on to my bedclothes. Fortunately as it turned out, Campers thought this was a mistake, and put lining in between the bunks and the hull. While pressing for economy of weight in such ways, at the same time, John suggested a second lavatory, or "heads" as we call it. He said that when the boat was going fast it would be impossible to use the one forward. This surely was a novelty to have two lavatories for a singlehander and I was surprised at his proposal because of his expressed desire to keep the weight down, but I agreed for the one reason that I knew it would provide me with a really adequate cubicle for hanging up oilskins, which otherwise I should not have had. This is a most important feature for long ocean racing.

On top of all this, there was the tremendous extra weight of the special self-steering gear in the very worst place, aft of the end of the stern of the boat. There was the extra weight of the levers which had to be added, and that was on top of the deck, also in a bad place. To return to the discomfort below, in the autumn of 1964, Angus Primrose, the partner of Illingworth and Primrose, came over to *Gipsy Moth III* lying at her mooring in the Beguile River, and Sheila and I spent several hours with him laying out the interior of the new boat. My principle was that everything should be the same as in the previous boat, unless there was a definite reason for changing it. We measured all the cabin furniture, settees and bunks, also the galley layout, and we noted everything down. Unfortunately, all this was wasted, because his notes and plans were lost. By the time this was discovered, *Gipsy Moth III* had been stripped and laid up, and the same work could not be done again. However, Sheila had taken over the galley layout, and the general decorating and furnishing, and nearly every week discussed the items with the head joiner at Campers. In addition to that a full size "mock-up" model was made of the galley, and the next section of the boat to it, which contained my swinging chair and gimballed table. Sheila took the greatest trouble over all the details; but in spite of all this she did not get what she had designed and asked for and half the things went wrong.

For instance, if you opened one of the cupboards under the galley when the boat was heeled, the contents would spill out on to the cabin floor, and when I got out on the ocean I reckoned the stowage of cutlery, crockery, bottles, jars and tins was the worst I had experienced. They all rushed and banged from one side to the other when the boat changed heel, making a noise out on the ocean which I can only compare with a country fair in full swing. One thing that was good was the stowage of the saucepans, frying pans and the like. The cupboards above the galley were set so far back that they were out of normal reach. The plate racks were in an inaccessible well behind the galley sink, put farther back than planned, and the water which splashed into this well stayed there until there was a carpet of mouldy muck at the inaccessible bottom, bits of which were brought up every time a new plate was fished out.

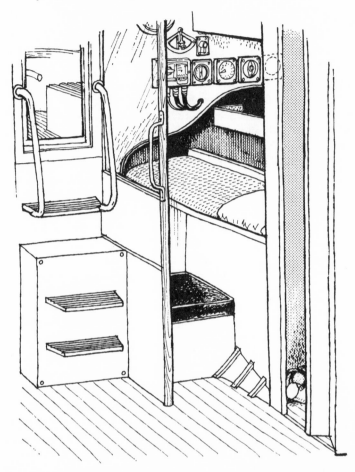

Pilot's berth—(head forward) facing instrument panel, showing seat cum boot locker. Folding door belongs to toilet—on the floor, the electric bilge pump. The panel with steps also forms access to engine. There is a half-glass partition between bed and steps.

When the galley drawers got damp—and they were always being splashed with the water squirting under the ill-fitting sides of the cabin hatch—they jammed, so that it was impossible to open them; for weeks a lot of things I wanted were locked up in this way in one drawer. There was nothing to prevent these drawers, when they were working, from coming right out of their openings, unless they were shut tight, and several times a whole drawer shot across the cabin, emptying the whole lot of cutlery on the cabin floor.

The main cabin was cramped. Sheila did not have enough room to get in and out of her bunk when the yacht was heeled, and the side of the bunk had to be cut away and hinged. There was not a comfortable seat in the cabin, and although the table was too small for my needs, it was difficult to squeeze past it if the yacht was heeled, even when the flap was down. Very little came out as we originally planned. Time was short.

As for the construction, the shipwrights' work was superb. The shipwrights were responsible for the six-skinned hull, and all the laminated frames and stem and stern pieces, and the keel. This hull stayed watertight throughout the voyage, and stood up to all the stresses and strains the boat was subjected to. The rest of the construction was a different matter. An immensely strong cabin doghouse was built of moulded laminations, with the armoured glass windows firmly bedded into it. But all round this doghouse, where it was joined to the plywood deck, leaked badly when I got out into the ocean. Similarly, the deck leaked all round where it was joined to the hull, with the result that the lockers were nearly all running wet. It became difficult to find a dry spot in any locker where I could stow gear which I wanted to keep dry. I tried to stow everything first in a plastic bag before putting it into the locker, but the trouble with these bags is that they sweat, and it is amazing how water from a locker running wet will find its way into a bag. I had trouble with the plumbing, too; the freshwater tanks continued to bring up clouds of fibrous, fungusy matter, presumably due to chemical action taking place on the inside of the tanks, or the pipes. The two fuel pipes, by which diesel oil was fed into the tanks in the keel for the motor used for charging batteries for the radio telephone and electric light, actually shrank and pulled away from the tanks when I was at sea, and presumably all the diesel oil would have spilled out into the bilge when the boat heeled if the tanks had not been narrow and deep, let right into the keel. I never could use the basin in the heads during the voyage, because, when the boat was heeled to port, if the lavatory was pumped out its contents were pumped into the basin, and there they stayed, however much pumping was done, until the boat heeled the other way, or until I mopped out the mess. As soon as I could I jammed the plug into the bottom of the basin, and kept it there.

When the builders came to fit the engine after the various alterations in plans, it was found that the propeller would be out of the water. The engine had to be moved forward into the cabin, thereby spoiling some lockers, and cutting down the available space.

I think it is important to mention these things, because they illustrate the sort of thing one has to try to foresee when planning a non-stop passage of more than three months' duration. If things go wrong on a three or six days' race, it is not a great hardship to put into port for mast or rigging trouble, while plumbing trouble, even if it results in loss of fresh water or fuel, would probably not do more than cause inconvenience or discomfort. The same failure of gear might well wreck a 14,000-mile voyage. My old *Gipsy Moth III* would have done well enough for the voyage, except for some constructional features. First of all, I wanted a flush deck, to give easy passage to breaking waves without risk to deck hamper. Secondly I thought I should have a stronger cabin top or doghouse. This was needed over the galley end of the cabin, partly because the floor rose up there, and partly because I wanted to be able to look around from the cabin. In *Gipsy Moth IV* this top was made immensely strong out of four skins of mahogany glued together over a mould, and the openings for the windows were cut after the gluing and moulding had been completed. It had rounded corners and edges, and would offer little resistance to a wave. Another feature of *Gipsy Moth III* that I wanted changed was the single-plank hull. I had a bad leak with this construction in the 1964 Transatlantic Race, which gave me a lot of trouble and cost me a lot of time. Such a leak, in the big seas of the Southern Ocean, might have opened up sufficiently for the boat to founder. *Gipsy Moth IV* was to have six skins of mahogany, the total only 7/8 inch thick, but immensely strong, and very light for all that strength. I also wanted a watertight bulkhead forward, eleven feet from the stem, which would give the boat a good chance of survival if she had a head-on collision with an iceberg.

One of the things I had asked of the designer was that the boat should be easily manoeuvrable with only the mainsail set. I had two things in view here; in the first place it is a great boon to a singlehander to be able to manoeuvre his craft easily, no matter how slowly, with only one sail set, and that must be the mainsail. I could take old *Gipsy Moth III* in and out of the moored yachts up the Beaulieu River with only the mainsail set, and I cannot recall ever touching anyone. The second point is that I reckon that if a yacht will manoeuvre easily with the mainsail only, she is likely to have a well-balanced rig when the headsails and mizzen sail are added, which means that she will require only a light touch on the helm. This is enormously valuable in a singlehanded yacht, controlled by a self-steering gear. It means that the load on the self-steering gear will not be excessive. Our first day of trials, by tradition, was for builder's trials, and I was not expected to take the helm. However, when I returned to the harbour and only the mainsail was set, I was given the helm. I sailed out towards the near by jetty on the east side of the harbour, and when within 50 or 75 yards of it put the helm down to tack. *Gipsy Moth IV* would not answer the helm. We were headed right for the jetty and getting closer every minute but I was so angry that I did nothing but call to John about this. He started the motor, pushed it into gear, speeded it up, and got the boat round that way. The design had failed me badly in this respect.

I had been worried when John increased the length of the design to 54 feet, because for one thing the bigger the boat the more sail is required in light airs, and therefore the more work is required of the singlehander in setting sails and taking them down again. John was soothing and countered my opinion by saying two things: firstly that this boat would be so light that only a small sail area would be required to drive it, and secondly that it was so big that it would be able to carry its sails much longer in the changing wind than would a smaller boat. I want to make it clear that the original design for *Gipsy Moth IV* had a displacement of 8 tons. When John pushed the size up, increasing the length to 54 feet, I reasserted that 9 tons (Thames Measurement) was the optimum size for a singlehander to get most efficiency, and most speed. When John asserted so positively that this boat would be so easy to handle, and that the extra size would give me greater speed because it would push up the theoretical maximum speed, I raised my limit to 9 tons displacement. The boat as finally designed was of 9½ tons displacement, which was already half a ton over my maximum figure. When the extra ballast had been added to the keel the displacement ended up at 11½ tons—no less than 18 tons Thames Measurement! The latter was double the weight limit I had intended from the beginning, and the displacement was no less than 37½ per cent more than the final weight I had agreed to. The sail area could not be increased any more, because each sail was already up to the maximum which I could handle efficiently. Therefore, I was now going to have a boat greatly undercanvassed in light airs; also she would need all sail setting in much less wind than if the hull had been of the size I really wanted. John's saying that she would carry her sail much longer than a small hull was true in a way, but drew attention away from the two facts which really concerned me—first, that because of the extra size I should have to set all sail much sooner, and secondly, that in a gale all the ordinary sail has to be stripped off to make way for storm sails, and I should still have all the work to do whether it was done sooner or later. With the bigger hull there would be more sails to strip off, and therefore more work to do.

I waited excitedly to see what speed I could get out of her in the Solent. At first I was disappointed, because she seemed slower than *Gipsy Moth III* in light airs, but she gave me a thrill when the breeze piped up to 24 knots and she reeled off 9 knots. This is certainly a thrilling speed for a singlehander. But there were two factors which I could well have taken more notice of; one was that she had to have all plain sails set to get up this speed in a 24-knot breeze, which meant that she would be undercanvassed with all plain sails in a lesser wind; and the other was that she heeled 30 to 40°. Being in the cockpit when sailing in the Solent one pays no attention to a heel of 35°—it just adds to the thrill of fast sailing. When it comes to working below at this angle of heel, it is a very different matter; and when the sailing is in big seas instead of the smooth waters of the Solent, an initial heel of 30 to 40° is unsafe. A big wave can push it over another 40°—and then what?

As speed was to be such an immensely important factor in my voyage, let me state some basic facts about it. Any kind of hull should be able to attain a speed (in knots) equal to 1.3 times the square root of the waterline length (in feet). For example, Joshua Slocum's *Spray* in the 1890s could attain a speed of 8 or 9 knots, though her hull shape would give modern yacht-designers the horrors. Her stem and stern were nearly up and down, so that her waterline length and overall length were nearly the same. Whatever the modern designer's views on *Spray*, the fact remains that she not only made fast passages—the 1,200 miles Slocum sailed in eight days in 1897 stood as a singlehanded record for seventy years, until about two years ago—but she was also a splendid seaworthy boat. There is no mention in any of Slocum's writings of her ever having broached to, and I am sure he would have mentioned this if it had happened.

A hull designed solely for speed, like a crack Twelve Metre, can have a maximum speed of 1.5 times the square root of the waterline

length. An off-shore racing yacht by a top designer will have a maximum between the two. The reason why the maximum speed is a
function of the waterline length derives from the wave-formation of
a yacht going at speed. A shorter yacht has to start coming up the
face of the wave sooner than a longer yacht would do. And, of
course, as soon as she starts climbing, her speed must stop increasing. The sheer radical speed of *Gipsy Moth IV* is, therefore, the
square root of 38½ feet multiplied by 1.3 at its worst, or 1.4 at its
best; that is, 8.06 knots, or 193.6 miles per day, or 8.687 knots and
208½ miles per day. While *Gipsy Moth IV* was building I had hoped
from what the designer had said that the theoretical maximum
speed would be greatly exceeded in a moderate breeze, say 15 knots,
at which most sailing is done, but now this hope was fading. I asked
Peter Nicholson, one of the best off-shore helmsmen in the world,
to come out one day. I thoroughly enjoyed watching his helmsmanship and particularly how close to the wind he could sail the
boat. The breeze freshened to over 20 knots when Peter was aboard
and I was convinced that I had been getting the maximum out of
the boat for that wind. I was sorry it was not a light breeze; I should
like to have seen him at work in light airs, to check whether the boat
was slow then or if I was sailing her badly.

BY NOW I had been planning this project for three years, and all
the early part of 1966 I spent preparing charts and navigation, test-
ing instruments, etc. Although I had planned to have only one port
of call, I must be prepared to go to the nearest port anywhere along
the route in case of a bad accident, such as being dismasted. I
wanted Great Circle charts, and Hydrographic charts, showing the
average winds and currents for the months of the year when I would
be passing through the area. I had to get a dozen Admiralty Pilots,
the sailing directions for the lands I was passing, and the seas that I
should be sailing through, the Admiralty Manual giving radio beacon details all around the world, and another volume giving the
time signals.

One of the reasons why I wanted speed was that whereas I
wished to reach Sydney at the beginning of December, I did not
want to be at the Cape of Good Hope one week earlier than necessary, because it would be early spring down there at the beginning
of September, when I could expect very rough conditions. I wanted
to leave Sydney by the end of December so as to round the Horn
before the end of February. This meant a fast turn-round at Sydney.

I reckoned that I should never be able to refit there in a month by myself. My only hope of getting away quickly would be to have Sheila and Giles out there to help me. I can't believe that there is a more hospitable city in the world than Sydney, and I reckoned that the social pressures and the amount of work to be done on the boat, with all the planning for the second passage, would amount to a terrific load for anyone in a great hurry. To finance all this I agreed to radio an account of the voyage, twice a week, once to the *Sunday Times*, once to *The Guardian*. This required preparation, not only the installation of the Marconi Kestrel radio telephone set and the provision of suitable aerials, but also the organisation of radio contacts with all the different countries along the route. This was tackled with great efficiency by George Gardiner of the Marconi Company.

In order to get these various things rolling I was forced to disclose my plans much though I disliked doing so. A press conference was arranged for March 22. The night before this I was asleep when the telephone rang. Sheila said, "Don't answer it," but unfortunately I did. It was Tony, who said, "The cost of the boat has amounted to 50 per cent more than I understood it was going to be. Can you find the extra money?" I felt an immense depression; my spirits seemed to sink to nothing. It was an almost intolerable burden since I was in the thick of preparations, and I had given no thought at all to the finance. It was a big sum for me to find too; considerably more than the originally-planned *Gipsy Moth IV* would have cost.

On top of that I had an even worse blow. The brass knob at the end of one of the curtain-pulling cords in our drawing room had swung back, hitting Sheila in the eye and bursting a small blood vessel at the back of her eye. The doctor said that in the circumstances it was serious, and that she must go to bed for a complete rest straight away, and certainly not attend the press conference. Sheila had been working far too hard for months, preparing the press release for this venture, helping to run our map publishing business of which she is a director, and working on the layout of the boat's interior and the provisioning for the voyage, while I was concentrating on the preparations for the voyage itself. Life seemed at low ebb. I was deeply worried about Sheila, worried and annoyed at having to set to at this stage to find so much extra money, crippled in one leg, and disappointed in the boat. I suddenly realised how much I should miss Sheila at the press conference, and I realised, too, how much I had leaned on her strength and her flair for handling anything in the nature of public relations. However, I was committed to the project, and it must go on.

Most of the summer months of 1966, before I sailed at the end of August, which ought to have been spent in deep sea trials of *Gipsy Moth IV*, had to be used, instead, for difficult business dealings. First of all, Colonel Whitbread, of Whitbread's the brewers, came to my rescue with a contribution towards the cost of the boat. He is an amazing man; I suppose that everyone knows him as one of the business tycoons of Britain, but besides that he has a remarkable diversity of sporting skills. The ones that interest me most are that he learned to fly in the same year as I did (1929), and still pilots his own plane (which I don't), and that he is a keen yachtsman. His contribution was made without any paper work or strings attached to it, a generous gesture which made me keen to repay it tenfold. Several other firms supplied gear for the boat or cash towards the building cost. The International Wool Secretariat paid for a one-seventh share of the boat.

When we started building, my cousin Tony had insisted that no firms should supply free gear or goods in return for advertisement.

However, to raise the money we were still short of, I had to approach all the suppliers, and ask if they would contribute in return for advertisement. Most firms refused, but some rallied round; for instance Ian Proctor presented me with a special discount for the masts and spars; John Shaw, as before with *Gipsy Moth III*, made up and gave me the stainless steel rigging wire which never failed me; ICI Fibres presented me with cordage and deck wear. All these business dealings not only caused me immense worry but also prevented me from carrying out the off-shore sailing and the much-needed sailing-drill which I had planned. As a result it was not till I was on the ocean that I discovered *Gipsy Moth IV*'s three major vices which spoiled my plan for the project and nearly wrecked the voyage.

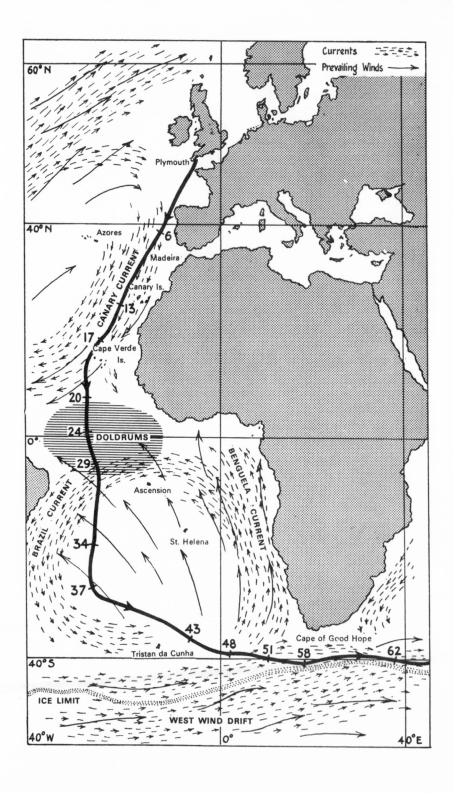

THREE

THE "OFF" AT LAST

IN SPITE of my anxiety about Sheila, the pain in my own leg, incessant worry over money to pay for *Gipsy Moth IV,* and realisation that I had not got the boat I wanted, I kept going. The project really did seem a great one, worthy of framing and panache. I would start from Tower Pier, London, and sail down to Plymouth with my family as crew, attempt to sail round the world with only one stop, and then sail back from Plymouth to the Tower of London. The clippers used to take a tug down the Thames, perhaps as far as South Foreland, and they might carry a pilot as far as the Lizard, so that my having a crew aboard as far as Plymouth would not be departing from traditional clipper practice. I had intended to walk down from my house in St James's to the yacht, and then walk back home again when I completed the voyage. Unfortunately, my damaged leg wouldn't let me walk on it, so that particular plan had to be abandoned.

For the rest, the essential things somehow got done, and preparations went ahead. The press conference was well received, and I was heartened by the immense fund of goodwill that ordinary people up and down the country seemed to feel for me in my venture.

I gave all the time I could to sailing trials of *Gipsy Moth* in the Solent, and although there were so many things about her that worried me—as they were to worry me throughout the voyage—gradually I worked her up and improved her performance. I discovered one reason for what I felt was *Gipsy Moth IV*'s crankiness—her mainmast, which was supposed to be only 47 pounds heavier than the mast of *Gipsy Moth III*, had turned out to be 162 pounds heavier.

There were things that comforted me, too. A friend came with me on one sail to calibrate instruments, and I was just starting a short sleep when he rammed a big light buoy head on. The only damage was that the stem was bashed in to a depth of about ¾ inch, about 12 inches above water level. It was amazing how well the construction stood the shock. My friend was very depressed and apologetic, but I was relieved at the strength of the yacht's construction. This incident made me worry rather less about icebergs!

Looking back to my journal over those days, however, I find most of the entries reflecting pain or worry of one sort or another. I do not wish to weary anyone with an account of my miseries, but the troubles I had then were germane to the voyage. I will sum up with a few extracts from my journal:

• • •

"May 10. Been hot-packing thigh. Very painful at times. Twenty-three days since I slipped on the saloon skylight.

"May 14. This has been a very depressing period, and I seem to get more miserable, not less. First, the worry about Sheila. Her living an invalid's life for three weeks is depressing, and on top I have all the worry of the finance troubles with *Gipsy Moth IV*. I can still barely walk. Several of my toes are out of control. I have aches like sciatica nearly all the time, with bad nights, unable to sleep for more than 1½ hours without waking to bad pain.

"May 19. F + D = fatigue breeds despair. Day trip to Gosport fatiguing—4½ hours travelling to and fro by train, 5 hours sailing, 1½ hours tidying up, added to strain of wonky leg.

"May 28. Clear sky after dawn—it promises a lovely day. Chores yesterday. Rigged anchor tripping line and buoy, washed more paint and moved the mizzen staysail halliard which was in a dangerous place, where I would grab it in place of a taut shroud and could easily go overboard.

"June 4. Everyone says I am not to worry, but it all ends in worry and work for me each time I seem to be getting ahead with my sailing trials. I suppose we shall sort it all out. On the bright side, a bound but uncorrected copy of my *Along the Clipper Way* arrived, and I was thrilled to read Masefield's race up Channel in *Bird of Dawning* again. What a superb artist!

"June 5. Today was exhilarating. I feel cheered up. A romping sail in a fresh wind put fresh heart into me, killed my depression and sense of futile failure, restored my confidence and optimism. It was badly needed.

"June 29. Pile of agenda not lessening. Time shortening.

"July 7. Two-day fast to get rid of the acid and fatigue due to all the financial scraping and worry. Thank heaven that Whitbread's have come to my help.

"July 11. Got through a tremendous amount today with post-fast energy. What I worry and get sad about is Sheila's present state. She seems so fragile."

• • •

That is enough. We lived through that period, although there were times when financial troubles seemed so overwhelming that I wondered whether Camper and Nicholson would release the boat to let me start at all. In the end, the finance was sorted out some-how. On August 12, with Sheila, Giles and Commander Erroll Bruce for crew we sailed the yacht to London for my start from Tower Pier, and the Reverend "Tubby" Clayton (of Toc H) held a service of blessing on board *Gipsy Moth IV*. We had a good passage back to Plymouth, where *Gipsy Moth IV* lay to a mooring off Mash-ford's Yard at Cremyll, for a thousand and one last-minute jobs to be done. The time of departure was drawing very near. It was good to be at Mashford's again, the starting point of all my singlehanded ocean sailing.

SHEILA AND Giles helped me to sail *Gipsy Moth IV* from the mooring at Mashford's to the Royal Western Yacht Club's normal starting line off Plymouth Hoe. I had the usual sinking feeling before a race. Sid Mashford in his launch took off Sheila and Giles, and after that I was alone. I ought, I suppose, to have experienced a sense of thankfulness, or at least relief, that here I was after all the years of planning, actually at sea with my great adventure before me, but the truth is that I was kept so rushed manoeuvring the yacht that I did not have much time for feeling of any sort at all. I was tacking to and fro behind the starting line, waiting for the eleven o'clock gun; and short-tacking a 53-foot boat keeps a one-man crew fully occupied. However, I managed it without too great an effort. I had a jib and the mainsail set, and by timing the tack right, letting go the jib sheet at the right moment, and hauling it in the other side while steering with my backside against the tiller, I could avoid the grind of using a winch.

I crossed the line as the gun fired and was off on my 14,000-mile sail. It was a sparkling, sunny morning and I added my big staysail and the mizzen as I made my way out of Plymouth Sound. Eighty-eight minutes after the start, Eddystone Lighthouse was abeam, and I had been making good 7¾ knots. I turned in for a short sleep, and immediately got a dollop of sea on to my shoulder in the bunk from one of the ventilators. I cursed it heartily.

I set a course which would take me clear of the main steamer lanes. At nightfall I hauled down the White Ensign, and also the little pennant which the *Cutty Sark* had presented to me, and which I was flying in the starboard rigging. I lit my "Not Under Control" lights—two red lights, one several feet above the other on a staff, which fitted into a socket in the stem. This would warn any other vessel which might expect me to give way to it when I was asleep that *Gipsy Moth* could not change course, or slow down. I was feeling queasy and off my feed: I was not sure if this was due to sea-sickness, or to a hangover from the excellent party we had the night before. Perhaps it was both.

At midnight I flashed my torch and hooted four times at a small steamer, which kept on a collision course. She finally altered course to pass astern. I got an hour's sleep at 01.30, but was woken at 03.00 by pain in my leg. A deck leak was dripping into my bunk near the foot, and I rigged a plastic bag, with string at the four corners, to make a sort of tent over the place. At 05.00 a gale squall had me out, to furl the mainsail and drop the staysail genoa, thus reducing the sail area from 940 feet to 440 feet. I got pretty wet in spite of a one-piece deck suit, and it was quite hard to get a foothold on the heeled deck. At 07.00 there was a rough sea with a 24- to 32-knot wind, and I still had only the mizzen and a jib set. I had no appetite, but had been actually sick only once. By noon I had made good 190 miles in the first 25 hours of the voyage. I got a sextant fix from the sun, and finished hoisting the mainsail and the staysail genoa by 13.30. I found that the windward tiller line from the self-steering gear had stranded. This was the start of almost endless trouble with making the boat self-steer, though mercifully I did not then know it. These troubles were not the fault of the self-steering gear; the load on the rudder was so great that a tremendous strain was imposed on the tiller lines connecting the self-steering gear to the tiller.

I was still too near the tribulations of the land for the peace of the sea to find me, and I was still feeling feeble and unbalanced on my feet. The cabin, I am ashamed to say, was still a muddled dump. By evening *Gipsy Moth* was slowed right down, slamming badly, and scooping up the foredeck full of sea. It was very uncomfortable and sickening, and my head was aching. One big slam set *Gipsy Moth* aback. I thought the self-steering gear must be broken but it was all right. I dropped the jib and decided to jill along until conditions improved.

I had no feeling of romance about the voyage yet but, of course, seasickness is very anti-romantic. I was ready for a good sleep that second night, but ran into an extended fishing fleet on the edge of the Continental Shelf. And just at that time there was a heavy squall, so I had to keep a lookout as well as I could, in pelting rain and a strong wind. I must say I cursed those fishermen. I think they were tunny fishermen, although in the dark I could see nothing but their lights. I did see a single tunnyman next day, with his brown sails and the long poles for his fishing lines.

I could still eat nothing, but at noon on August 29 I managed to get down a little food—my first meal since leaving Plymouth two days before. It had been a bad morning. I was having great difficulty in handling the self-steering gear, and the boat. A 35-knot squall from the north-west had set *Gipsy Moth* griping up to windward, overpowering the self-steering gear. I dropped the 300-foot jib and, after a rest, hoisted the 200-foot working jib. I had not fastened its tack to the deck, and it flew up the stay to the masthead. However, on slacking the sheet right off, it came down again. I left it on deck, I am sorry to say, and although I knew well enough that what should be set were the working jib, storm staysail and trysail, I decided to wait a while and try instead to get some food inside me, for I feared that lack of food was making me short of strength. I could not manage much, but I think that the effort to eat did me good.

It was rough going, but my third night brought bright moon-light from a full moon (or nearly so), in a clear sky, with a few fair-weather clouds. But there was still 30 knots of wind. At 06.00 in the morning I turned out for a 40-knot squall from the west, and dropped the mizzen, which at once gave the self-steering more control. My one-piece deck suit took several douches well. That after-noon I rigged and hoisted the trysail, finding it a tough job, with my bad balance, and feeling weak and lethargic. It was difficult to stand firm in the wind, which was still blowing at 30 knots, and plenty of sea was coming over the boat. After that the tiller line which I had rigged for the self-steering gear parted again. I rove a 1¼-inch plaited nylon line to replace it. This line had been *Gipsy Moth III*'s jib sheet, and I hoped that it would stand the great strain. It was so hot working that I had to take off my shirt under the deck suit.

My leg continued to hurt and I could not sleep in the quarter berth because of the pain in my leg when I lay down. I tried the cabin bunk but had no luck there either, and finally slept a little sitting up on the settee.

Next day I got down to some housekeeping, and wrote in my log:

. . .

"12.50. I managed a wash up at last, chiefly of glasses used when drinking with John and Helen Anderson on Friday evening last. I would like a shave, but can't do everything at once. I am going to switch all clocks over to GMT for convenience."

. . .

I had sailed 556 miles in the first 4 days, and a spell of bright sunshine made me feel better. I went on with my housekeeping, hanging out clothes to dry, and tackled various deck-jobs, working in shorts only, which was very pleasant. I sent the kedge anchor down, and secured it in the forecabin. This made the foredeck much clearer for working. I had had a big nylon net specially made which I had fitted on the deck amidships for stowing bagged-up sails, and now I rigged an extra line over the top of this net for security in bad weather. I spent some time scrubbing several ropes—the main sheet, jib sheets and pole guys—using detergent to get off the oil or tar which had fouled them in Plymouth. They were brand-new sheets which I wanted to keep clean. I felt ready for tea, and ate some of Moggie Sinclair's excellent cake.

It was still rough going. I reflected that the *Cutty Sark* would have loved this weather, which meant such heavy going for me, but then her hull was 5 inches thick, compared with my 7/8 inch. Everything in every cupboard rattled and banged, and I noticed with dismay that the bulkhead forward of the heads was cracked, with a jagged line showing where the plywood had parted under stress. This must have happened in one of the big slams that the yacht had undergone. I hoped it had not weakened the structure of the boat, because John Illingworth had specially stressed to me the importance of these bulkheads for strength.

Soon after this I made another worrying discovery—I found that I had left behind my tables for reducing sun sights between 40° N and 40° S by means of the modern short method. This meant that I should have to use the long, old-fashioned method with logarithms through 80° of latitude. I realised suddenly how much a project like my voyage depended on a host of details being satisfactorily attended to before the start. I had another scare—I have written various manuals on astro-navigation, but just couldn't remember any of the formulae. I thought I had not brought with me any navigation manual which would give me the mathematics for solving the spherical triangle using the old log method. I imagined myself stuck from 40° N to 40° S without the means of working out a sun sight for longitude! Fortunately, I found that I had put on board the textbook on *Navigation* by Wing Commander E. W. Anderson, Ex-President of the Institute of Navigation, and that, of course, would give me the method. And I always carry with me Norie's *Tables of Trig Logs*. All the same working out sights by the old logarithm method was going to be a chore.

By the night of August 31, I was clear of the main steamer lanes, which was a relief, though I was still near the route marked from the Channel to Recife, in Brazil. I reckoned that this was not an overcrowded route. I was past the latitude of Cape Finisterre in northwest Spain, and hoped for a northerly airstream.

At 11.30 on September 1, I logged, "Having all meals in the cockpit: that's something that never occurred in the Transatlantic solo races. Enjoyed my first shave for five days, and an all-over wash." Soon after this cheerful entry, however, tragedy struck—I got up a nice thirst, and I couldn't draw any beer from my keg! I wondered if I had left the pressure on, and the beer had escaped in rough seas. The koala bear given to me by Sheila Scott, who had just become the first British woman pilot to fly singlehanded round the world, fell flat on its face when I discovered the tragedy of the beer. It was not, in fact, as bad as it might have been. I think I must have made a mistake with the gas cylinder valve, for I found later that I could get beer again.

I crossed the parallel of 40° N and on September 3 I had to use the long Haversine formula for reducing my sun sights for the first time on the voyage. The result was obviously all wrong. I double-checked all my working of the formula, and could find no mistake. Finally I took another sun shot and worked that out afresh. As soon as I started working on it I found that I had used the Greenwich hour angle and the declination of the sun for *September 4* instead of *September 3*. What a blunder! A mistake of this sort shows why one becomes apprehensive after navigating for two or three months by the sun without any sight of land for a position check.

Next day—Sunday, September 4—I had the first good sleep of the voyage, the first good sleep, it seemed, for months. I slept well for four hours without my leg's waking me up. Of course this four hours' sleep was not the only sleep I got; I would drop off for a few minutes from time to time, and sometimes for an hour or so, usually just about dawn. But four hours at a stretch was a wonderful relief. At noon that Sunday I reckoned that Madeira was 210 miles distant, and I gave myself a sluice down of Madeira sea water—a lovely pale indigo—from a bucket on the after-deck. I had a salad lunch with bread and cheese and beer. It was a halcyon day. In the afternoon I read some passages of Conor O'Brien's story and Ann Davison's in my book, *Along the Clipper Way*, and much enjoyed them.

After viewing the chart I reckoned that I should gybe 90 miles after my noon position. I continued to have trouble setting the self-steering gear, and I tried hanging two anchor cable swivel links as weights on the windward tiller line. These swivels weighed 1¾ pounds, and I reckoned that they would give a constant pull on the windward tiller line of about that amount. The only bother was that when the tiller was brought up to windward by the self-steering gear, these swivels sagged down and began banging on the cockpit seat. I wondered if I should *ever* get the self-steering gear to work troublefree. However, it was wonderful sailing, and lovely weather, with a warm breeze on my bare skin—sheer delight.

I picked up the aero beacon at Funchal, Madeira, and got a bearing of it, which agreed with the plotted position. At 01.40 on September 5 I was 77 miles from Porto Santo. It was a lovely moonlit night. The swell had eased, and the dark surface of the sea was sprinkled with gleaming white horses. In the morning, when I was breakfasting in the cockpit, I saw my first flying fish.

At 11.00 that morning I could see Porto Santo dead ahead, faint but unmistakable. I prepared a hoist of my number, GAKK, allotted to me as the nearest thing possible to the registration letters of my Gipsy Moth plane in 1929, GAAKK. By lunchtime the island of Porto Santo was abeam. *Gipsy Moth* was galloping downwind in bright sunlight and a brisk breeze, sailing at 7.8 knots. She was only making good 6.7 knots, however, so must have had the tide against her. I feared that I had boobed in sailing through the group of islands, and that I might lose the Trade Wind in the shadow of the islands. The clippers must have had reason for passing to the westward and windward of the Madeiras. I had hoped to make for Point Barlavento, the easternmost extremity of Madeira, but the wind backed and I could not make it on that gybe, so headed for the little semi-desert island of Deserta Grande, a long island 1,446 feet high, with its greatest width less than a mile. I planned to gybe

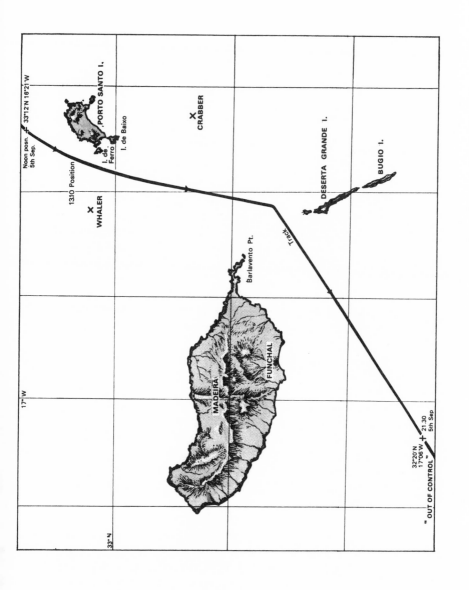

when I got near it. There were one or two ominous cracks and I wondered if the pole carrying the big genoa was feeling the strain. I eased the outhaul to reduce the compression load. The truth was I was carrying too much sail for that wind.

I saw two boats with huge, high, pointed prows. One appeared from round the south end of Porto Santo. It had its mast laid horizontal fore and aft, and was plugging dead into the wind, using its motor. It was full of crew, and I inferred that it was a whaler. Then I came across a crabber half way between Porto Santo and Madeira. It had only one man on board, and it, too, was plugging into wind. Though they took no notice of me, they gave me a feeling of being crowded here, of being in an enclosed space between these three islands. Yet it was more than 15 miles between Porto Santo and Madeira.

When I was below there was a loud crack which I couldn't account for, and when I went on deck to investigate I found that the spinnaker pole had bent in the middle. This was a bad business, because it looked as if very little more would be needed to break the pole in half, and I could not use the starboard side pole on the port side. I dropped the poled-out sail and got the pole inboard with some difficulty because of the heel jamming in the track. I started straight away trying to devise some way of straightening the pole again but I could not see how it could be done.

By evening I was past the eastern end of Madeira, and was sailing some miles south of Funchal. But by 21.00 that night I was in trouble. I was in the lee of the island, and although it was about 8 miles away, I was being struck by minor squalls from wind eddies whirling down from the 6,000-foot peaks. I had my first experience of *Gipsy Moth*'s being out of control, and I didn't like it. I had a desperate feeling when I couldn't move the tiller; the sails were pressed right down, and the boat was tearing through the water out of control. Gradually I got the mainsail down, followed by the mizzen. Then she was under control again, but almost immediately the wind died away to a complete calm. These whirling gusts were repeated time after time. I longed to escape from the wind shadow of the island. "No wonder," I logged, "the clippers kept outside Madeira. What a fool I have been! And I am worked out." During the intervals of being becalmed, the self-steering wind vane, released, rotated, swinging through whole circles. A clipper under these conditions would be in pretty serious trouble. With each burst of wind I gained a few miles to the south-west, and finally got clear of the island, determined if possible to keep well to windward of any other groups of islands on the voyage.

After losing 4 hours in calms, I got a true wind again, and for the first 2½ hours after midnight averaged 7 knots. My leg kept me from sleeping in a bunk for the first part of the night. Heavy deck-work seemed to inflame it.

With morning the wind became a light north-easter and I rigged out a spinnaker pole to port with a big genoa outhauled to it. On the other side I had a jib and a staysail.

Before I left Plymouth, someone, anonymously, had sent me some orchids, with the hope that they would last all the way to Australia. I logged at the time that I did not think they would last beyond Madeira, and they didn't, giving up the ghost as I sailed past the island. I was sorry to see them go, but had expected it. The loaves I brought from England all went mouldy. I cut off the mould and mildewy outsides, and started to rebake them in the oven. Unfortunately, I left them there for 54 minutes while I set the mainsail, and they were spoilt by burning. Even more bothersome (for I could bake more bread), I found that my garlic was attacked by mildew, too. I saved as much as I could of the garlic by putting the bulbs in the cockpit in the air and sunlight, for I attach enormous importance to garlic and usually ate a clove a day. I had been advised to do this for the good of my lung. One does not often get a chance to eat as much garlic as one wants without bowling over anyone who comes near!

The boat rolled madly with a following wind, and the din of banging blocks, or bottles, tins and crockery crashing from side to side was terrific. I had a lot of chores waiting to be done, but I also needed a rest. It was at this point that I began to suspect that some tablets of a glucose preparation that I took to give me extra energy might be impairing my appetite, for I seldom felt like food, except at breakfast time, and had rather to force myself to eat. I shall be referring to these tablets again.

Though it was hot on deck, I could not resist the pleasure of sunbathing. I sloshed on plenty of Nivea cream for my shoulders and knees, but in the end had to wear a cotton coat because of sunburn—perhaps I ought to have covered them up more. An hour before midnight I started to gybe, and it took me until an hour and a half after midnight to complete the job. I had to drop the pole to starboard and the big genny outhauled to it, also the pole to port and then rehoist sails on that side for a wind now coming in from abeam to starboard. I was tottering with fatigue when I finished, but was up again at 04.35 to retrim. Then, at 07.00, I was woken again to find the ship headed north back to England, sails all aback, pressing against the mast or rigging.

At noon that day (September 7) the temperature in the cabin was 81° Fahrenheit, where it felt quite cool! The heat on deck was grilling. A sudden shift of wind sent *Gipsy Moth* heading towards Newfoundland. The yacht had at this time four stays, going from the stem to the masthead. I had wanted only two stays there, but the architect had talked me into having four. When, after trials, I said that I should like to remove two, he asked me not to. Later, I understood why. Meanwhile I cursed having the four, because I had to drop the big genny which was set on the foremost of these stays, and rehoist it on another one. I spent an hour or two tinkering with the self-steering gear, but it was really too hot to work in the sun.

Every day was getting hotter. On September 8 I logged: "I have to be careful to cover up before going out under the high sun; I take everything off as soon as I am below." The day's run was only 96 miles and of that 17½ miles was due to the Canary Current, which is an extension of the Gulf Stream, branching off round the Azores, and flowing south-south-westwards past the Canary Isles.

That day I found out why the port side pole had jammed in the mast track. I noticed that the track had been twisted and pulled away from the mast for a foot or so. The cracks I had heard must have been the rivets popping, and not the pole cracking as I thought at the time. I was still using this pole, but taking care not to overload it, and watching it like a cat watching a mouse, for fear that it would bend more, or double up completely. "If this track goes," I logged, "I shall be poorly placed, because I did not bring any metal repair tools or gear. The tracks for these poles should have been fitted further abeam the mast, to take the thrust from them against the mast, instead of tangential to it."

In the afternoon I made various improvements for better gearhandling. Success in singlehanded sailing depends on easy gearhandling, and being able to keep the boat in control all the time. Some of the improvements I made were to fit blocks, so that the mizzen boom vangs could be led into the cockpit; blocks amidships for leading the after-guys of the poles back to the mast, where I fitted two camcleats to the deck on each side of the mast to take the boom guys. This arrangement enabled me to hoist a boom while all the time keeping control of it from where I stood at the mast. All the same it was quite a feat of juggling, because I had to control, at the same time, the foreguy, the aft-guy, the topping lift, the uphaul of the heel of the pole, and the downhaul of the pole heel, also the outhaul of the clew of the sail to the end of the pole and the sheet from the cockpit to the clew. (As the pole foreguy is paid out, for instance, the aft-guy needs taking in the same amount.) I have only myself to blame for the frightful number of operations involved in a gybe, for I designed the rig and layout of these poles myself. When I am working with normal efficiency, they do enable me to hoist and keep control of the two big running sails. Also, with this gear, I can drop the sails without much trouble if hit suddenly by a squall, whereas if I set a spinnaker of the same size as these two running sails (1,200 square feet) as is the usual practice in a racing boat in off-shore races, I should soon be in big trouble. Even yachts with big full crews usually get into trouble with their spinnakers.

In spite of all this fine talk about improvement, I got landed in a super-shemozzle that night. I had finished a gybe, and was looking forward to a peaceful noggin of brandy in the cabin, when along came a squall. It was not a severe one, but with more than 1,600 square feet of sail set, *Gipsy Moth* began to get out of control—that is to say, the self-steering gear could not hold her on course, and I could not take the helm as well as drop the sails. It was all very well galloping along at 9 knots, but no good if this was in the wrong direction! So I decided to drop the big genny which was poled out to starboard. I stupidly overlooked a step in my standard drill—a bad slip-up while working in a near gale-force wind. I let go the halliard and brought the luff of the sail down the topmast stay, and now had the bunt of the sail partly muzzled by my body and arms right in the stem of the boat inside the pulpit. The mistake I made was that I had left the running part of the clew outhaul cleated up at the mast, instead of bringing it forward with me to the pulpit. I had to leave the pulpit and let go the bunt of the sail, so that I could release this outhaul. The clew and foot of the sail stretched 20 feet outboard to the end of the pole, and this part of the sail filled out with wind to the shape of a banana, and began flogging madly up and down in the near-gale. Then I made a second blunder. I should have robbed a furled headsail near by of its sail tie, and used this to secure to the pulpit as much of the big genny as I had managed to smother in my arms. But the wind was freshening fast, the situation was getting serious, and I decided that the best thing to do was to dash for the mast and slack away the outhaul with a run. Before I got back to the pulpit, the sail had caught the wind, bellied out, and blown round to the leeward side of the stem. That sail is a piece of Terylene the size of a room 20 feet by 30 feet, and once it gets out of control it is a really tough proposition for a singlehander. When it was round to the leeward side of the fast-moving stem, the water caught it, and my heart sank with it as it disappeared under the stem and the ship sailed over it. My lovely sail, so essential to this project, ridden under the keel! I must slow up the ship as soon as possible, but first I had to slack away any ropes holding the sail to the windward side of the boat. The strain on all this gear from a huge bag of Terylene under water, in a speed of 8 to 9 knots, must have been terrific. I let the outhaul fly. The rope disappeared into the sea like a thin snake. I then let go the foreguy to the pole; this allowed the sheet from the cockpit to the clew of the sail to pass under the keel. Now, the sail under water was held only by the hanks fastening it to the forestay. It should be streaming freely in the water, and no more harm should happen to it.

I dropped the big genny on the leeward side, then the mainsail, and lastly the mizzen and, with the boat nearly stopped, I first housed the pole on deck, and then began hauling the sail inboard foot by foot until it would come no farther. I was puzzled by this until I realised that the sheet was still fast to the winch in the cockpit on the starboard side, and was holding the clew under the keel to the weather side of the ship. I let go of the sheet, and got the rest of the sail inboard. This may sound simple enough, but it was no fun at the time. It was dark and blowing hard, and it was all hard work. I was immensely pleased to find later that though both sail and sheet had plenty of red anti-fouling paint on them from the keel, the sail was intact. But I was depressed at losing a night's sailing. The boat was too big, no doubt of it. I felt that I had had to put out a much bigger physical effort than I thought I was normally good for. I went below and had my brandy at last, but I had no appetite at all, although I had had only a sandwich for lunch. However, I could not bear to lose the good wind, so I donned my lifeline again and hoisted the big port-side genoa once more. The yacht began moving, and I went below to try and get some sleep.

But my leg ached too much to sleep. The rolling was bad without the mainsail, so I decided to have another go. I went on deck yet again, and rehoisted the mainsail. I finished the whole operation at 14 minutes before midnight. The giant shemozzle itself had lasted

3¼ hours. There was a time when I had thought sailing would be no good to me because it provided no physical effort and exercise! At that moment, that seemed a pretty good joke.

At noon on September 8, I had been on a latitude level with the westernmost of the Canary Isles, but after my experience of Madeira I had given them a good berth of 30 miles. By September 9 I was well past them, and headed for the Cape Verde Islands, determined to pass well to windward of them, too. The sea here gave a curious impression of being like a desert, a Sahara, lifeless and empty, instead of teeming with fish and bird life as I believed it to be. The water was pale blue-black, like diluted blue-black ink.

That night it was dark at 19.30—I was getting near the tropics. Two hours after midnight I logged that it was a very black night in spite of some stars visible. "Lovely quiet sailing but she needs that mizzen staysail for speed. I can hardly drag my feet along for fatigue, so will sit tight a while yet." That night I had twice as much sleep as on any previous night and figured that another such night would set me on my feet again. The pain in my leg had nearly gone. Noon brought the end of my second week at sea. I was disappointed in the week's run, only 886 miles, making an average so far of 128.9 miles per day.

After noon I poled out a 300-foot jib for the first time. It took a lot of adjusting of guys, lifts, outhaul, etc., the object being to fill the leeward big genoa with wind. Here I had my first experience of *Gipsy Moth*'s broaching-to. She was running downwind, with the wind on the quarter, when two waves swung the stern round and brought her up head to wind. After that the poled-out jib was aback, and the self-steering gear could not bring the boat under control again; no wonder, because it took a big effort from me with my foot on the tiller and my back to the side of the cockpit to bring the boat back on to her original heading. However, it was the first time that I had seen the speedometer needle come against its stop on the dial which was at 10 knots. Three and a half hours later I recorded: "Great sailing in the sunlight and I love to see that needle come against the stop at 10 knots!"

On September 10 I made up and cooked a nut roast for dinner, but it wasn't a great success; I think the nuts were too old, and perhaps a little sour. It was a great thrill to be in the cockpit, the first time that I had been consistently rising to 10 knots in a small boat. The course was dead downwind. *Gipsy Moth* averaged 7⅜ knots for 8 hours.

At midnight that night I logged:

• • •

"Roughish going," and 1½ hours later my log read, "Most puzzling: I was woken by a shattering shock, and got the impression that things were jumping about in the cabin due to it. I thought of what could have caused it, the mast broken, the main boom adrift and banging the cabin, a pole come down from aloft. I dressed in full war paint—shorts, lifeline, harness and cap—and went on deck to find out the worst. I could see nothing wrong at all. I inspected everything right up to the stem. I believe *Gipsy Moth* must have sailed full tilt into a whale, and got away with it. Very fortunately there was no more water in the bilge. I suppose it could have been a dream or a nightmare."

• • •

An hour and a half later I logged: "The wind has eased, but the boat seems to be going very fast; looking over the side it is hard to focus on the white water rushing past. It is like looking out of the window of a train at things a few feet away rushing past."

On September 11 I sailed into the tropics, and had a good day's run of 194 miles, the best so far of the passage. It was very hot, 82° in the shade, and later, in the dark, it was awe-inspiring on the foredeck when doing 10 knots; it gave the impression of a runaway horse. The white water rushing past was shot with brilliant dots of phosphorescence. But it was difficult to sleep with the rough riding. Two hours after midnight (September 12) I was again worrying about *Gipsy Moth*'s tendency to broach-to. I logged:

• • •

"I got worried about *Gipsy Moth*'s griping up to windward after a wave had slewed her stern to leeward. There is the strain on the pole gear as the poled-out jib is taken aback, a big strain on the self-steering gear fighting to get the boat back on course, and then there is the risk of the mainsail's doing a Chinese gybe [that is when the top of the sail is twisted over on the starboard gybe while the bottom half of the sail is still on the port gybe] when swinging the head back on to the old course."

• • •

I dropped the mizzen sail, which I thought might be a big factor in causing the boat to broach-to. At 03.15 that early morning, I logged: "Rough riding. I wish I could sleep the first part of the night. It is good time wasted too, because I need to use the daytime to make up sleep shortage. Thank heaven I am not beating into this wind instead of running before it!"

I had a change of diet for breakfast later that morning—fresh flying fish. I found one in the cockpit, another in the sail net amidships, and two more on the foredeck. They were delicious fried in butter, tasting somewhat like a herring with a flavour of mackerel.

By noon of September 12 the day's run was another good one, 174 miles. I logged:

• • •

"What's to do first? Wash up, shave and wash, set the mizzen, take the sun shots, work up the dead reckoning, or prepare tonight's radio transmission? The answer—you will have guessed — I had a snooze. After all, I have just finished a meal of four flying fish and four potatoes and it is 82° Fahrenheit in the shade."

• • •

To show how rough the going was, it took me 28 minutes to get 6 sextant shots of the sun that day. I reckoned that I was moving out of the south-west-going Canary Current into the west-going North Equatorial Current, and was well in the middle of the north-east Trade Wind belt. I didn't have any luck calling up London that night, but managed to get through the following night and radioed a report to John Fairhall of *The Guardian*.

An hour after midnight on September 14 a flying fish landed on board at the sail bags under the nets amidships, while I was on deck there, though I did not see it actually alight. I returned it alive and kicking to the deep, which must have been a surprise for it. At 08.42 in the morning I logged: "I have just realised that all last night I had not a twitch of pain from my leg. How wonderful, and yet how ungrateful that I should nearly let this pass unnoticed, when it changes my present life immensely." I collected ten flying fish round the deck that morning. I was sorry that I could not return them alive like the one in the night, and since I could not save them I breakfasted off them. (One flying fish, cooked, is not very big.)

FOUR

MY SIXTY-FIFTH BIRTHDAY PARTY

SEPTEMBER 17 brought my 65th birthday. I had a big time with a freshwater wash, followed by opening Sheila's birthday present, a luxurious and most practical suit of silk pyjamas. I shed a tear to think of her kindness and love, and all the happiness we have had together since 1937. I started celebrating my birthday by drinking a bottle of wine given me by Monica Cooper and other members of our map-making firm for a birthday present. That was at lunch time. In the evening I wrote in my log:

• • •

"Well here I am, sitting in the cockpit with a champagne cocktail, and I have just toasted Sheila and Giles with my love. Full rig, smoking, smart new trousers, black shoes, etc. The only slip-up is that I left my bow-tie behind, and have had to use an ordinary black tie. I have carried this 'smoking' (my green velvet designed and built by Scholte before I met Sheila in 1937) six times in *Gipsy Moth III* across the Atlantic, intending to dine in state one night, but this is the first time I have worn it in a *Gipsy Moth*. No dining in state, either. I don't get hungry in these 85° F heats until the middle of the night, or early morning. But why worry, with my bottle of the best presented by my own Yacht Club, the Royal Western Yacht Club, by that old satyr Terence (I always expect him to pull a pipe from some hidden pocket and start serenading Cupid), my dear Coz's brandy to make the cocktail, a lovely calm evening, hammering along at a quiet 7 knots on, extraordinary pleasure, a calm, nearly flat, sea. I will turn on some of the music Giles recorded for me. I meant to ask him to get a recording of Sheila and himself talking together, but forgot, which is not surprising, because the amount of thinking and planning for the voyage was unbelievable. A thousand items to remember or see to.

"This must be one of the greatest nights of my life—right in the middle of this wonderful venture—just passed by 100 miles the longest six-day run by any singlehander that I know of, and a great feeling of love and goodwill towards my family and friends. What does it matter if they are not here? I would not love them as I do in their absence, or at least I would not be aware of that, which seems to be what matters.

"People keep at me about my age. I suppose they think that I can beat age. I am not that foolish. Nobody, I am sure, can be more aware than I am that my time is limited. I don't think I can escape ageing, but why beef about it? Our only purpose in life, if we are able to say such a thing, is to put up the best performance we can— in anything, and only in doing so lies satisfaction in living.

"Is it a mistake to get too fond of people? It tears me to shreds when I think of Sheila and Giles being dead. On the other hand, I keep on thinking of the happiness and pleasure I have had at various times with them, usually when doing something with them. That first voyage home from America with Sheila, just the two of us, keeps on recurring to me, all the little episodes, and the joy and comradeship of it. The same with the third passage back, with Giles. I wonder if I shall ever enjoy anything as much. I see that action appears a necessary ingredient for deep feeling. This sort of venture that I am now on is a way of life for me. I am a poor thing, incomplete, unfulfilled without it.

"It is too dark to see any more. Think of me—as the sky darkens, music playing, the perfect sail, and still half a bottle of the satyr's champagne to finish.

"Darkness came, alas, a bit too quickly—sudden nightfall is one of the bad features of the tropics. I love those long northern twilights."

• • •

For all that darkness came too soon, that was a magic evening. I had much to celebrate, not only my birthday, but my record run of the previous week. How often does a sailing man sit drinking champagne while his craft glides along at 7 knots? The horizon looked a clean straight line, and the departing sun suffused some clouds with an orange glow. The moon was on its back above the sun's exit. That, I think, was about the first time on the voyage that I was at all sentimental—up to then it seemed to have been all technics and worry. It seems odd that it should take about three weeks of a voyage before one can begin to enjoy it, but so it is, or seemed so then to me.

I COULD have done without a celebration hangover at 2 A.M., when a sharp squall of wind laid *Gipsy Moth* over on her side. I staggered out of my bunk with difficulty, as I was on the lee side of the boat and was still pretty full of brandy and bonhomie. I started looking for clothes, getting the best footholds I could at the side of the boat and on the bunk, but with a shot of panic in my vitals I realised that this was a serious emergency; there was no time for clothes. I grabbed a lifeline harness and put that on as I climbed into the cockpit. *Gipsy Moth* was pressed over on her side, with the sails dipping in the water and out of control of the self-steering gear. No wonder at that, because after I had released the self-steering gear from the tiller I could not move the tiller even with a tiller line to help. The situation was serious, because if she went over further and the sails got completely below the water, the companion being wide open, the water could easily rush in there and the boat founder. *Gipsy Moth* was carrying every square foot of sail I had been able to set. I let go the mizzen staysail (350 square feet) with a run, and hauled it into the cockpit, which it half filled, until I could get at the mainsheet and pay off the main boom. Slowly the boat righted, and I was able to turn her downwind and engage the self-steering gear again to control her. This enabled me to get forward to drop the big 600-square-foot genoa. That left the staysail genoa and the mainsail. After the squall eased I waited a few minutes because of the heavy rain, and by 03.17 I had added the big jib and the mizzen. I was tempted to reset the mizzen staysail, but did not want to be turned out again that night for another shemozzle with the boat out of control, so left it down. As I turned in again I made a note that I must devise a better arrangement for the tiller lines.

I was woken by the boom banging and the sails slatting in a calm, with *Gipsy Moth* headed nearly east. There were tropical showers drifting about, an overcast sky, and a glassy look about the sea surface. But it looked finer ahead. My leg started hurting me again, and I wondered, did I sprain it, or pull the old strain, hauling on the halliards during the night? I comforted myself by thinking that perhaps it was due simply to the champagne.

I felt no inclination to put away my glad rags of the previous night, but it had to be done, so I tidied up. Then I decided to bake some bread, made the dough and got the Primus under the oven going. It was not all that successful, for a series of squalls followed the calm, and perhaps the yeast jibbed at so much movement. I did the actual baking job at a mean angle of heel of 30°.

My noon position (6° N, 23° 45′ W) on September 18 put me within 6 miles of exactly the same Great Circle distance from Plymouth as is Newport, Rhode Island. In the 1964 Singlehanded Transatlantic Race it took me 30 days to cover this distance, and now it had taken 22 days. That was a good thought, in spite of the squally, uneven weather. But I was still in the Doldrums and there was no sign of the tropical rain showers coming to an end. They could be seen in every direction. It was very tedious, the endless changing of the helm and trim before and after each squall. I was up and down to the deck all day, as each squall went through, like a damned jack-in-the-box. Of course it was the pounding and bashing in a rough sea which I had to worry about; I didn't think that wind would damage the gear. I was feeling the physical strain of the incessant changing of sails at intervals throughout the day and night and cursed having a boat so much bigger than I had wished for, which was causing me the extra labour.

That night I found a Mother Carey's Chicken (Wilson's stormy petrel) on the deck and moved it to a more comfortable berth on the weather side where it was more level than down on the lee side and the bird had more to hold on to. It felt woolly, and was a game chick, always good for an attempted peck. It flew off the deck in the end but seemed unhappy. A flying fish landed near me as I was working on the foredeck.

On September 19 I was headed by a southerly wind, and I was only able to make good a track of ESE. I could have done a little better on the other tack, but I preferred to make easting in preparation for being pushed westwards by the South-East Trade Wind which I was due to reach at any moment.

Early in the morning of September 20 I decided to tack and, after I had finished the tack, I spent half an hour trimming the sails and the self-steering gear. *Gipsy Moth* was hard on the wind to a 22-knot breeze. I was having a lot of trouble trying to keep her headed close to the wind. *Gipsy Moth* was pounding severely, and every now and then a succession of three or four waves would knock her head closer to windward until she ended up pointing dead into wind, and stopped. At 10.40 that morning I reckoned that I had sailed into the South-East Trade Wind belt at last. I set a 300-foot jib in place of the storm jib. I complained in the log:

. . .

"I must be very feeble as it seems such a big effort; also I find it a great disadvantage having completely lost balance control in my feet. Anyway, enough for the ship for a while and now a turn for the Inner Man. A lovely fine day, blue and white; what a wonderful change."

. . .

In the evening I set the mainsail in place of the trysail for the South-East Trade Wind. It was a lovely evening, and lovely sailing. *Gipsy Moth* was now on the wind doing 5½ knots, and headed south by west. It was now that I experienced one of the big setbacks of the voyage.

Let me explain the situation. From where I was then at 4° N and 21° W the old clipper way curved slightly westward down through the South Atlantic to Ilha da Trinidade from where the curve changed gently to the south-east, passing close to Tristan da Cunha Island to reach the Greenwich Meridian at 40° S. The distance along this route from where I was to where the clipper way passed south of the Cape of Good Hope was roughly 5,000 miles or 7.14 knots for 700 hours. The first 1,500 miles of this clipper way passed through the South-East Trade Wind belt. South-east was the direction of the Cape so both the clippers and *Gipsy Moth* would be hard on the wind for at least the first 1,500 miles. I had felt quite sure that this was one point of sailing on which *Gipsy Moth* would excel, and I had checked that she would sail nearly as close to the wind as a Twelve Metre in a 30-knot wind in the comparatively smooth water of the Solent. I had based my plans for a 100-day attempt on sailing much closer to the wind in this belt than the clippers could have done. In other words I had planned to cut the corner and save no less than 800 miles on the way down to the Cape. I trimmed up the ship carefully to sail as close as possible to the south-east wind. The wind had dropped to a gentle and ideal breeze and the sea had moderated. The waves were now quite small—ripples, I felt like calling them—but I found that they made *Gipsy Moth* hobbyhorse in such a way that three waves in succession would each knock ¾ knot off the speed. The first wave would cut the speed down from 5½ knots to 4¾, the second to 4 knots and the third to 3¼ knots. If there was a fourth or fourth and fifth they would bring the yacht up head to wind and it would stop dead. The only way of avoiding this with the self-steering gear in control was to head off the wind another 20°. This meant that I could not sail any closer to the wind than the clippers, and the plan that I had set so much store on collapsed in ruins. This hobbyhorsing was the first of *Gipsy Moth*'s nasty tricks that I was to suffer from on the voyage.

It was a tiresome and trying period of the voyage. If I kept *Gipsy Moth* going fast on the wind, she slammed damnably into the seas, which worried me for the safety of her hull. Yet I had to keep going as fast as I could if I was not to fall hopelessly behind the clippers. I could make no good radio contacts, and I had trouble trying to charge the batteries. I could not get a good charge into them. At night I was troubled by cramp in my legs which would hit me after I had been asleep about two hours, and would let go only if I stood up. This meant that I never got more than about two hours' sleep at a time. It was hot, and I sweated profusely; I wondered if my body might be losing too much salt. I decided to drink half a glassful of sea water a day to put back salt.

On the morning of September 21 I awoke to find the ship headed east with all the sails aback. While I was asleep hobbyhorsing must have brought the ship's head up into the wind, and after she had stopped she must have fallen back on the other tack. I released the main boom so as to let the mainsail come over completely and slowly wore the ship round downwind back on to her course. At noon I saw a tanker, the last ship I was to see for two months. This was at 2° 19′ N, 21° 43′ W. She was the *African Neptune*. She turned and followed me, and came close up to leeward. I am always apprehensive when a steamer comes near the yacht in the open sea. If she comes up to windward of the boat she takes all the wind away and the yacht loses control. The ship drifts slowly downwind, and the rolling yacht is liable to damage her crosstrees and rigging against the side of the ship, as happened to David Lewis in the 1960 Singlehanded Transatlantic Race. However, the *African Neptune* was well navigated and I need not have worried. The captain asked me if there was anything he could help me with by way of luxuries, etc., which I thought nice and kind of him. At the time I was trying to make the bilge pump in the cockpit work, and I had the pieces scattered around. On seeing the ship approach I went below to dig out my "number" GAKK, a hoist of flags; also a signalling lamp, and a loud hailer. I tried speaking to them with the signalling lamp but they took no notice of that. After the steamer had disappeared in the distance I tackled the bilge pump again. There was a lot of bilge water due to seas washing over the deck and swilling down the navel pipe, where the anchor chain emerges at the deck. I feared that I should have to dip the bilge water out with a bucket if I could not repair the pump. In the end I discovered the trouble, which was that one of the rubber flap valves in the bilge pump was not fitting properly. I fixed this up, and the pump worked. Puffed up with my success, I then had a go at the beer keg. It was terrible in that heat to think of all the beer in the keg lying inaccessible. I looked for an air-lock or a kink in the pipe down to the keg in the keel but could find nothing wrong there. I came to the conclusion that the CO_2 cylinder had leaked and there was no pressure to force the beer up.

That evening I logged:

• • •

"What I cannot understand is why I almost never have an appetite. Here it is 9 P.M. and $1\frac{1}{4}$ hours after dark, and I don't feel the least hungry. I had only two slices of wholemeal with trimmings for breakfast, one slice and one Ryvita with dates and cheese for lunch. Nothing for tea."

• • •

I crossed the Line on September 22. That was fascinating. I went up to try for some sun shots at local noon, and first I was looking for the sun's reflection in the mirror of my sextant to the southward, as usual. I was amazed to find it in the north-east, then realised that I had overtaken the sun, sailing southward, and that it would pass to the northward of me. I started "shooting." As the sun passed the meridian I had to swirl round as fast as I could—one minute I was facing north-east, and it seemed only seconds later that I was facing north-west. It is very difficult shooting in these conditions, because the way of telling if you are measuring to the sea vertically in line with the sun is to swing the sextant gently, like a pendulum, until you find the direction in which the height of the sun above the horizon is least. This pendulum sweep moves the sun's image in a flat arc above the horizon, and you must decide where the sun's image "kisses" the horizon.

For some days I had been having a private race with the sun which was on its way south for the northern winter. I won by the narrow margin of 22 miles because the sub-solar point—the point vertically beneath the sun on the earth's surface—was 22 miles north of the Equator at noon that day. I stowed away my North Atlantic charts and fished out a set for the South Atlantic. It was a thrill changing from one ocean to another.

Navigating with the sun passing nearly overhead it was wise to get some star sights as well, and fortunately I had a fine, starry night. I was wondering what was the bright star near Canopus, when I noticed it moving! How awesome those satellites are—I mean, the thought that man has put them up there! I think it is the star-like brightness which is most impressive.

It was now that *Gipsy Moth*'s second vicious habit began to take effect. Now and then when the wind eased I would log that I was having some lovely sailing, but alas a few minutes or hours later there was sure to be a complaint about the difficulty of keeping *Gipsy Moth* to her heading. The log is littered with entries such as, "*Gipsy Moth* keeps on edging up to the wind and slowing up then," "I feel she is too much heeled, labouring and pinned down," "The self-steering could not settle down and keep to a heading: too much weather helm," "I see she is sailing too free now; I must have another go at her, drat it!," "I could not stand the violent slamming which built up when the wind increased above 20 knots and the 40° heel is pretty excessive," "I think the vane must be slipping in some of the big bumps," "*Gipsy Moth* is sailing 65° off the true wind." (She ought to have been sailing within 50° of the true wind at the most.)

From now on, except when the wind dropped and the sea moderated, I had an almost endless struggle trying to keep *Gipsy Moth* to a heading close-hauled. I thought at the time that it was due to the self-steering gear being unable to hold the tiller. Eventually, however, I discovered the trouble. I was standing on the deck one day looking forward, when the wind increased suddenly in a puff from 20 knots to 25 knots. The boat heeled over more, and to my astonishment I saw the bows slide over the water downwind about 30°. It was like a knife spreading butter, sliding over a piece of bread. What had plagued and puzzled me became quite clear; there was a critical angle of heel for the boat. If the hull came a degree or two more upright it would start griping up to windward and slowing up. If, however, the hull heeled over a degree or two more than this critical angle, the forepart of the boat slid off to leeward, the boat lying more on its side had quite different sailing characteristics, and would romp off at great speed on a heading 30° downwind. On this heading *Gipsy Moth* went at racing speed, but of course this was unfortunate if the heading I wanted was 30° different. When I did discover this trick, it explained something else which had puzzled me. Normally, when sailing hard on the wind if you want to ease off 5 or 10°, the drill is to slack the mainsail sheet, and the heading will at once ease off a few degrees downwind. With *Gipsy Moth IV* it was necessary to do exactly the opposite; to head a few degrees *away* from the wind it was necessary to harden in the sails! What happened was that this changed the angle of heel, and she would romp off downwind at a great pace.

On September 23 I lunched off my first crop of cress grown on the premises, and very good it was, too, with Barmene, some mayonnaise, a little garlic and some raisins. I was determined to grow some more cress, but was worried by the appalling lethargy which seemed to swamp me. Anything that required remembering and doing twice daily (watering cress, for instance) seemed a burden. It was hot, too hot to stay on deck long during the heat of the day, and pretty hot below—83° at 5 P.M. It would have been nice below if I could have opened the skylights, but spray showered in at once. Added to all this, I found it a treble burden to do anything at all at a constant angle of heel between 20 and 30°. I refreshed myself by pouring buckets of sea water over me in the cockpit.

I could not stand the violent slamming which built up when the wind increased above 20 knots, and the 40° angle of heel was excessive. But I told myself that I had got to get used to this, for these South-East Trades are no zephyrs.

I decided to sort out my fruit, to remove anything that had gone bad. I found that I still had seven oranges, twelve apples, thirteen lemons and about a dozen grapefruit (but I forgot to count the grapefruit). Very little had gone bad. The fruits were in good nets, each piece wrapped in its own bit of tissue paper.

I tried, and failed, to call up Cape Town. The Cape Town operator said that he could hear me at Strength Two, and I could hear him faintly at times, but then a woman started a very loud strident talk, which drowned everything.

There were good moments too, though. The night of September 23–24 was lovely, and I felt that I could stay in the cockpit all night. *Gipsy Moth* was sailing beautifully, making 6⅔ knots. The moon's shadow was a perfect curve on the well-setting mainsail, and the water was smoothish, which meant little slamming. I reckoned that we should be on the wind for another 1,250 miles.

I had a triumph in getting my old electric clock to go again. I first had this clock in *Gipsy Moth II* in 1957, and it wintered each year in my bedroom at home. But it had stopped going. I turned the pressurised silicone spray into the regulating hole at the back and gave the works full blast. That started it again, and I hoped that it might have a new lease of life. I thought of Joshua Slocum and his one-handed clock which he boiled in oil.

September 24 was the end of my fourth week at sea. I had sailed 3,887 miles at an average speed of 138.6 miles per day. I broke my usual rule of not drinking until evening. It was a maddening day of setting and resetting sails and I could not get *Gipsy Moth* to hold the course I wanted. In the end in disgust I left her to it, and went below to have a late lunch, or early tea, of a gin and lime and my last bit but one of the Scottish Cheddar, some of the best cheese I have ever come across. I finished the fresh butter. I had kept the English brand till last, and none of it ever went rancid, which I thought pretty amazing in the tropics.

I had more trouble with the self-steering. The tiller line stranded, and I fitted a new one with some difficulty—it was like trying to control a half-broken horse without a bridle. I tinkered with the corner block, trying to improve the lead, but the difficulty was that as soon as I got on to the end of the counter *Gipsy Moth* would first try to shake me off, bucking to shake my teeth loose, then she would bring herself up into the wind until I had to make a rush for the tiller to avoid getting aback or in irons. I tallowed the tiller lines where they were chafing most, and wished I had thought of this before. I tried again to contact Cape Town by radio, but again a powerful woman's voice on the Cape Town frequency blotted out everything.

On Sunday, September 25, I was woken suddenly by the table clock capsizing on my belly. This stirred me into getting to work. *Gipsy Moth* was lying quietly, and although there were some heavy black clouds about, they were only a few. I unreefed the mainsail, and set the genoa staysail in place of the smaller one. Then I tackled a job that I'd been dodging for some time—the eggs.

I could not stand it any longer; either the cause of that stink would have to go overboard, or I should. So I turned out the box, and found sundry smashed ones, which had reached a nearly audible state of putridity. I was worried about my eggs. The beeswax coating which a friend had proposed for some of them seemed a big failure; the yolks were stuck to the shell inside, and some of the eggs had black spots, which I took for mildew, inside. However, I had an omelette from what I could get out of two, and it seemed pretty fair. The trouble with eggs is that one's imagination makes one feel sick at the suggestion of a bad egg, though it may be quite hale and hearty in fact. I tidied up the box, throwing out all broken or obviously bad ones, and hoped for the best.

The wind at this time seemed to blow up to Force 6 or so every night; I noticed that the barometer would drop two or three millibars in the afternoon, and then rise again after dark. On that Sunday night it blew up in the usual way, and I wondered if my full rig would ride it out. The going became "slammy" with a wind increase from 20 to 24 knots, but I decided that this was due to a black cloud passing overhead, and that the blow would not last long. It was a pity to disarrange the rig if it could be avoided. So I left things as they were, and all was well. The change in temperature as we sailed south was noticeable, and I began sleeping under a woollen blanket.

It was not comfortable sailing in the strong winds. Big "slams" would slow the boat right down, and then she would pinch up to windward as if the self-steering had been "forced." I thought, indeed, that this was what was happening, and I would go and give the self-steering a downwind twitch. I felt that I needed both a monkey and an elephant for supplementary crew—the monkey to tackle things when *Gipsy Moth* was heeled to 35° or more, and the elephant to take the helm when it got out of control in a squall.

On Monday night (September 26) I had just settled nicely in my berth, absorbed by Maigret and *La Grande Perche*, when there was a big bang astern. A big sail flap followed, and I thought that something in the self-steering gear had burst. I got on deck as fast as I could, but it was no weather to be there without a safety belt. I was relieved to find that it was only a tiller line which had broken. I robbed one of the spinnaker pole guys, and rigged that hoping that the old rope had just perished and that the new rope would hold. It was quite a long job, in a strong wind and rough sea, but I got it done and got back to my berth feeling so sleepy that I could hardly keep my eyes open. I was not allowed to sleep for long—*Gipsy Moth* was getting such a bashing that I could not stand it. I went on deck again and dropped the mainsail, and then I did manage to get a bit of rest.

I got up after a couple of hours, intending to go on deck and get the mainsail up again, but I decided to have a cup of hot chocolate first. The wind increased to 25 knots while I sipped my chocolate, so I hoisted the small staysail, and left the main down. That morning might have seen the end of the voyage as far as I was concerned, for I had a narrow escape in a nasty, though rather absurd, accident.

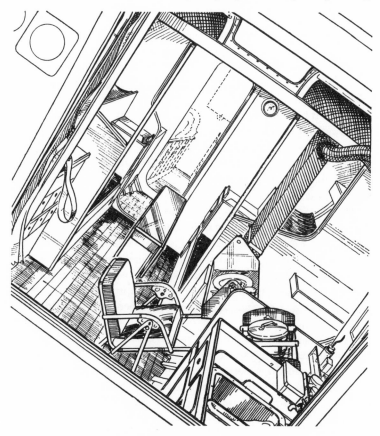

This is the cabin at an angle of heel of 35° to starboard. I once spent eight days heeled to port continuously like this.

The weather continued dirty, and *Gipsy Moth* was much thrown about. I went to the heads (lavatory) and the door was twice thrown open, and I pushed it shut. Without warning the door burst open again, smashed back downhill from behind me, and the handle struck me a crack on the forehead, sending my spectacles flying. The blow cut my head about two inches above my eye, and left me feeling nearly stunned. Amazingly, the spectacles were not damaged, and some dabbing with disinfectant seemed all that the cut needed. But my escape seemed a miracle—supposing that handle had caught me on the eye, after smashing through my glasses!

My big event next day was a shave. I could not use the mirror in the heads, because there was no means of keeping myself in position for shaving when *Gipsy Moth* was heeled over. So I used a bucket sitting in the lounge with a hand mirror. I mention this because some think that it is only a matter of picking up a razor to shave when sailing, and wonder why yachting men are so slovenly!

The heavy-duty bearings in the self-steering gear seemed to be clanking a lot, and I worried a good deal about the gear. There was so much of it to go wrong.

In spite of the efforts I had made to sort out my eggs, all was not well in the egg box. I couldn't stand the smell in the saloon, so I humped the box to the cockpit, and found a niche for them in the afterhatch. Fourteen dozen eggs, apart from whether they are bad, make quite a lumpy package to handle gingerly in roughish going. I believe that this big package (too big) was dropped en route to the boat or before sailing, and that the smell came mostly if not wholly from cracked eggs. Those eggs survived only a few days longer. The smell grew worse and worse, and finally I dumped the lot in the ocean, and watched the box dwindle to a speck as we sailed on. It isn't often one has to throw away the best part of fourteen dozen eggs. They were a loss.

Winding up the story of my eggs, I have got a little ahead of events. An odd thing happened in the afternoon after my shave. I decided to pump the bilge to check that the pump was working. I didn't expect to pump more than a few strokes, for I glance at the bilges regularly, and there was hardly any water there when I looked that morning. I began pumping more or less automatically and went on in a sort of daydream, until suddenly I became aware that I had been pumping for a long time. I thought that maybe one of the pump valves was not working properly and that I was just pumping the same water to and fro, so I went forward to hunt for a stick to poke the end of the pipe. I found water running out of the heads! I must have left the inlet seacock turned on when I gave up trying to shave there, and transferred myself, razor and shaving things to the cabin. The open seacock had been quietly filling up the boat ever since.

On my 32nd day out (September 28) I was 1,940 miles from where I should cross the Greenwich meridian at 40° S. *Cutty Sark*, on her 32nd day, was 1,900 miles from where she crossed the meridian. So I figured that the *Cutty Sark* was only some 40 miles ahead of me after 32 days. The weather grew much colder, and I began wearing woollen shirt and trousers below deck. I felt that the Antarctic was creeping up!

After my encouraging calculation about the *Cutty Sark* on September 28, the 29th began badly, with the discovery that the port aft settee locker was well flooded. I decided that this was due to the main boom flogging during a sail change which had caused the boom downhaul to draw an eyebolt partly from the deck. The mishap was a pity, because the locker was full of books, and they were all messed up. I took the precaution of pumping the bilge again, and found it took 35 strokes to clear it. I hoped that it was water from the heads which had not found its way aft when I had pumped out the day before.

After this work with the pump I noticed that I kept having to hitch up my pants. I measured my waist, and found that it was down to 30¾ inches—pretty ladylike, I thought. I had certainly lost weight, which didn't surprise me, but I wished that I could find more appetite for food. I enjoyed some of my meals, but there were many days when I had more or less to force myself to eat. I stood myself a gin, which was a mistake, for I found that gin usually seemed to bring a squall and hard work on deck.

This gin ran true to form, bringing a gale from 160°, roughly SSE, and a horrible sea. The gale came at me from where I wanted to go, so there was not much that I could do about it for a while. I tried to stay in my bunk, but was forced out by cramp in my right leg. Wary of the troubles that seem to be in store when I drink gin (or champagne) on board, I gave myself a brandy, hot, "with," for a change. I can't remember what Jorrocks meant by "with," but I think it was sugar and lemon. Anyway, mine was a very good drink to hearten a fellow. The gale moderated a bit, but there was still a rough sea, and we jogged along under reefed mizzen and spitfire jib. The brandy stimulated me to do some deckwork, and I greased and oiled two winches which had refused to work during the night. I also fixed another cord to the self-steering gear. This was most necessary work, for the winches and the self-steering gear had given me hell in a shemozzle during the night. What happened was that I did not think it would pay to tack, so turned in, to be awakened by the flap when the boat tacked herself. In the darkness the rattle and flap was enough to panic an elephant. I whipped on a lifeline harness round my waist, but had no time to dress, and arrived on deck barefooted in pyjamas. As the headsails were aback, I decided to accept the situation and leave the yacht on the port tack. Neither winch would work. Then the self-steering gear jibbed. The steering oar lay hard over to one side, and my most herculean hauling couldn't centre it. I had to fiddle with tiller lines to get the boat sailing again while I dealt with the self-steering. This was difficult, because while the self-steering was connected to the tiller, the load on the tiller was very great, and it was hard to cope by using tiller lines. And all the time I was struggling with torches, my powerful one to try to see what was wrong with the self-steering, and an ordinary one for the usual deckwork. At some time during all this, an empty bottle, left on the cockpit seat to dry for paraffin storage, was knocked off on to my toe (it gave me a black toe). This last incident did me good, for it emphasised the absurdity of taking it all too seriously. But I could scarcely be surprised at losing weight.

TOP: *Trials in the Solent, before reballasting.* (EILEEN RAMSEY/CHICHESTER ARCHIVE) BOTTOM: *Alone—sailing down the Channel.* (*SUNDAY TIMES*/ CHICHESTER ARCHIVE)

Top: *7½ knots and heeled over 35 degrees.* (CHICHESTER ARCHIVE) Bottom: *A glass of beer.* (SUNDAY TIMES/CHICHESTER ARCHIVE)

Showing the starboard pole with the 300 sq. ft. jib rigged instead of the 600 sq. ft. genoa. (CHICHESTER ARCHIVE)

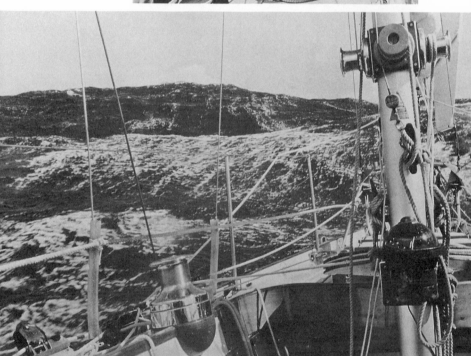

Top: *A wash.* (Chichester Archive) Bottom: *Snapshot from the cabin.* (Chichester Archive)

FIVE

WHISTLING FOR WIND AND RAIN

ON OCTOBER 1, five weeks out, I began to feel hungry again, and had a wonderful breakfast. I had slept well, and woke feeling properly rested. I went on deck and changed up the storm jib to the working jib. This gave me an appetite, and I found a flying fish on deck, provided for my breakfast. I cleaned and cooked the fish, and that breakfast stays in my memory. The menu was:

1 grapefruit (about one-quarter thrown away because of going
   bad)
2 potatoes fried up with the flying fish
2 slices of wholemeal toast with butter and marmalade
1½ mugs of coffee

When I had "rested" that lot, I went up and set some more sail. Between the 32nd and the 35th day out I had lost my good position relative to the *Cutty Sark*. She had terrific runs on her 33rd, 34th, and 35th days out compared with me, and from being only 40 miles behind her on the 33rd day I was 352 miles behind on the 35th. This was dispiriting, and sometimes I would feel really black despair for a while, when the whole boat seemed hopelessly too big to handle in troublous conditions. Being turned out of my bunk from sleep to cope with a crisis involving a lot of dirty hard work on deck made things seem at their worst. I used to think how different it would be if one were on watch in a crewed-up boat, waiting and ready to deal with any fresh conditions, however tough. These moods passed, and I always felt better when I managed to get a few hours of sound sleep. That would transform me, and I would cheerfully tackle any jobs that needed doing. I would water my garden, and sow seed in any vacant patch where I had cut the cress. There was music, too—how wonderful life can seem with the right circumstances *and* the right music! I would get Giles's tape-recorded concert going, and feel that I had been taking life too seriously, and worrying about things that didn't really matter.

The South-East Trade Wind held beyond its normal limit, giving me headwinds when, according to the averages, I should have had at least three days of north-easterlies, which, of course, would have enabled me to romp ahead instead of having a gale in my teeth.

In the evening of October 1 I was still in the South-East Trade Wind belt and I complained in my log that "it seems as if I am doomed to travel south for ever." It was a black night, and when I first went on deck the sky was as black as the sea, but my eyes gradually detected a difference. "Those deckhands on the clippers," I wrote, "had to know the ropes; no lights aloft for them. If one is on watch, it is amazing how much one can see in the black after a while, but those clipper crews had to turn out of their bunks in a hurry at times, just as I have to do; all hands on deck." But four hours later I sailed out of the Trade Wind. I could scarcely believe my eyes when I read east of south on the compass. For the first time since crossing the Equator I could head for the Greenwich Meridian at 40° S. I was then 300 miles south-east of Ilha da Trinidade.

The wind piped up to 24 knots and I thought that we were in for a blow from the north-east, so I eased all sheets and took two rolls out of the main. But I was wrong, because the wind dropped back to 18 knots. But *Gipsy Moth* was going nicely, and it was so wonderful to be laying the required course that I just stopped worrying. A bad mishap this day was that I lost my biggest and most important screwdriver overboard, trying to make some more jammed Lewmar gear work, this time the stop for the mainsheet slide.

On the night of October 2 I saw the Southern Cross for the first time since 1938, when I was coming home with Sheila from New Zealand. That was a thrill, though in the meantime one of the four stars of the Cross had become faint, which marred the handsome constellation.

I was now in a lonely part of the ocean which few ships use. I saw a large bird about 75 yards off—I think it was an albatross, but it might have been a mollyhawk. I hung up in the cabin Sheila's lovely silk scarf, with pictures of horse carriages on it. It looked gay and brightened the whole cabin.

On Monday, October 3, I sounded the freshwater tank and found that I had only 21 gallons left, plus half a jerrycan (about 2½ gallons) which Giles, my son, had made me take as a reserve. To be on the safe side and have a little in hand, I ignored this in my calculations. My diminishing water supply was worrying, but not critical. When I started I knew that I had not enough water on board to see me through the passage to Sydney; I had allowed myself enough for all reasonable needs for six weeks, relying on getting enough rain to fill my tanks before there could be any real chance of running short. But I underestimated my use of water, particularly for the twice-daily watering of my cress-garden. And so many things needed water—baking required it, and all dried vegetables, egg and milk powder wanted it. I could cook potatoes in sea water but not rice. With my underestimation of consumption, I seemed, too, to have overestimated the chances of rain, or at least my ability to catch it. Rain had come with the squalls from time to time, but not in catchable quantity, apparently. I realised, too, that I had made a mistake in my plans—the sort of mistake that can completely upset a long passage in a small boat, though it wouldn't matter at all for a passage of only a week or two. My water-collecting system relied on collecting rain from the mainsail by means of the hollow boom, from which I could pipe it into the tank. What I failed to take into account was that rain usually comes with a strong wind, when the mainsail is not set; or, if it is set, then salt spray is probably flying as well as the rain, thus ruining the water for drinking purposes. I ought to have made arrangements to pipe the water off the *mizzen* sail instead of the mainsail, because the mizzen is carried in rough conditions long after the mainsail has been dropped.

It is normally reckoned that a man can live well enough on half a gallon (four pints) of water a day; that is, of course, for drinking and preparing food—it allows nothing for washing oneself or one's clothes. Half a gallon a day was the old sailing ship allowance. At this ration my 21 gallons would last me 42 days—it seemed almost inconceivable that there would not be rain to help me out within that time. But I couldn't be *certain* of rain, and I was shaken to find that I had already been so long at sea without catchable rain. How long would my 21 gallons have to last? There was no knowing; suppose for some reason rain just didn't come, or I couldn't manage to catch rain? I hoped to be in Sydney in 100 days, which meant at least another 65 days at sea, but I might take 120 days, or 140. Or I might be dismasted, my radio put out of action, and drift for months in these unfrequented seas. Perhaps this was unlikely, but it could happen. I decided to make do on less than half a gallon a day, and to record every pint of water I used. If I could manage on a quart a day, I should have enough for 80 days.

As if to comfort me, there was a sharp rainsquall during the night, and at breakfast next morning I found enough rain in a jug I had left in the cockpit to mix an egg-powder omelette. Later that morning rain came again, and I hurried on deck to rig my plastic rain-collecting pipe from the boom. At once the rain stopped. Noon brought another sharp squall, again I rigged my rain pipe and collected about one pint of brackish water. I studied every drop as it flowed from the sail to the boom and into the collecting pipe, and I soon saw that the method of collection needed modifying. Rain ran off the mainsail into a trough by the mainsail slide track, but there were rivet holes in the track, and a lot of rain was being wasted by running through these holes. Between squalls I worked out a method of correcting this, and when the next squall came I managed to collect a bucketful (about 1½ gallons). Again it was brackish, but this seemed unavoidable, because of salt in the spray that came with the squall, and of salt from earlier spray on the sail. However, the water was drinkable if I did not drink too much at one time, and it could be used for cooking. I felt sure that about two hours of good, steady rain would clear the salt, and fill my tanks with fresh water.

But two hours of good steady rain did not come. There was some rain, but either it came in squalls with too much spray to make it worth collecting, or it came with high winds that forced me to take in the mainsail, so that there was no means of collecting it. By October 14 I was down to 16 gallons (plus the half-jerrycan of Giles's reserve). Considering that I had "won" 1½ gallons in the squall on October 4, that meant that I was still using rather more water than I reckoned. I rationed myself more strictly.

Though concerned for water, I was not worried about food, for my food was lasting well. True, I was using up some of the things that I liked best. I finished my last grapefruit, and my last orange. As I enjoyed that last orange I reflected that it had come from South Africa, and so had had nearly a round trip. On October 14 I ate the last of my potatoes, and much regretted that I had not brought more, for they are one of my favourite foods, and had kept well. The loss of my fourteen dozen eggs was a sad bereavement, but I had powdered eggs. I had powdered potato, too, but both egg powder and potato powder needed water before I could use them, so that I was rationed in their use. Looking back, I am sure that the real trouble about my feeding at this stage of the passage was that I was being starved of protein, had I known it.

Those rainless days had compensations, for they were mostly pleasant weather, with clear skies and calm seas. I was frustrated at not being able to sail faster, but I could be philosophical and enjoy the weather. I saw lots of birds, and always enjoyed watching them. I appointed myself a judge at a birds' sports day, and awarded first prize for graceful flight to the Cape Pigeons. I saw several albatrosses, but in that part of the ocean they were small birds, none bigger than about 4 feet across. They must be beginners, I thought, with the big birds all away, nesting. There were a number of chocolate-brown birds that followed the yacht. I think they were a kind of petrel that clipper sailors called "Cape Hen." Sometimes they would settle on the water together, and chitter-chatter away, looking very much like hens. But they were not as domestic as they looked, and I saw one of them attack a Mother Carey's Chicken.

I was half-excited, half-alarmed when a big mammal swam fast across the stern. At first I thought it was a killer whale. These fierce creatures kill other whales by jumping on their backs until they are exhausted. I wondered what I would do if a killer whale started jumping on *Gipsy Moth*. It was not a pleasant thought, and I kept a Very pistol handy, hoping to scare him off. Whether he was a killer whale or not, I don't know.

All this time, as well as being concerned about water I was worried about current for my batteries. I had an alternator, but could not get a proper charge from it. And to charge at all, I used too much fuel. The second week of October I had only ten gallons left; not enough, I feared, to see me through. Priority in using the batteries must go to the radio, so I rationed all other use of electricity severely, and did not allow myself electric light. There was something wrong with the charging system, and it was hard to know what I ought to try to do. On October 7 I had found two short-circuits, one between heavy-duty wires and the alternator casing, the other three inches away between two light wires entering the alternator. I badly needed technical advice on how to correct these things, or whether I ought to disconnect the alternator altogether and connect the batteries directly to the generator. But radio contacts were so poor that it was as much as I could do to report my position, and I could not get through what had to be a fairly complicated message about the behaviour of the generator and alternator. At last, after nearly a month of poor or frustrated communications, I made a good contact with Cape Town and sent a message to John Fairhall of *The Guardian* explaining my troubles with the machinery and asking him to get advice from the makers for me. On October 14 the replies came.

I was on the radio telephone for over an hour, and finished with limp nerves. The speaker at Cape Town had a low, deepish voice, and it was terribly hard to hear what he said as he read out a long telegram from John Fairhall with top advice from the motor engineers. It seemed very complicated, and took ages to get the words correctly to me, some technical words which I did not know the meaning of, or which were not associated with neighbouring words in the text. I turned in tired and depressed, but was up at 06.45 next morning, to the cheerful sound of rain. It soon stopped, but not before I had been able to make a pot of tea with freshly caught rain. After deckwork and sail trimming I tackled the electrical work. One sentence in John Fairhall's telegram asked if I had checked the drive belts for the alternator for tightness. I hadn't, because at Plymouth the alternator had been taken out on purpose to get the belts running true and taut. I searched through all the maker's handbooks, and found a test for showing whether a belt was tight enough. Mine were not. Sid Mashford at Plymouth had given me a special tool for tensioning the belts, and I decided to tighten them all to specification before having a go at dismantling the alternator. I started up, and got 22 amps charge. There was tremendous joy in the ship! I had found the cause of the trouble. At the same time, I felt a proper Charley for not having spotted it. The truth is that I hate motors on a sailing ship and resent them, and therefore neglect them.

The electrical drought and the water drought ended together, and that evening I lay comfortably in my bunk, reading by electric light and listening to the lovely sound of rainwater running into the tanks. I had the luck to find among my books a Maigret which I had not read. I am a great fan of Simenon; I think his creation of personality and atmosphere is hardly equalled. Unlike those dreary American novels with miles of detailed description making one cudgel one's brain to get a feeling of personality, Simenon achieves a powerful result with a few words. I regretted only that I had not brought my French dictionary, as there were occasional words of modern idiom or slang that I did not know.

In spite of my worries about water and the batteries I felt fitter, and found myself less exhausted after hard work than at the start of the passage. Then I was in a feeble, unfit state, and I found it amusing to reflect that I had spent a month in the South of France in February on purpose to get super-fit. Too much planning often goes wrong and upsets things. I suppose one must do things in one's stride without great extra effort for the successful achievement of an objective. I would talk to myself in this strain from time to time while I was doing things. I had a return of cramp in my leg, and decided that this was due to neglecting my daily drink of sea water. It is important that one should have enough salt, and the body soon feels the lack of it.

Calms were the very devil, and sometimes it could feel quite creepy as I sat or lay alone in the cabin. The little noises seemed to be in a deathly silence in vast space, the bulkhead at my shoulder creaking, a block creaking. Day after day I waited for a big wind switch to a westerly. This was when I felt the lack of a crew, to take advantage of every light air, to tack again and again to get the best heading. There were limits to the number of tacks that I could make, because I had to get some sleep. And tacking was a laborious business, for without a helmsman every change meant altering and resetting the self-steering gear.

In eight days (October 5–12) the *Cutty Sark* had gained 1,140 miles on me. My luck seemed to be at the ebb, and I had the worst possible sailing conditions (barring storms) for speed. The wind would be either dead ahead, coming from precisely where I wanted to go, or light zephyrs alternating with calms. I thought wryly of the *Cutty Sark* down south in the big winds, going like smoke.

I felt that I had made a big tactical blunder, getting myself on the wrong side (north side) of a huge high-pressure system. I had to travel as near southwards as I could, to cross the centre and to get east-going winds; anything with some west in it would do. I felt like a fly in the middle of a huge spider's web. I also felt that I had been stupid, for this "high" was well known, and fully shown on the US Hydrographic Chart, and on the pressure chartlets of the Admiralty Pilot for Africa. But though I felt a fool to have got into this "high," I comforted myself with the reflection that it is very easy to see the right thing afterwards; had I tried to avoid it, it would probably have moved to where I did go, etc., etc. I found it hard to get the hang of that gigantic weather system. I tried to determine what shape the "high" was, and just could not make it out. Judging by the winds that sometimes came it would seem that I was really passing south of a "low," but how could that be with the pleasant, sunny weather and a barometer reading of 1035? It was all extremely puzzling.

Gipsy Moth ghosted along, the tiller often needing my handling; I wished I had my old Miranda self-steering from Gipsy Moth III for work in those light airs. Gipsy Moth sailed on, and mostly in the right direction, though once I came on deck and found her headed back north-west! She sailed through several oily smooth patches of sea, about thirty yards across, with bubbles dotting the surface here and there. I don't know what they were. If one can call a "high" a hole, what I wanted was to get out of that hellhole as soon as possible, reckoning that I must find more wind once across the belt of calms and fickle airs. So I did all I could to keep up the yacht's speed, unless the heading was wildly astray from where I wanted to go.

From time to time this relatively gentle if frustrating existence would be interrupted by squalls. They seldom lasted long, but were fierce, and I would have to take in sail. When the squall had passed, I would have to put back the sail I had just taken in, for I was determined not to lose speed by carrying too little. Sail setting and changing went on all the time, and once I totted up that I had handled 4,700 square feet of sail that day. Here is a fairly typical extract from my log (for October 13):

• • •

"0605. Port pole and sail down and pole housed. Speed 5.4 k.

"0610. Mizzen staysail down. Speed 4.2 k.

"0627. Gybed. Speed 5.1 k. on other gybe.

"0643. Mizzen staysail hoisted for opposite gybe. 6 k.

"0705. Big genny rigged on starboard side dropped. I had to drop it because five or six hanks were off the stay. Changed sheet to port-rigged genny and hoisted that.

"0747. Starboard spinnaker pole rigged and sail rehanked. One damaged hank repaired. Sail hoisted O.K., but difficulty with self-steering. Took some time trimming it before it would hold the ship to course. The load on each tiller line has to be adjusted carefully.

"0807. Mizzen staysail dropped and rehoisted because of twisted tack pennant. Poled-out sail trimmed.

"0810. Gybing completed. I hope a wind change does not require me to do it all again! Now a sun sight, and then I hope for some breakfast, for which I am full (or empty!) ready.

• • •

I was lucky that day, for the wind held fairly well until noon. But then it started backing, and at 13.00 both the poled-out genny and the mizzen staysail had to come down. As I handed the genny and housed the pole, the wind veered, so that a poled-out sail would have been just the thing! Crestfallen, I was wearily contemplating going through the whole process once more, when the wind backed again, and justified dropping the sail. A poled-out sail only just holding the wind and occasionally set aback is no sail to have up when one is singlehanded and in need of rest.

That Benguela High or whatever it might be called meant slow sailing, but it also gave me some good sleeping, and I would wake from a sound sleep feeling much refreshed and ready to tackle anything. I would scrub the galley stove, sweep the galley floor, and hang out all my towels and dishcloths to be aired. One day I gave myself treacle pudding for dinner. I had the pudding in a tin, but it required 40 minutes' boiling. However, I was set on it, so I gave it the full time, and finished off the whole pudding with plenty of golden syrup. Meals did not always go so well. The day after my orgy of treacle pudding I dined more modestly on a slice of bread and jam, and in the middle of my bread and jam—while my knife was in the bread—a breeze got up, whang! Before I could get into the cockpit *Gipsy Moth* was aback, and I had to tack and sail west until I could tack back. My modest dinner took a long time that day!

The ending of my fears of water shortage, and the restoration of the alternator which gave me back electricity, brought a new spirit of optimism to the voyage. *Gipsy Moth* seemed to catch it, for after the worst week's sailing of the voyage we crossed 40° S and the Roaring Forties began at least to coo, if not yet to roar. It was time to "turn left," for 7,000 miles of running down the easting on the clipper way, one of the greatest sails in the world. Seven thousand miles in a straight line (rhumb line)—there are not many places in the world where that could happen.

SIX

THE ROARING FORTIES

WORKING UP my sights at noon on October 18 I found that I was well over half way to Australia—at noon that day I had sailed 7,300 miles, and had 6,570 miles to go to Sydney Heads. As if to celebrate this achievement the day changed like magic from grey with misty low clouds and overcast to a bright blue clear sky, with a darker, but still bright, blue sea. Sunshine, however, did not free me from work. I had trouble with the genoa hanks which were always coming unfastened, and the big sail had to come down so that I could refasten them. I had to leave this operation with the sail down, because just before the hanks unfastened themselves I had been making ready dough for baking, and I had to rush to get it into the baking oven before it fell flat. I left the bread safely baking and went back on deck. I changed the big genoa for the 300-footer jib, and found that the yacht went better for the change. The wind was veering, and the mizzen staysail had to come down to sail nearer to the wind. Dropping that mizzen staysail I was nearly lifted off my feet—it is amazing how the strength of the wind can creep up without one's noticing.

There were thousands of prions flying about. These are lovely birds, silvery white seen from below, and a soft whitish grey seen from above. They swoop fast over the waves, resembling swallows. I never saw one pick up anything, but there must be something in the sea for them to eat. They did not seem interested in *Gipsy Moth*—probably they thought her an incredibly slow and clumsy bird. A school of porpoises played around the bows while I was struggling with the sail, but I made rather a noise with the mizzen staysail as it came down, and in a flash they disappeared.

When all the sails were trimmed *Gipsy Moth* was on a close reach, and went beautifully. It was pleasant sailing through that sunny afternoon and evening, because the sails and blocks were asleep, and for what seemed the first time for many days my ears

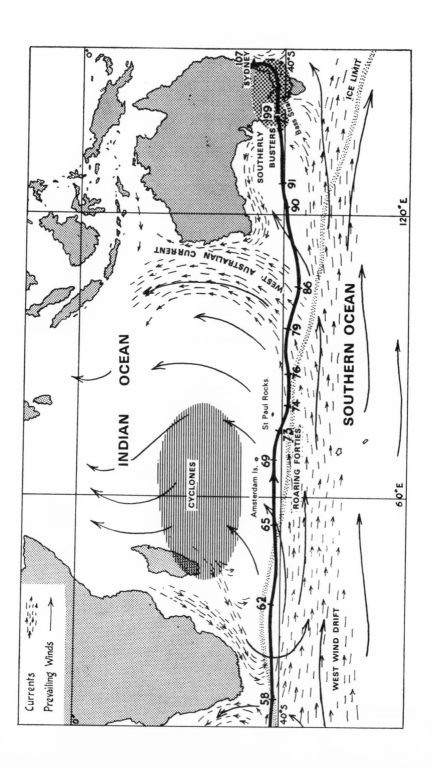

were not assailed by the cacophony of barking blocks and cracking sails. The ship sailed as if she were satisfied—to me this is like being on a good horse, riding fast, but within her strength.

I put away my South Atlantic charts, and got out the charts for the Indian Ocean. There were not many straight charts, but US Hydrographic Office pilot charts, British Met Office current charts, a gnomonic chart, and plotting chart sheets. It was quite a thrill to shift from one ocean to another. It is not often that a yachtsman changes oceans in one voyage!

I was rounding the Cape of Good Hope, though well to the south of it, and the weather grew more boisterous. The Forties really were beginning to roar, with strong winds increasing suddenly to gale force. I was bothered still with cramp in my leg, and began to suffer from lack of rest. On the night of October 19–20 at 2.30 A.M. I fell into a sound sleep for what seemed the first time for ages, but just after 4.30 A.M. I had a rude awakening. A dollop of water from a wave coming on board landed on the head of my bunk, and it was followed quickly by a second and a third. It was my own fault, for leaving out the top washboard of the companionway into the cabin, but this did not make it any more pleasant. I got up at once, dressed, dropped the spitfire jib, and turned dead downwind, because I thought *Gipsy Moth* would run dead before the wind under bare poles. Conditions were rugged on deck, with a lot of wind and water, both sea and heavy rain. I had to make sure of a good grip handy all the time, because of the rolling, and the seas pitching into the hull. After dropping the sail I felt seasick, and went below again to lie down, and try to get some more sleep. It was no good. No sooner had I undressed from my deck clothes than *Gipsy Moth* broached to, and I had to scramble into all my deck gear again and get back on deck as quickly as I could. *Gipsy Moth* had been slewed round broadside on to the waves, and she refused to answer the helm to take up any other heading. I noticed that the self-steering vane had apparently slipped, and was no longer trying to turn the rudder. I decided to stream a drogue from the stern, in the hope of bringing the stern to the wind. This I did, after collecting a shackle, a swivel, some rope from the afterpeak and the drogue from the forepeak. It didn't work; the yacht had not enough way on her to give the drogue the power to haul the stern round.

Gipsy Moth under bare poles in a gale would do nothing but lie ahull, broadside on to wind and waves. I was convinced by what had happened that she could not be made to run downwind under bare poles in a seaway. The rudder could not control her without a storm jib on the foremast stay. This was a serious setback; it meant that her slowest speed running downwind in a gale would be 8 knots. I had never even considered that such a thing could happen! *Gipsy Moth III* had steered easily downwind under bare poles, or even with the wind on the quarter, and the American-designed *Figaro* had steered lightly and easily when we brought her up the English Channel one night under bare poles in a strong gale.

It was damnably uncomfortable. The wind went up to 55 knots, and the yacht was thrown about in all directions. Water kept forcing its way under the cabin hatch whenever a wave hit the deck. My sextant, which I stowed for safety in a cabin berth—fortunately in its box—was thrown out on to the cabin floor. I had one wave come right over me when I was in the cockpit; the water felt oddly warm, and the wave did not seem to strike with much force, I suppose because we were not moving. The air was biting cold with hail.

The self-steering vane was damaged. It had sheared the bolt and pin holding it to its upright mast or shaft, and I thought it remarkable that it had not blown away altogether. I could make no attempt at repair then, because it was impossible to work on it in that high wind and very rough sea. All I could do was to lash it up temporarily.

The storm went on all day. From time to time the wind would seem to ease a little, and I would go on deck to see if I could do anything with the self-steering gear. In one such interval I managed to dismantle the self-steering oar and haul it inboard, because it was getting such a pounding from the waves. It seemed amazing that the vane had not taken off into the air. But always after these lulls the wind came back again, and I could make no start on repairs. The seabirds got very excited about the drogue churning up white water astern. Watching their flight against the strong wind took my mind off my own miseries. They seemed to creep up the sides of the waves uphill, very close to the water. At three o'clock in the afternoon the birds lost whatever entertainment they had had from my drogue, because the warp attached to it parted, and the drogue went.

A big breaking wave struck *Gipsy Moth* and turned her right round, so that she faced north-west. I could do nothing to get her back without setting a sail, and it was too rough for making sail. I felt that it did not matter much which way she was headed because although we were being flung about all over the place, it was hard to tell if *Gipsy Moth* was moving through the water at all.

By that time I had not had anything to eat for twenty-four hours, and still I did not feel hungry. I scribbled in my log: "It is the queasiness which kills appetite, I think. This is not my merriest day, but it might be worse. It is very cold out."

By nightfall I managed to get the yacht going again. At last the wind lulled for long enough to enable me to raise the little spitfire jib, and I gybed round. I contrived a very temporary repair of the self-steering with cordage, but it was not doing a job—the self-steering oar was still on deck. I set the tiller to take advantage of the fact that *Gipsy Moth* liked to lie beam on to the wind, and I left things at that until next morning. It was still appallingly uncomfortable, but we were sailing. The seas were impressive. If I looked up while working on deck I felt that I had to hang on for dear life. It seemed impossible for the monster rolling down on top of us not to submerge boat and all. But always *Gipsy Moth* rode up again. Some waves I called "strikers"—they would slam into the yacht viciously. I think these were waves which started to break about 25 yards from the boat. They looked about 100 feet high, some of them, so I dare say they were about 40 feet. They treated the boat like a cork, slewing it round and rolling it on its side. I would trim the self-steering gear and go below, only to find the heading 40° off what it should have been, so back I would have to go, to retrim the self-steering gear. I decided that the big waves, slewing the boat through an angle of 45–60°, must make things impossible for the self-steering gear.

Gipsy Moth's third vice was taking effect; she could not keep to her heading at the top of a wave face, but whipped round and broached to, lying broadside on to the wind and the waves. Sometimes the self-steering gear could bring her back on to her right heading, but often when the wind vane was suddenly swung 60° across the gale force wind, the pressure on it was too great; if the safety clutch had not given way, the vane must have broken. Broaching-to was the danger that was most dreaded by the clippers. Slewing round, broadside on to a big Southern Ocean storm, they would roll their masts down, and, if the sails went into the water, they were likely to founder, as many did. Leaving the danger aside (which, anyway, I did not consider as great for *Gipsy Moth* as for the clippers because *Gipsy Moth* ought to survive a knockdown which would cause a clipper to founder) those broachings seriously threatened the self-steering gear. To cut down the broaching, I was forced to cut down the amount of sail that I would have carried in north-

ern waters. This was a big setback to my plans, because I had reckoned on making long runs in the westerlies down south. I had
hoped, before I started the voyage, that a long light boat, which
Gipsy Moth was designed to be, would knock off runs of 250 miles,
day after day. I am not a designer myself, and my opinion as to the
cause of this trick of *Gipsy Moth*'s may not be of value, but I did
have a long experience of the boat and, in my opinion, her tendency
to flip round as easily as a whip is cracked was due to her having too
short a forefoot, and no grip on the water there, combined with an
unbalance of the hull which required an excessive load on the tiller
to activate the rudder.

There were leak drips everywhere, and I made a list of them:

LEAKS
Doghouse post over sink
Doghouse post over Primus
Doghouse join about Primus v. bad
Post above head of quarter berth
Cabin hatch lets water in freely, both sides (according to heel)
All bolts holding companion hatch cover leak
Foot of quarter berth under outboard edge of the cockpit seat
From deck beside head of portside berth in cabin
Starboard forward locker—everything wet through
Seacock in cloakroom
Both ventilators when closed

I had to force myself to eat something to keep up my strength,
so I had a chew at some mint-cake. It was not a very successful
meal, for in biting on a piece of the mint-cake a tooth broke in half.
Luckily my tongue recognised the bit of broken tooth as not mint-
cake, and I did not swallow it, but recovered it in the hope of later
repairs. Nigel Forbes, my dentist, had given me a dental repair kit,
and now had come the time to use it. But I could not tackle den-
tistry then and there, because it was still too rough. I cleaned and
scraped the broken bit as per instructions, and wrapped it up safely
to await a session in *Gipsy Moth*'s do-it-yourself dental chair. I made
myself a cup of tea and turned in.

I was up two or three times during the night to tend the tiller
lines. I wanted to try to keep heading 90° off the wind, but I did *not*
want a gybe. There seemed to be a devil of a lot of strong wind
about, but I was able to snooze a bit, after a fashion. Around six
o'clock in the morning *Gipsy Moth* did gybe, and began rolling

madly. I found that she was headed WNW. It looked cold and unfriendly outside, but I had to get on with repairs to the self-steering—clearly I could not go on like this. It took me an hour to dress, make tea, collect my tools and generally screw myself up to make a start. The rolling was frightful, and I felt as feeble as a half-dead mouse. I turn to my log for some two hours later:

• • •

"0909. Well, there we are. The vane is repaired, the self-steering oar in the water and in charge of the ship, the mizzen and genoa staysail are set. Of course the wind has dropped now and more sail is needed to move, but I am on strike and intend to have some breakfast first. After a 40–50 knot gale the sea is monstrously lumpy, and it was no picnic repairing the vane sticking out beyond the end of the boat. But it might have been a lot worse. The coffee is made, here's to it."

• • •

That day I had a successful radio transmission with Cape Town, and felt much the better for it. Throughout this part of the voyage I was harassed by poor radio conditions, and it was always an immense relief to get through a message to the newspapers that were helping to make my voyage possible. When I failed to make R/T contact I would worry about it, for I hated not being able to do what I had said I would do. In poor conditions even a successful R/T transmission could be a strain. It might take an hour and twenty minutes to get off a 250-word cable. That used to take the stuffing out of me.

With conditions a bit better I felt some return of appetite, and my log records a notable meal on Saturday, October 22:

• • •

"Ai, but that was good, that breakfast! A mug of hot chocolate and sugar, dried bananas and wheat, onion pancake (aimed at omelette with dried eggs!), home-baked wholewheat toast and lime marmalade, mug of coffee."

• • •

I got out my dentist's repair kit, and spent an hour having a go at my tooth. I succeeded in cementing the broken piece on again, but in doing so I cemented in a fragment of cotton wool from a cotton wool pad I had put in my mouth to keep my tongue away from my tooth while I was working on it. I left the bit of cotton wool in the repair—I felt I dared not pull it for fear of pulling off the piece of tooth I had managed to stick on.

I found a handsome six-inch squid on deck. It had attractive, variegated colouring rather like tortoiseshell, not at all like the pallid ones I had met before. It seemed just the thing for a good bouillabaisse, but I couldn't face eating it.

Birds continued to bring much interest to my life. The prions would cavort madly round the yacht. They seemed to like flying through the wind shadows of the sails—I suppose the turbulence must be unexpected and intriguing. I threw out some old wheat grains, but they did not appear interested. When emptying my gash bucket of scraps I would bang it on the rail, and that would bring along the Cape Hens (white-chinned petrels). They would alight and pick over the scraps. I had a feeling of meanness every time this happened—compared with the waste from a liner, my vegetable scraps, perhaps no more than a dessertspoonful, because I harboured my stores carefully, must have disgusted them.

At this time, too, I began to meet *real* albatrosses; not that my earlier albatrosses, or the birds I called albatrosses, weren't real, but they seemed tiny compared with the big fellows I met now. One beautiful bird soared by with a wing-span that must have been at least eight feet across.

Alas, my tooth-repair did not hold. I tried it out at supper time, and it was no good—the broken bit simply came off again as soon as I tried to bite. Perhaps the best dentists do not mix cotton wool with their cement. I had another shot at cementing, this time without cotton wool fragments, but the repair was no more successful. In the end I got a file and filed down the jagged edges of the piece of tooth still in my jaw, and left it at that.

What had I expected from the Roaring Forties? They are not seas that many yachtsmen frequent; indeed, few ships of any sort go there now, because with steam and the Suez Canal the modern route to Australia is quite different. From my reading of the clipper logs I had an impression of a steady, surging wind, strong, driving ships day after day on towards the east. Of course, life is never quite like the tidy pattern that imagination makes of it. The clippers had great passages, and it is these that stay in the memory, but they had days (and weeks) of exasperating frustration too. Then one can gain a quite misleading impression of the seas from the logs of big ships—compared with *Gipsy Moth*, *Cutty Sark*, *Thermopylae* and their peers were all enormous. A gale that forced me, singlehanded, to lie ahull, at the mercy of wind and sea, to them might have been a good sailing breeze. I knew enough of singlehanded sailing in small boats to have assessed these things rationally, but rational assessment, and emotional preparation for the reality of something in life, are by no means the same. From my reading, and study of the clipper passages, I had expected the Forties above all else to be *steady*. That is just what they were not—it seemed luff and puff, luff and puff all the time. But it was luff and puff with a difference, nothing gentle about it; the difference, one might say, between the playful games of a kitten, and the gambolling of a tiger cub. The squalls with which the weather, as it were, changed gear, were not a nice gentle change from, say, 20 mph in a car to 25–30 mph. They were like a fierce racing changing from 20 to 90–110 mph. Another thing which I find hard to describe, even to put into words at all, was the spiritual loneliness of this empty quarter of the world. I had been used to the North Atlantic, fierce and sometimes awesome, yes, but the North Atlantic seems to have a spiritual atmosphere as if teeming with the spirits of the men who sailed and died there. Down here in the Southern Ocean it was a great void. I seemed planetary distances away from the rest of mankind.

Just as I was getting ready for breakfast on Sunday, October 23, I had a bad shaking. In England before I left, Sheila Scott had given me a toy koala bear, and it lived on a perch beside my Marconi set. It was always falling off its perch and that morning, as so many times before, I went to pick it up. I was holding the bear with one hand and making my way across the cabin from handgrip to handgrip with the other, when a violent lurch caught me between handgrips and threw me hard against the table. When I picked myself up a place in my ribs under my right arm felt very sore. I thought some ribs must be broken though I could find nothing wrong. The same old lesson was driven home to me forcibly again—*never to move about below without one handgrip, or at least an eye on the next one, so that it can be grabbed instantly if the boat lurches.* Those lurches, as a beam wave caught her, made *Gipsy Moth* move like a whip cracking. I consoled myself for my sore rib with the reflection that I might have been much more seriously hurt, and that the accident would have done good if it made me remember the lesson about holding on.

When I had recovered from my shaking and had some breakfast I went on deck to replace the trysail with the main. The wind seemed lessening, and I felt that *Gipsy Moth* needed the main. I did not like that main, it was my least favourite sail. For one thing, it required too much brute force to handle, for it was always pressing against a shroud or binding on a sheet; for another, I had to trot to and fro from mast to cockpit about six times during the hoisting. First I had to slack away the vangs as the sail began to rise; then to alter the self-steering trim to head more into the wind so that the head of the sail would not foul the lower aft shroud; then several times to slack away the sheet as the sail went up. After that the lower shroud runner had to be released, and the shroud tied forward to another shroud. Why, then, did I use the mainsail? Well, it was double the area of the trysail and had much more drive, and when I did get it up and trimmed, it set better. Furthermore, it was my collecting-sail for rain, and I needed more rainwater in my tanks. But man is adaptable, and before the end of the voyage I had devised a method of raising the mainsail in a Force 6 when going downwind with no trouble at all!

That evening I was involved in a silly accident to the rigging. I had the starboard levered shroud, which was slacked off, tied forward to another shroud with the lever released, so that the wire should not chafe the mainsail. Gradually the tie worked its way up the two shrouds, until it nearly reached the lower crosstree. As a result, I could not tauten the shroud with the lever when I needed to. I tried for half an hour to get down the tie with a boathook, but I could not shift it. Then it got dark, and I decided to leave it until daylight, when I intended to go up the mast to free it. During the night I worried about the safety of the mast with an un-tautened shroud and at 01.30 in the morning I got up and shone a torch on the mast. It looked quite unmoved, but I dared not come up closer to the wind, which I wanted to do. At 05.30 I went on deck to tackle the shroud, and determined to have one more try at freeing it before climbing the mast. I got my long burgee stick (5 feet 6 inches) and taped a foot-long carving knife to it. The knife had a sharp, narrow blade—I had carried it on board various boats for at least ten years, and this was the first time I had ever used it. By standing on the main boom, I could make the knife just reach the nylon tie binding the two shrouds together. I sawed and stabbed at it with the knife, and after a somewhat lengthy process I contrived to cut it through.

While I worked at the shroud, *Gipsy Moth* galloped along on a grey-green sea. There was too much heel for comfort, but I left the mainsail up, because I expected the wind to veer and free the boat, and I went below to try for a little more sleep. Alas, I was wrong, for instead of veering the wind backed, and soon *Gipsy Moth* was hard on the wind coming from the south-east. I sweated up the main to get it setting better, and felt most unfairly treated, because according to the US Pilot Charts a south-east wind should have been pretty rare in that area of sea. I wrote in the log: "What an indignity to have to cope with an east wind in the Roaring Forties."

For the next twenty-four hours the wind went on backing, with intervals of light, fluky airs, or all but calm. I was up and down at the sails, constantly fiddling at the trim to get the best out of the yacht, and became drowsy and doped with fatigue. At last, during the morning of October 25, the wind began to return to the west, and as it did so, it increased in strength. Suddenly, there was a major crisis. I suppose I should not have let myself get caught, but due to fatigue I was not at my best for dealing with emergencies. As I was trying to eat some breakfast, a particularly fierce squall struck. I grabbed my padded coat and rushed into the cockpit—still in my "indoor" slip-on sheepskin boots—to turn downwind and run before it. With so much sail set I could not move the tiller, even with the help of cords after I had disengaged the wind vane. Later, I realised my mistake; I had released the self-steering vane, but I ought to have released the self-steering tiller lines to the rudder quadrant as well. I was pushing the tiller against the immense power of the self-steering oar locked to one side. I redoubled my efforts with the cords, and suddenly the tiller responded. Before I could check the turn, *Gipsy Moth* had gybed.

The boom came over with an almighty "wham," the vang tearing a stanchion out of the deck. As it came across, the mainsheet slide shot across the track rail, and tore out the permanent stop screwed to the end of the rail. The slide holding two parts of the mainsheet came off the rail or horse.

I gybed back again, because of the headsails being on the other gybe. I did not notice that when the boom crashed over to starboard the first time the topping lift from masthead to boom end had hooked up behind the upper crosstree. It was amazing, and a great tribute to the rigging and spars, that the crosstree did not carry away when I gybed back. All this time I was still in my "house" boots, bareheaded, and without a safety harness. Fortunately I had stowed away a spare harness in the cubby hole at the side of the cockpit. I struggled into this, took off my boots and dropped them into the cabin, thinking that I might as well keep them dry. I could not leave the cockpit in those boots, because without non-slip soles they would have been dangerous.

As soon as I had the tiller lashed so that it should give me sufficient time before gybing or tacking, I went forward along the deck in bare feet. I dropped the mainsail, letting most of it (the bunt) fall into the water—the boom was way out abeam. Then I dropped the genoa staysail, and the jib, in each case securing the halliard after removing it from the head of the sail—I did not want halliards winding round the crosstrees! I let the sails lie, partly in the water. As I left the cockpit I had freed the mizzen halliard, hoping that the sail would drop of itself. This it did not do, and was damaged. I told myself: "Never mind. It might have been much worse."

When I turned to the main boom I noticed the topping lift hooked up to the weather crosstree. First I furled and tied the sail in three places to reduce windage—it was blowing a stiff 45 knots— and then I brought the boom inboard by hauling on the weather vang. As soon as I could reach the end of the boom I freed the topping lift from it, and dropped the boom on deck, lashing it there. After that I hoisted the spitfire jib, and engaged the self-steering as soon as *Gipsy Moth* started moving again. I hurried over this for fear that the self-steering gear would be damaged while *Gipsy Moth* lay ahull. Waves knocking the gear from side to side shook the whole boat with shuddering bangs.

One's thoughts at these moments of crisis are sometimes curiously detached. My chief personal worry during the gybe and the troubles that followed it was that, without a cap to protect them, my spectacles would blow away. I had intended to have a washing bout that morning, and I reflected that at least my feet were getting their wash in advance.

SEVEN

OVERCOMING DISASTER

I BEGAN to understand why these lonely seas are called "The Roaring Forties." It is the noise of the wind in the rigging. I would not call it a roar exactly, but I know of no other way of describing it—a hard, compelling noise that seems unique to those latitudes. In the days of the clippers, with their forests of masts and rigging, the noise must have been awe-inspiring.

My sense of spiritual loneliness continued. This Southern Indian Ocean was like no sea I had met before. It is difficult to paint the picture with words of what it was like down in the Southern Ocean in those spring months. I have sailed across the North Atlantic six times, three times alone, and experienced winds up to 100 miles per hour (87 knots) there, but looking back it seemed so safe compared with this Southern Ocean stuff. This Southern Ocean was totally different; the seas were fierce, vicious and frightening. The boat was under big accelerations from the powerful, monumental waves. It was hard to say what the speed was. From the deck it seemed slow, but the foam on the water and the whole water surface were moving fast themselves, which made it difficult to judge.

The squally weather was beginning to form a pattern. Phrases such as this kept on recurring in the log:

• • •

"A 45 knotter threatened to flatten *Gipsy Moth*. I did not know if it was the start of another gale or what."

"There is a big sea running, and a big one coming under the boat slews her stern round now and then."

"It was so still below after dropping the genoa that I went up into the cockpit to see if we had stopped. It was still blowing 30 knots of wind, and we were sliding along at about 6½ knots."

"Rolling and strong sideways accelerations."

"Pretty rough going with strong winds."

"The moon shines bright between clouds as if to stress how ordinary all this is for her."

"Banging and slamming and throwing about all over the place—probably due to two or three different seas overriding each other."

• • •

The incessant squalls had one unexpected quality—often the sun would continue to shine brightly while the wind whipped the sea to fury. Somehow this didn't seem right. An Atlantic squall usually comes from a grey sky over a grey sea. The bright sunshine was good, but it seemed odd, and out of place. Why should the sun be out there enjoying himself, when conditions were so rugged for the rest of us?

The near-calms were the most exhausting ordeals for me. Time after time the ship would go about, with all the sails aback. I would have to wear round, and retrim the mainsail and mizzen. These near calms seemed to last seven or eight hours, and usually occurred at night. I would be up and down to the cockpit time after time for retrimming, and I would be lucky to get more than a couple of hours' sleep during the night. Each swell passing under the boat brought its own little wind during a near calm. First, the swell pushed the ship so that the sails were all aback as the crest passed under, then it made a wind from the opposite direction after the crest or summit had passed.

Aback, aback, aback—this is the constantly recurring entry in the log. Each time involved wearing the ship round and retrimming at least the mainsail and the mizzen, then half an hour to an hour coaxing the self-steering gear to take charge again. I attributed this trouble to the unbalance of the sails or hull, or both. A slight change of wind force would completely alter the balance, the boat would head off in a new direction, and the rudder was so hard to move that the self-steering gear could not cope with it. On October 29 the log reads:

• • •

"It is heartbreaking to have a lovely sailing breeze and fine sunny weather, to be sailing well off the wind and able only to do under 5 knots. The sea surface is pretty smooth really, yet *Gipsy Moth* splashes down, sending out great sheets of spray at the bows, and slows down for 3 rocks on 3 little waves. It is like a charging elephant being stopped by a fly whisk."

• • •

The seabirds continued to fascinate me. The albatrosses' legs and feet shook and shuddered each time they flew into the turbulent wind shadow downwind of the sails. In a storm, the birds seemed to climb very slowly up the face of a wave, as if walking up it. I wondered if they could get up *only* by using their feet or if they had to use their wings as well. Whenever I could, I tried to feed the albatrosses. I liked watching them alight. They would put down their feet to act first as an air-brake, and then to stop them on the water.

Twice I entered the Forties, and was driven out by a gale. A 50-knot squall going through was like the infernal regions, with great white monsters bearing down out of a black void, picking up the boat and dashing it about. I hated the feeling of being out of control. Once a wave broke in the cockpit, not seriously, but the immense power it showed was frightening. I wrote: "It requires a Dr Johnson to describe this life. I should add that the cabin floor is all running wet, and my clothes are beginning to get pretty wet too. Vive le yachting!"

On November 2 I could not understand why *Gipsy Moth* nearly gybed time after time. Several times I reached the companion just in time to push the tiller over (leaning out from the cabin) at the gybing point. If she had gybed in that wind with the boom right out, there would have been chaos and damage. Then the boat would come up to wind until the wind was abeam. I began to fear that something had broken in the self-steering gear, so put on a coat and went to investigate. I found that the self-steering gear was not connected to the rudder at all; the link arm between the wind vane and the steering oar had pulled out of its socket after shaking out the safety pin somehow. I was thankful it was no worse. That day my speedometer packed up. At first I was surprised how much I missed it, but as things turned out it did not matter much, for I found that my dead reckoning was as accurate as it had been when the speedometer was working. As a matter of fact, it was more accurate, because the speedometer had been underregistering at low speeds. Perhaps this was because the little propeller of the speedometer's underwater unit was getting foul with marine growth. After I had got over the feeling of loss when the speedometer failed, it was quite a relief not to have it. There was certainly more peace in not eyeing the speed all the time, wondering if it could be improved.

On November 3 I had been three days without a sun sight, three days of "blind going" as the clipper navigators called it. This was just what I hoped would not occur when I was approaching Bass Strait, with no position fix since Madeira. With strong currents during the gales, no wonder so many clippers were wrecked there. In the afternoon of the 3rd I got a sun sight for longitude. This gave a day's run of 227 miles, but again this depended on the dead reckoning being correct for the two previous days when the runs had been 155 and 138.

I wondered how much more speed I should have made if I had not got the high-powered radio telephone on board, and did not have to use it. My log is full of entries such as this: "Long R/T contact with Cape Town. I feel absolutely flattened out." Apart from the effort of transmitting and writing out reports, there was the matter of the great weight which had to be carried to operate the telephone. There was the weight of the radio telephone itself, which was four feet or so above the waterline, and therefore badly placed for the stability of the boat. Then there were the heavy batteries, the alternator for charging the batteries at high amperage, fuel for the charging motor, earthing plates down to the keel of the boat, two backstays rigged with big insulators top and bottom for transmitting aerials. On top of all this was the negative effect of transmitting; time after time I would delay sail setting because a radio telephone schedule was coming up during the next hour. Altogether the effect on the performance of the boat was considerable.

November 3 brought the first real fog of the passage, with visibility down to about 100 yards. I had both flames of my Aladdin stove lit and full on, trying to dry out the inside of the boat which was oozing water everywhere. My rain-collecting system went on sending down water collected from the fog—no smoke particles there! It rained a good deal when it wasn't foggy, and by November 4 I had collected 27 gallons of fresh water in my tank. That made me secure as far as water for drinking and cooking was concerned, but did not give me enough for washing clothes. I could sit for hours watching the rainwater trickling through the transparent pipe leading to the tank. It gave me great pleasure and satisfaction. I can't explain why; I think some primeval instinct must have been involved.

I was fagged out, and I grew worried by fits of intense depression. Often I could not stand up without hanging on to some support, and I wondered if I had something wrong with my balancing nerves. I felt weak, thin and somehow wasted, and I had a sense of immense space empty of any spiritual—what? I didn't know. I

knew only that it made for intense loneliness, and a feeling of hope-
lessness, as if faced with imminent doom. On November 5 I held a
serious conference with myself about my weakness. When I got up
that morning I found that I could not stand on my legs without
support, just as if I had emerged from hospital after three months in
bed. I was exhausted after a long struggle with the radio on the previous evening, and a long-drawn battle with the mainsail during the
night finished me off. Then I thought, "Husky young men on fully
crewed yachts during an ocean race of a few days have been known
to collapse from sheer exhaustion. I have been doing this singlehanded for more than two months. Is it any wonder that I feel
exhausted?" That cheered me up a bit, and I made two resolutions:
firstly, to try to relax and take some time off during each day; secondly, to eat more nourishing food. Because I was so tired I was not
eating enough. I logged: "I must go more for things like honey,
nuts, dried fruits. I ought to bake some more wholemeal bread."

My oven was a camping one which fitted over the Primus, and
it baked very well. But I had rather got out of the habit of baking,
which was a mistake, because I enjoyed my bread, and always felt
that it did me good. But conditions were usually so rough and I felt
such lassitude that often I did not have the energy to prepare the
dough and bake. After my resolution I did bake more regularly.

Breakfast was my best meal, partly, perhaps, because I felt more
like eating after getting some sleep, but partly, too, because breakfast always seemed important as a ritual after coming through the
night safely—candy for the kid. So deliberately I took more time
over my breakfasts. I was often up at dawn, and at it all day until
dark without a let-up, followed probably by three or four dressings-
up in deck clothes during the night. So I sat for as long as I could
over breakfast, and sometimes went back to my bunk for a snooze
after it. My bunk was the most comfortable place on the yacht, but
I had to give up the quarter berth which I liked best because of
leaks. My sleeping bag and everything else got so sopping that I was
driven out to another berth in the cabin.

Those first weeks of November were hard going. There was constant rough work on deck in huge seas, and I was constantly afraid
of another accidental gybe, which might have brought grave damage. I was fortunate that my earlier gybe had not done more
damage than it did—I felt I had been lucky. Apart from the deck-
fittings, which I contrived to repair or replace from my bosun's
stores, the only real damage had been to the mizzen staysail. That,

too, was mendable, and although sewing was difficult in the rough conditions, I managed to restore the sail.

I think that the patent hanks on my headsails caused me more cursing than any other item of equipment on the boat. Almost every time a sail was hoisted, some of them came undone. On November 8 I logged that it was quite a job getting the big genoa down because the wind was piping up, and all the hanks except four were unfastened, so that the sail began flogging as soon as I started to lower it. There was one hank left at the head of the sail, but with the strain on it that tore free of the sail. I would have given a lot to have the good old-fashioned hanks on my sails.

On the evening of November 9 I was transmitting to Cape Town for *The Guardian* and got half my message through when the lead came off the aerial. I was still able to hear the operator and he could hear a few words from me, which I think was amazing with no aerial at all, and a 2,500-mile transmission! Part of the message which they got wrong was that I liked having birds around me, but that they made me realise how completely I was alone. The message went through, "*because* they make me realise how I am completely alone!"

In 10,000 miles of sailing I had not seen a single fish in the water, only flying fish in the air, and on the deck. A few squid landed on the deck at night. The prions were my favourite birds then—most beautiful dove-grey birds with pointed wings, flying like big crazy swallows. They would play above the top of the mizzen mast, flying up to it and hovering there in the updraught, before turning and streaking downwind. I think it must have been a prion that I saw one midnight, flying silently round the yacht like a white ghost. The Cape Hens were the quickest to settle on the water, to examine the scraps I threw to them.

Sheila, on her way to meet me in Sydney in the P and O *Oriana*, sailed from Aden on November 10, and I looked forward to being able to talk to her on the radio telephone. I tried two or three times to call up *Oriana* but without success. I was bothered about this, because I knew they were expecting me to call them and feared they would worry if they could not pick me up. But making unanswered radio calls was an exhausting strain, and *Oriana* became a sort of nightmare. I felt that I ought to tune in to try to contact her twice a day, but I also felt that it was nonsense to be trying to reach a ship still some 3,000 miles away. I decided to wait and not to try again until *Oriana* was nearing Fremantle in Australia. After my last futile call on the night of November 11 I wrote:

• • •

"No luck with *Oriana*. I don't think I shall try till they are near Fremantle. It wears one down with uncertainty. I'm sure Sheila would understand that. I think she is the most understanding, sensitive woman I know."

• • •

On November 11 I got all my dispatch for the *Sunday Times* through to Philip Stohr in Cape Town, but it took me 1 hour 20 minutes. This made an inroad into my charging fuel, which was already running short.

Next day I pumped the bilge and found that it took 257 pumps to clear the water. I had last pumped on November 9, when it needed only 57 pumps. I wondered where all the water came from—257 pumps represents a lot of water. It had been heavy weather all the time, and I decided that the total of all deck leaks could probably be enough to account for the water; a lot of water always seemed to get in through the doors of the dinghy well. Still, 257 pumps *was* a lot of water. I added to my tasks the job of keeping a more frequent eye on the bilge, in case there was a leak below the waterline. In spite of my resolution I had another go at trying to call *Oriana* but not a squeak could I hear.

It grew steadily colder. My fingers used to get frozen with any work on deck, and on November 14 a squall brought hail instead of rain. The hailstones rattled on the skylight like piles of white peas. I had a good contact, however, with Perth radio, and got through a 412-word telegram to *The Guardian* quite easily. I asked them to tell *Oriana* that I had tried to get her, and to say that I would call again on November 16 and 17 at 14.00 hours.

THURSDAY, NOVEMBER 15, brought disaster. I woke to a 40-knot wind—a heavy weight of wind, but no worse than the rough weather over most of the past weeks. The burgee halliard parted, but that was small beer. At 12.15 I went aft to make what I thought would be a minor repair to the self-steering gear, and found that the steel frame holding the top of the steering blade had broken in half. There were two steel plates, one on each side of the top of the blade, to hold the blade and to connect it to the wind vane. Both had fractured. The oar blade was attached to the ship only by a rod used to alter its rake. It was wobbling about in the wake like a dead fish held by a line. I expected it to break away at any moment, and rushed back to the cockpit. I let all the sails drop with a run as fast as I could let the halliards go, so as to stop the ship and take as much strain off the gear as possible. Then I unshipped the blade, and got it aboard as quickly as I could, before the fitting which held the rod broke off and I lost the oar. The sight of the self-steering gear broken beyond repair acted like a catalyst. At first I turned cold inside and my feelings, my spirit, seemed to freeze and sink inside me. I had a strange feeling that my personality was split and that I was watching myself drop the sails efficiently and lift out the broken gear coolly. My project was killed. Not only was my plan to race 100 days to Sydney shattered, but to make a non-stop passage there was impossible, too. Then I found out that I was not really crestfallen; it was a relief. I realised that I had been waiting for this to happen for a long time. I went below and stood myself a brandy, hot. Now my thoughts began whirling round in tight circles, as I thought about what had happened, and searched for the best course of action. I went back to the stem and studied the breakage. Two steel plates, 27 inches long, 6 inches wide and 1/8 inch thick connected the wooden steering oar to the rest of the gear. These had both broken clean across, where a strengthening girder had been welded on to the plates. I considered all the pieces of sheet metal on the boat that I could think of, wondering if I could make a repair. The best bet seemed to be the swinging frame of the Primus stove, but it was not nearly as strong as the original metal that had broken and, besides that, I had no suitable nuts and bolts for bolting it to the broken pieces. The self-steering gear could not be repaired on board—I was well and truly in trouble. If I had had a normal boat I could have trimmed her up to sail herself, but experience so far had convinced me that *Gipsy Moth IV* could never be balanced to sail herself for more than a few minutes. The bald fact was that she could only be sailed from now on while I was at the helm, otherwise she must be hove to while I slept, cooked, ate, navigated or did any of the other many jobs about the ship. I should do well if I could average 10 hours a day at the helm; that would give me 60 miles a day at 6 knots. Taking calms and headwinds into consideration, I should do well to make good, on an average, 50 miles per day. I thought I was 2,758 miles from Sydney which was a long way, only 200 miles less, for example, than the Great Circle distance from Plymouth to New York. It would take an age to reach it, 55 days at 50 miles per day, perhaps 3 months. On top of the 80 days I had spent on the passage so far, it seemed out of the question. The only course open to me was to head for the nearest place where I could get a repair. The nearest suitable place was Fremantle. Even that was 1,160 miles away which would mean a very long time at the helm. I worked out a course for Fremantle.

I started work. I hoisted a small sail and after rigging a line from the tiller to the side of the cockpit I played with the adjustment of this until I got the boat reluctantly to keep roughly to a heading. It was not the best heading, but it could have been worse. I logged: "How I shall get her to steer on any heading that is not nearly abeam I can't think at present. I'll have some lunch and try again with more sail, etc. Of course this 37-knot wind is pretty strong." Later I wrote:

• • •

"Life is going to be pretty good hell I imagine for the next fortnight or so. I have been out to the tiller several times in the past two hours, once to prevent a gybe when the wind dropped, another time because the wind had increased, making the boat gripe up to windward. Tomorrow I must try to lead tiller lines into the cabin so that I can steer from there. Otherwise I shall go barmy if I have to dress up each time I have to adjust the tiller. At the moment the wind direction is the best possible, because beam to wind is the boat's natural lie. What I shall do to make her go downwind I can't think at present. I am going to turn in for a sleep while I can."

• • •

It was a stinking night, and I was called out several times to find the boat headed west instead of east, with all the sails aback. On one of these occasions I lay drowsy in my berth reluctant to get up again, and I noticed that although the sails were aback, the boat was forging ahead slowly and—a most important fact —*she kept a much steadier course than when she was sailing in the right direction with the sails all drawing.* At the time I took these facts in without really being aware of them. They imprinted themselves, as it were, on my subconscious self.

At 6 A.M. I started the job of trying to make the boat sail itself in some way or other, so that I should be able to eat and sleep without having her stop dead. It looked desperate by breakfast time, when I had been trying for an hour to balance the sail pressure, etc., against the pull on the tiller. However, I had a good breakfast, even though I absent-mindedly dipped into the coffee jar instead of the marmalade pot. Some time during breakfast I recalled that *Gipsy Moth* had held a steady heading when she had been turned round facing west with the sails aback. This was a strange fact; surely I might be able to make use of it? During breakfast, when I was trying hard to squeeze something out of my brain, I had an idea. I devised something and by 10.20 I had the boat sailing herself, on course, and downwind. She was not going very fast, but by then there was only an 8-knot wind (thank Heaven). An albatross gravely insulted my efforts by swimming or paddling along a few yards astern, to keep up with *Gipsy Moth*.

All that day I was experimenting. I unshackled both the storm sails and changed them over, so that the smaller sail was on the staysail stay, then I hove the clew of this small storm staysail to windward, so that the sail was as she would be if the ship had turned right round and the sail was aback; then I linked the clew of this sail to the tiller by means of blocks on each side. After a lot of trial and error, the result was as follows:

When the yacht was on course, the sail was aback, and wind pressing on it pulled the tiller sufficiently to windward to counteract the tendency of the boat to turn up into wind.

If the boat *did* begin turning off course into wind, the pressure on the sail increased, with the result that the pull on the tiller increased, making the boat turn off the wind again.

If, on the other hand, the boat started turning downwind, this steering sail would presently gybe, as it were, and the wind would press on it from the other side, thereby exerting a pull on the tiller in the other direction to leeward, with the result that the boat turned towards the wind again.

Luckily the wind had fallen light that morning, and all day I was working in a gentle breeze of between 7½ and 10 knots. By noon I had sailed 91 miles on course for Fremantle since the self-steering gear broke. At 17.30 I logged: "Nearly becalmed. At least *Gipsy Moth* has steered herself all day which I regard as an achievement starting from scratch, even if it isn't right for other conditions."

My chief anxiety now was not to embarrass Sheila. Her ship was due in at Fremantle next day, and I had to get a message to her before then, so that she would not continue on to Sydney while I put into Fremantle. That evening I had a bad contact with *Oriana*. Her operator seemed to hear me better than I could hear him. I kept on repeating: "I am on my way to Fremantle, I am putting into Fremantle." The contact was too bad to explain why. I logged: "Poor Sheila, she will wonder what is happening."

That night was dark and it was raining. I saw a *strange* thing, bright blobs of phosphorescence up in the air passing the boat. As my eyes got used to the dark I realised that these bright patches were actually *in* the water, and the high waves had made them appear to be up in the air!

By noon of the 17th I was another 81 miles on the way to Fremantle. But I was getting increasing fits of depression and sense of failure; I had set out to sail non-stop to Sydney. The prospect of putting in at Fremantle stuck in my gullet, and finally I decided that I could not stomach it. At 3.45 that afternoon I altered course back for Sydney.

All day I worked on my self-steering system, watching the effect on my steering arrangement and the tiller of any change in the heading, or in the wind strength, or direction. By the end of the day the heading required was dead downwind to a 33-knot wind, but my system was coping with it, though with a loud clatter of ropes and sails flapping.

I was now anxious to get another message through to Sheila, so that she would not get off at Fremantle while I sailed on to Sydney. I tried calling up *Oriana* again that night, but had a rotten contact. Altogether I tried five times on the 16th and 17th to contact *Oriana*. I thought they were hearing me, even if I could not hear them, and I repeatedly said that I was headed for Sydney again, and was not going to Fremantle. I asked for Sheila to speak to me on Perth Radio when she landed there.

My system took a minor squall pretty well, and I was pleased with it. The day's run to the 18th was up to 111 miles. I felt happier than I had been at any time previously during the voyage. I had been waiting for the self-steering gear to fail, and apprehensive all the time that I should be helplessly stuck with a badly balanced boat. That I had been able to rig up gear to make her sail herself was deeply satisfying. I hate turning back; I hate giving up; and I hate being diverted from my course; it was a seaman's job to get over difficulties. I think this compensated for my chagrin at failure of the 100-day project, which did seem impossible now for two reasons—firstly, because the steering sail was depriving me of one of my best driving sails when on the wind, and secondly, because part of the steering sail was actually acting *against* the forward movement of the boat, pulling against the other sails. I knew I had set a very high target with 100 days, but I believed that I stood a fair chance of achieving it if the self-steering gear had not bust. At the time that happened I had 2,758 miles to go and 20 days left of the 100. In the previous 20 days I had sailed 2,920 miles.

On the night of the 18th I had a long radio session with Perth, and explained the whole situation during 80 minutes. Just before midnight I was called out by a minor shemozzle, to find all the sails aback, including the mizzen staysail. "And that," I logged, "is something to have aback." I had set too high a standard for my steering system, asking it to control the boat with the mizzen staysail set in a light wind which was something the self-steering gear itself had often failed to accomplish.

The fourth day's run with my system produced 138 miles and I began to warm up my hopes: could I possibly do it in 100 days after all? Of course there were a lot of miles lost in the first three days which I should have to make up, and that would be a big handicap. Again I kept at it all day, fiddling with the system and ironing out minor troubles.

The petrels and one or two albatrosses stayed with me, and they would come from quite far when I banged my scrap tin before emptying it—to call them to dinner. Then they kept on flying round close, for more scraps. I loved watching them. To make things better still, that evening I made contact on the radio with *Oriana,* and had a long talk with Sheila. It was a joy to hear her, and to be able to talk directly to her. This cheered me up immensely, and I wrote in the log:

. . .

"I have been leaning over the garden gate, in this case the washboards of the companionway, looking out at the hazy moon and the water sliding by; I am more at peace than at any time before on this passage. I think that the damned self-steering gear was a constant worry to me, waiting for it to bust. Now we seem to be really sailing and I feel happy."

. . .

On the 20th I had got the day's run up to 168 miles. My system could keep the boat pretty steady on a heading downwind, or across wind, but for a wind half way between them the going was very tricky.

Next day I could only jog along in a 40-knot gale. There had been a quiet roar in the rigging all day and I had trouble getting the steering sail to control the boat when there was only one sail drawing. I logged: "My experience of these gales is that you can't set sail again seriously until the noise in the rigging, a mild roar, one might call it, eases." I was feeling very feeble physically again; it seemed as if the gale had taken the stuffing out of me. I meditated why, wondering whether my feebleness was due to the incessant effort of holding on and straining to keep a position without being thrown, or to damp, not enough food, or the nervous strain tensing up for the next time the hull was hit, thrown down or over. The day's run dropped to 82 miles.

I could not hoist the trysail right the way up, because the loose end of the broken burgee halliard was twisted round the trysail halliard and everything else aloft. I was afraid to use the winch, and there was too much wind to wiggle things free. I do not get on well with burgee halliards, and logged: "It could easily happen that that burgee halliard stops everything from moving up there! Curse it, this has always happened on every ocean crossing I have done. I should get rid of the damned thing before I start."

My great interest every day of the voyage was to get an accurate sun fix, so that I could know what the ship had sailed during the past day, and ponder on my tactics for the coming days. On November 22 I recorded:

• • •

"I got four shots at the sun with some difficulty, and then a surfing wave took charge of the boat. The crest coamed into the cockpit giving the sextant a real sea bath. However, I rinsed it in warm fresh water with some detergent in it. Just after I finished, a 45-knot squall hit the boat. I was sheltered in the cabin helping out the tiller in overpowering gusts. The hatch was only open an inch to allow passage of the cords to the tiller, but the rain was so heavy that it was driving 7 feet into the cabin through that small crack. I put on a raincoat and a hat standing in the cabin."

• • •

That afternoon I dropped the jib, and stopped the ship. All the battens had been torn out of the working jib, and the sails were taking a beating. It was hard to stand on the deck. Waves were coming into the cockpit, and hail sounded like rifle fire. It was also very cold, and my hands were half numb. The seas, squirting through the closed hatch, had swollen the woodwork in the galley so that I could not open two of the drawers there. That was irritating, because there were several things I wanted in those drawers.

In the evening I got *Gipsy Moth* sailing again, but I had to come to the rescue of the steering system several times next day, both to prevent a turn downwind from becoming a gybe, and a turn up into the wind from stopping the boat. Undoubtedly the system had its disadvantages. I could not use the mainsail, because the boom would have fouled the steering lines from the sail to the tiller. And the cockpit was so full of lines that it was dangerous to set the mizzen staysail. The boat was like a birdcage. It was difficult to make way along the deck, and when I came out of the cabin it was easier to crawl under the tiller than to move over it.

But I was improving all the time, and on November 24 I logged:

• • •

"Still driving hard through grey-green seas, and grey sky of low overcast. The rig seems to be spoiling me, keeping course at 7 to 7½ knots all through the night, except for periodic roarings in the rigging and bashings of waves over the deck when a wave throws the boat's head off to the north-east or even further to the north; but each time so far, after rough going for a few minutes, the steering sail has brought her back on course. It is 9½ hours since I touched tiller or rope. Long may it continue; it smacks of the marvellous to me!"

• • •

I got quite a thrill when I found suddenly that I was well past the western end of Australia, which I might not have noticed if I had not run off the end of the chart of the Indian Ocean. Perhaps I should add that I was then 500 miles south of the land, so that there was no likelihood of charging into it because of not noticing that I was passing it. It was exciting to dig out the chart of Australia. I was now only about 1,200 miles from Bass Strait which was a daunting (if exhilarating) prospect after no sight of land since Madeira.

I still had no log or speedometer, but I found my dead reckoning much better than expected. One gets used to judging speed. For instance, the previous day's run was 158 miles by sun fixes, and my dead reckoning run, based on judging the speed at intervals, was only 3½ miles short of this.

An extraordinary thing happened after I had finished my radio telephone dispatch on November 25. As the light over my chart table had failed temporarily, I connected an inspection lamp at the end of a lead to give me light to work the telephone. I hung this lamp on the wire lead to the speedometer. Suddenly the speedometer began to work again. I found that the wire leading to the speedometer had snapped (probably it had been damaged when the radio telephone was being fitted), and the weight of the inspection lamp somehow managed to connect the two ends again inside the insulating cover! I had tried that particular connection between the wire and the speedometer about eight times, but never thought of the wire itself being snapped. Now I had a speedometer again (though I didn't actually repair the lead until next day). I was glad to have it, for I should need it among the islands of Bass Strait, but I reflected ruefully that my peace of mind would probably be less.

I fitted up a tackle with two blocks from the tiller to the windward side of the cockpit, and the running part of this tackle led into the cabin. On the lee side of the tiller I had at first a plain line leading from the tiller to the side of the cockpit, and from there into the cabin, but later I found that this was insufficient, and rigged a second tackle with two blocks on that side too. These two tackles were invaluable; they enabled me to control the tiller and help out the steering sail from the cabin, without having to dress up in deck clothes and go on deck. For example, on November 25 two smashing waves broke right on to the boat, picked it up and swung it round through a change of heading of no less than 140°. The steering sail might have brought the heading back again in time, but not without a lot of sail flogging. (It's a wonder any sail can survive flogging in a 45-knot gale!) By hauling on the weather tackle, I brought the heading back on course quickly without going up into the cockpit.

That evening a big swell began running in suddenly from the west; big, I would say 50 feet. There were a number of Mother Carey's Chickens about, which nearly always forecasts a storm, whatever meteorologists may say to the contrary. I could see them picking things out of the water while on the wing, but not what the things were. An hour before midnight a wave gybed *Gipsy Moth,* and put her aback, headed south. The steering sail could not move the tiller with the sails aback; nor could I with the tackle and the tiller line into the cabin. So I had to dress up in hard weather rig, and *still I* could not move the tiller by hand. I had to sit down on the lee side of the cockpit and, with my back to the side of the cockpit, and both feet on the tiller, I was able to move the rudder slowly and turn *Gipsy Moth* downwind, and gybe back on to course. It was really rather a splendid night. There was a bright moon, with some silvery clouds, and there were white manes to the waves. *Gipsy Moth* tore through the water at a good 7½ knots. Shortly after midnight I was woken up again with the ship aback, in a very unpleasant squall. I had to stick this one out in the cockpit, nursing the tiller to keep *Gipsy Moth* near downwind until the squall blew out. It was wild rocketing downwind, and I was very cold with only pyjamas under a quilted coat and trousers. As soon as I got a chance I put on a sweater and safety harness, and dropped the working jib. I hated losing the good speed, but a ship out of control is hell. At 5.30 in the morning I was woken again by the ship aback. I logged: "My steering sail, let's face it, will not control the boat in winds of Force 8 (35 knots) or more. It has not the power to work the tiller to bring the heading off the wind after a wave slew. That helm needs the strength of an elephant, anyway."

That was not my lucky day. Besides being turned out so often to rescue the helm, my drawer full of electrical spares, fuses, valves, etc., shot out, and on to the cabin floor. Next, all my rolls of chart fell from their nest close under the cabin ceiling on to the cabin floor; then I delved in the clothes locker under my cabin bunk, and found everything there running water, except what I had put in plastic bags. At noon I was in the middle of some sun shots when a big breaking sea surfed *Gipsy Moth* along with it until *Gipsy Moth* broached to on the starboard gybe, sails aback again. I felt that I needed a tent pitched in the cabin to keep things dry.

Two and a half hours later I logged: "Well! that was a near go." I was standing facing the companionway, and looking at the speedometer repeater dial above my quarter berth, to see if it was working properly. Suddenly the needle shot up hard against the stop at the limit, 10 knots, and stayed there. For a second or two I thought that the speedometer had bust again. Then the boat went over on to its side and, looking out, I saw that *Gipsy Moth* was on the crest of a big breaking wave. This breaker slewed the boat round broadside to it, knocking her down forward, so that the masts were horizontal, pointing in the direction in which the wave was going. From where I stood on the side of the bunk I could see the mizzen mast lying flat along the surface of the boiling, seething surf. I would say that the boat was travelling sideways at a speed of 30 knots. There was nothing I could do. I was not frightened; I watched interested. Would the masts dip in? If they dipped a few more degrees below the horizontal they must dive into the water, and inevitably the boat must then roll over. They didn't; the surf passed leaving *Gipsy Moth* broached to. She righted herself, and presently the steering sail brought her back through 90° on to her previous heading.

On November 27 I was 710 miles from Cape Otway, and I decided that I must adjust the lead of the steering sail lines so that I could hoist the mainsail again. I had to have it, because I could not now pole out either of the big running sails. I had robbed the main boom of its topping lift tackle for one of my tiller lines, and had to rig up another. There was a pale greeny blue sky like I have known before a terrific wind in Europe. There were also some strongly developed mares' tails in a straggly line across the sky. But these indications misled me, for the big wind did not arrive.

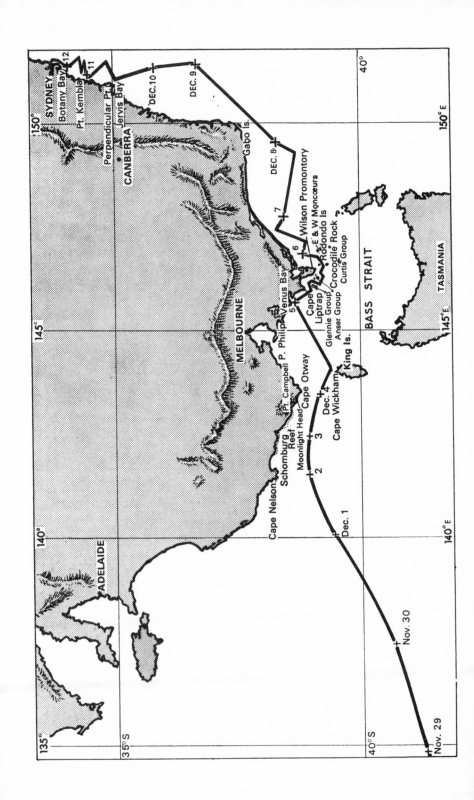

An albatross flying overhead dropped a personal bomb, which hit the mizzen sail fair and square, decorating it with a string of red blobs. Lucky shot! I rove a new tiller line to the steering sail and took the strain on it so that I could adjust the present one, then I did the same with the leeward line. The lengths of the steering lines, and the amount of play or movement of parts of this steering system were most critical, and fine adjustment made all the difference to its effectiveness.

Next day the wind returned to roaring in the rigging, and I dropped all sail except the storm jib and steering sail, content to jog along on course at 4 knots only. Some Mother Carey's Chickens were only 6 feet away from me when I was working at the stem; I had never seen them so close before. I watched them bouncing off the wave surfaces with their chests, and sometimes hitting the water lightly with first one wing tip and then the other as if they were flicking bits of fluff off a hot plate with their wings.

On November 29 I had sailed for 14 days since the self-steering bust, and had made good 1,808 miles, an average of 120 miles per day. This was good going because, quite apart from my self-steering difficulties, I was missing one of my best driving sails. Alas, it was not good enough to reach Sydney in the 100 days. I still had 1,057 miles to go and only 6 days of the 100 left. I was depressed because I had had a bad night, unable to sleep through being thoroughly rattled by the radio telephone, and the pressure being exerted on me through it for news, etc. After three months of solitude I felt that it was all too much; that I could not stand it, and could easily go mad with it. All this is weak nonsense, I know, but that is how I felt when I was twisting about in my bunk trying to clear my brain of all the thoughts and images attacking it. I told myself that I must try to be tolerant with the demands being made for air photography, telephone talks, etc., etc.

An hour after midnight on November 30 I was forced out of my bunk by a bad cramp. I always got cramp if I stretched my legs on waking, but I couldn't stop myself from doing it when still half-asleep. Fortunately, standing upright freed the bound muscles, which were as hard as wood, and very painful. I was always frightened that a muscle would break under the strain. A small drink of sea water usually prevented another attack—maybe I needed salt after losing so much during hard deckwork.

That afternoon I sewed up the seam of the mizzen staysail which had given way. It was a delightful sunny day for a change, and warm enough for me to sew in the cockpit. When I set the sail, the steering sail could not control the boat with it up, so I had to haul it down again. Then I set the big 600-foot genoa instead of the 300-foot jib. *Gipsy Moth* was doing 9 knots easily at times, but when the wind piped up the steering sail could not control the boat with that sail set either, and reluctantly I had to drop it again. What was so frustrating was that the wind dropped to near-calm almost to the second as I dropped the sail, and I could have carried it thereafter! If the wind had acted purely out of spite it could not have been more successful. I think there might have been a chance of controlling the boat if the trysail had been dropped, but it was getting dark, and I had a damned radio telephone appointment coming up. So I left the big sail down and rehoisted the 300-footer.

When on the foredeck in the dusk, after I had bagged the big sail, I was startled by what seemed a human scream close to the boat. I swung round to see whatever it could be. It came from an albatross! There were two of them, sitting on the water about 10 feet

---

* Rex Clements in his book *A Gipsy of the Horn* relates an oddly similar occurrence.

"One dark, moonless night just before we got clear of the 'forties', there occurred a most uncanny experience.

"It was about four bells in the middle watch, the 'churchyard' watch, as the four hours after midnight is called, that it happened. Suddenly, apparently close aboard on the port hand, there came howling out of the darkness a most frightful, wailing cry, ghastly in its agony and intensity. Not of overpowering volume—a score of men shouting together could have raised as loud a hail—it was the indescribable calibre and agony of the shriek that almost froze the blood in our veins.

"We rushed to the rail, the mate and the men too, and stared searchingly into the blackness to wind'ard. The starbowlines, who a moment before had been sleeping the sleep of tired men in their bunks below, rushed out on deck. Shipwreck would hardly bring foremast Jack out before he was called, but that cry roused him like the last summons. If ever men were 'horror-struck' we were.

"Even the old man was awakened by it and came up on deck. Everyone was listening intensely, straining their eyes into the blackness that enveloped us.

"A moment or two passed and then as we listened, wondering and silent, again that appalling scream rang out, rising to the point of almost unbearable torture and dying crazily away in broken whimperings.

"No one did anything, or even spoke.

"Nobody slept much more that night and thankful we were when the grey dawn broke over the tumbling untenanted sea.

"This was all. In bare words it doesn't sound very dreadful, but it made that night a night of terror. For long enough afterwards the echoes of that awful scream would ring in my ears, and even now it sends a shiver through me to think of it.

"Who and what it was that caused it we never learnt."

I wonder if this might also have been an albatross?

from the boat. They were courting, I think, facing each other, and one had its wings raised in a V with curved sides. It was too poor a light to see more.*

At 6.40 in the morning of December 1, the wind backed to the south-east and *Gipsy Moth* came hard on the wind for the first time for about a month. "I expect," I logged, "that it is going to give me a headache before I reach Sydney." How right I was!

EIGHT

BASS STRAIT

THE NOON position on December 1 showed that the current, probably following the wind, had set me 36 miles north of the dead reckoning position. The day's run was 140 miles, the last good run I was to have for many days. Now began a tough phase of the passage.

The heading I was on would run *Gipsy Moth* into the coast between Cape Otway and Cape Nelson 100 miles to the west of it, and this would be a lee shore. So I dropped the 300-foot jib and hoisted the working jib instead to harden up to the wind. *Gipsy Moth* at once started slamming, but I felt that I must endure it. By 20.00 that night the pounding became terrible. I felt that it could drive one mad, the tension waiting for the next crash. In the Forties I had usually been able to ease the heading until I was broadside to the wind or even downwind. Here I felt it would be a mistake running down on a lee shore. Actually it was still 90 miles away, but it seemed very close after the big stretches of ocean that I had grown used to. I dropped the working jib and set the storm jib in its place, and also reefed the mizzen. This cut the speed from 5½ to 3½ knots with the same heading, but it made existence tolerable by cutting down the pounding.

At midnight the sea got up, and was really socking the boat. I hove the storm jib to windward, dropped the trysail and lashed the helm right down to leeward, jogging along at 2 knots hard on the wind. At 06.00 in the morning of the 2nd I resheeted the storm jib and hoisted the mizzen sail.

At noon I had had a day's run of only 68 miles. I had had a single sun shot at 10.24, which confirmed the dead reckoning position, that I was some 35 miles from Cape Nelson at noon, and was heading into a bay of a lee coast. I had poor visibility, and a gale, increasing, with the possibility of a really bad blow, the way the barometer was moving. I had a low coast which would be difficult to pick out lying ahead of me. I wore the ship round on to the other tack and headed SSE. I expected to have to stay on this heading until the wind veered enough to let me into Bass Strait. *Gipsy Moth* was making only 3 knots owing to the steering sail being aback, but at least the pounding was cut down and I felt I could relax. It was fairly rough; I had to clean my sextant twice to get the one shot at 10.24, then I had to give it a freshwater bath because a big wave crest drenched it.

I had got stuck with what I had always hoped to avoid, having to enter Bass Strait in a gale with bad visibility and no position check for 12,000 miles. I was on edge about this, for sextant observations of the sun, moon or stars will give an accurate fix only if there is no blunder in working out the sights. I reckon to make some blunders in, I should guess, about one observation in ten or twenty, usually something quite silly, like using the wrong date in the almanac, or copying down the wrong figure from a 6-figure logarithm. Fortunately I nearly always realise when a mistake has been made somewhere; I seem to develop an uncanny instinct for smelling out an error. But, aware of having made these blunders, I could not help feeling nervy when approaching land and relying on astro-navigation for not hitting rocks or an island in the dark when the last positive position check was 12,000 miles back. Suppose there had been some consistent error running through all the astronomical observations, an undetected error in the sextant, or in the time, stop watch, the tables, the almanac . . . . I had expected to get a check from the radio beacons in Bass Strait; but when I tuned in to the frequencies listed in the latest Admiralty Signals Manual I could not pick up any of them—I did not know then that all the Australian frequencies had been changed. I searched the whole range of frequencies on my D/F radio set and picked up Mount Gambier airfield beacon on a frequency totally different from the one in the manual. I then began searching the frequency band for the Cape Otway and Cape Wickham beacons. The trouble was that these came on only at intervals of 30 minutes.

To make matters worse it was a head-on gale so that I was having to beat slowly to windward. At 5.30 P.M. I tacked again, and once more was headed for the coast, later in darkness and still a gale with bad visibility. The plunging and pounding of the boat could drive a man crazy and when I called up on the R/T that night I felt it was like trying to use a telephone when standing on a dodgem at a fair.

At 09.40 next morning (December 3) my dead reckoning position should have been within soundings for my little echo sounder, which had a range of 50 fathoms. But the echo sounder recorded no signals, so I assumed I was a couple of miles to the west where the chart showed a depth of over 50 fathoms. If that were right, I was still 19 miles off the lee coast.

Besides not being able to get a sun sight my navigation was complicated by not being able to pick up any of the radio beacons listed in the latest Admiralty manual. At last, by searching the frequency band, I located Cape Otway on 314 kcs instead of the 289 given in the manual—the latest available when I left. I also managed to find Cape Wickham's frequency, and I got a rough fix from the two. My run to noon of December 3 was only 53½ miles.

The fix from the Cape Otway and Cape Wickham bearings put me 12 miles from land, 23 miles west of Cape Otway, but 5 miles north of it. This was at 12.30, and I kept on popping out to see if I could see land ahead. I didn't want to tack until I had seen it, and also I was hoping that the wind would veer and let me weather Cape Otway without a tack. I kept on taking bearings of Otway and Wickham, but they were not good because the compass was so cranky in the southern hemisphere. Two hours and twenty minutes later I sighted a long cliffy stretch of coast dead ahead. The farthest I could see was a point away to the east, which I thought was Moonlight Head. I thought *Gipsy Moth* was headed for Oliver Hill, 3 or 4 miles west of Moonlight Head which was where I expected to be, but I could not identify the coast positively. If it was Oliver Hill, then I was only 16 miles from the Schomburg Reef, where the famous (or notorious) skipper, Bully Hayes, lost his clipper. Land was about 3 miles off when I tacked.*

I reckoned to stay for four or five hours on the port tack, to get clear of the shipping lane. At 17.00 there was a standard "Southerly

---

* According to an Australian newspaper, when I tacked off the coast to the west of Cape Otway on December 3: "An Australian fisherman who set out in his crayfish boat yesterday to take fruit, champagne and beer to the English yachtsman was beaten back by 40 m.p.h. winds and waves estimated at 30 feet. After struggling through the gale for 50 miles, the bottles were smashed, the fruit was pulp and everyone aboard the 50 foot motor boat was seasick." I wonder where he started from.

Buster" cloud formation along the coast astern, a long, low roll of cloud, purplish blue. I wondered if it was as vicious as it looked, and whether it would come upwind and attack me. I wanted to set more sail, but that roll of cloud scared me off it. According to radio bearings at 22.00 I was still 31 miles from Cape Otway and in a steamer lane, for I had just seen three steamers one behind the other. Those steamers would have been a good help to my navigation if I could have been sure what steamer lane they were on; unfortunately—this was one of those little slip-ups which bedevil a long passage—I had left behind my copy of the Admiralty's *Ocean Passages of the World* and therefore I could not tell what route the steamers would be on if they were making for Fremantle.

I had to get further south to be well clear of the shipping lanes when I tacked. At midnight I logged that the steamer lane was nearly as crowded as the English Channel; three more steamers were passing then, and I had had to turn downwind to avoid colliding with one. It was about a mile away when I went up to tack, and I thought it was far enough off to give me plenty of time. That was the first steamer I had been close to since the South Atlantic; this is the only excuse I can offer for mistiming my tack. As I came round I realised that I was on a collision course with the steamer, and I began bearing away to pass astern of it. The steamer must have been wondering what the devil I was doing, and, having a conscientious and good navigator on board, slowed to a stop. I wish all steamers would be equally chivalrous towards small boats. I bore away under its stern, feeling a proper Charley. I suppose it had taken me longer to tack than I had expected, and also the steamer had been going fast.

Now I could see the loom of the Cape Otway light. I got a bearing from it, but I could not tell how far away it was. I put it at 20 miles. I decided that the coast I had seen could not have been Moonlight Head. Altogether I was fussed up in a hard way till midnight, what with steamers, uncertainty of position, dirty weather and wind still occasionally up to gale force. I could not turn in for a sleep when headed for the land when I did not know how far off it was. So I laid down on my chart the limits of error in my position, and from this deduced that no matter where I might be within these limits, I could safely sail for a certain number of hours on the port tack before I risked running into King Island. In working this out I made due allowance for the treacherous currents round King Island which the Admiralty Sailing Directions warned about.

December 4 was a green-grey day, with rain, bad visibility, and wind still heading me from the south-east. I was going very slowly because of the terrific pounding. In spite of all this sailing and navigation, I still had not got into Bass Strait! The day's run was again miserable at 52 miles. *Gipsy Moth* would get up speed to 5½ knots, then slam on three or four waves in succession, and end up stopped. They did not need to be big slams, only just enough to start her hobbyhorsing, which would stop her dead. I had had no sun fix for three days. According to an afternoon radio fix, which I could not rely on, I had been set 10 miles south in four and a half hours since noon.

At 16.30 I reckoned that I was 8 miles north of Cape Wickham, at the north end of King Island. I thought this was close enough, and tacked on to an ENE heading. It was reported to me afterwards that the Cape Wickham lighthouse keeper said he sighted *Gipsy Moth*. This surprised me, because I should think that I would have seen the lighthouse before he could sight me. However, he may have picked me up on a radar screen.

This would explain what happened an hour and a half later, when an aeroplane found me, and made a number of passes over *Gipsy Moth*. I thought it was smart work on his part in the murk with cloud down to 200 feet. Each time he turned to make another pass he disappeared in the murk. The joke was that he must have known my position *exactly* whereas I still did not know it.

An hour before midnight I logged, "The wind and the sea have eased, thank Heaven. I just cannot understand how a boat holds together under such battering." I spent a lot of time that night trying to get radio beacon bearings. The clearest signal was from an air beacon on King Island. I had difficulty in getting good bearings because the compass needle swung about so wildly. This showed up another little slip I had made before starting the passage. I ought to have remembered to get a compass with the needle counterpoised for the Southern Hemisphere's magnetic dip. Also I discovered that the fluorescent lights in the cabin upset the radio bearings, and this was a nuisance, because it meant that I had to turn out all the lights in order to get readings of any value at all.

With daybreak of the 5th the wind fell light and also backed, thereby heading me worse than ever. On that day my hundredth day ran out. I reported:

• • •

"In the last four days I have made good only 279 miles, plugging into a head-on easterly, mostly of gale force. It was equivalent to beating up the English Channel for four days against a gale for a third of the time, and a Force 4 wind for the rest. Twice I had to heave to when the boat was being pounded too hard by the seas. It was thick dirty weather, and I did not get a positive position check until I reached Cape Liptrap at noon today."

• • •

I felt that it was time to make port, for I had finished my last onion. At 10.38 next morning I sighted land ahead. By noon, the day had begun turning into a hot summer's day. The day's run was 106 miles. I tacked when 3 miles off shore. I was in Venus Bay when I tacked away from the land, and from Venus Bay I had to beat to windward to pass Cape Liptrap, and make for Wilson Promontory. There were islands all round the promontory—the Glennie Group, the Anser Group and the Rodondo Group. Fortunately the weather stayed clear and there were two lighthouses, but even so it was tricky work for a singlehander getting through the islands in the dark. I had to check every mile of every tack, and the only sleep I got during the night was one catnap of less than two hours. However, I consoled myself with the promise that the head-on wind would be favourable for me as soon as I got round the promontory and headed ENE for Gabo Island.

I deluded myself. At 06.30 on the morning of the 6th, I was passing Rodondo Island, south of the promontory. This interesting-looking island was only about ½ mile wide and 1,150 feet high, really a big rock. I approached Rodondo to within a few hundred yards. It was exciting and strange to look at the rock and soil after living on the water for so long without a close sight of land. This little island was a tough-looking bit of the earth though, a barren-looking rock, like the crown of a Derby hat rising high out of the sea.

I kept on the port tack until I reached another island, seven miles east of Rodondo, and then tacked again. But the wind promptly backed further, and once more headed me. By noon I had made good only 62 miles during the day spent rounding Wilson Promontory.

I had still 449 miles to go to Sydney. I was not only headed, but the wind was merely a light breeze, so that it looked like a mighty long time before I reached Sydney. "It is a sobering thought that with a faint breeze from ahead I could take 8 days to do the 400 miles," I logged, "but it might be a lot worse."

On the 7th I was nearly becalmed in the night. However, I consoled myself with the thought that if I could once get round Gabo Island, the wind direction would give me a fair wind. At 08.00 in the morning I set the big genoa. It drew well, and put up the speed, but it made tricky work for the steering sail. A steamer, the *Illowra* of Newcastle, gave me a foghorny welcome with much waving, but she also gave me a scare by coming up on to my stern when I was wandering about according to the shifty wind. I logged: "Any nervous tension makes me feel as weak physically as a babe."

That noon I was 35 miles off the coast at the Gippsland Lakes District, and ghosting along in light airs when I was caught by some fishing boats full of reporters. I heard the chug of a diesel motor, and peeped out of the cabin to find a boat-load of journalists and cameramen. I answered their hails and one or two questions, but declined when they asked me to pose for photographs. I did not wish to be churlish, and said I would appear if they waited ten minutes. They demurred at this, saying that other boats were on the way out, and would catch up on them. I said I was sorry, but it was that or nothing. The truth was that I had not had a shave, and wished to rush that through, as well as changing into some clothes which would make me look less like a tramp. After not seeing anyone for about ninety days, I was exuberant with friendliness, affable and anxious to please. Yet I dearly wished that no one had found me until I reached Sydney: I should have liked Sydney Heads to be the first land sighted since Europe.

Later, a trawler brought Lou d'Alpuget from the *Sydney Sun*, whom I had met at Newport, Rhode Island, when he was covering the America's Cup races in 1962. He put off in a rubber dinghy, and came near *Gipsy Moth*, saying, "I've brought you a present of some onions and a bottle of whisky." I said, "I can't take anything on board. I know from previous experience how strict the Sydney Customs people are, and they will make a frightful fuss if anyone comes near me before I have been cleared." I remembered from flying through Australia what sticklers the Australian Customs were for rules and regulations. Lou slowly strangled my argument by saying that a tremendous welcome was waiting for me, and the Customs would be waiving all formalities. It seemed churlish to refuse his kind offer, though in fact I was not drinking any whisky on the passage, having taken a dislike to it at this time. And sure enough, the Customs people, when I met them, although most friendly, were anything but pleased that a photograph of me receiving the whisky had been spread abroad.

Another boat, which I think was a fishing boat, came close so that a journalist from the *Melbourne Age* could throw me a newspaper. This boat misjudged the distance and hit *Gipsy Moth*'s stern only a foot or two from the self-steering gear, that is to say, the part still fixed to the stern which had supported the wind vane which I had removed. I tried hard to fend off the boat, and I think did save a lot of damage, but, in doing so, I crushed my elbow slightly. I cursed him, using an extremely rude word of only four letters. I have rarely seen anyone look so shocked—I thought his face went white. He said nothing at all. As his boat drew away, I looked to see what the damage was, and, recovering from my bad temper which I already regretted, I waved to him. I think this man ought to be a diplomat, because instead of reporting what I had said (though really it was quite unprintable), he reported that I had shouted, "You bloody Sunday driver!" Apparently this caused a lot of amusement in Australia, and it certainly amused me, because I had never heard the expression before in my life!

At noon that day I had had a run of only 59 miles. In the evening I tightened the belts driving the alternator from the auxiliary motor for the last time. There was a great noise and a smell of burning. These two belts were just not up to the job and one had come to bits. By now I had grown quite used to the head-down, feet-up task of adjusting the belts. I had thought it a desperate job the first time I did it in a seaway, with half the nuts having to be tightened up out of sight, by feel only. But one gets used to almost anything.

The current stored up in the batteries was all I had left, and I told Sydney Radio that from now on I could send or receive nothing but urgent calls. I asked for the frequency of the Gabo Island radio beacon which they gave me, also the Sydney Airport frequency. The Australian radio operators were a most friendly and efficient lot.

By now I had been beating into a headwind continuously for six days. When at last the wind freed it came light, and then I was being set back by the powerful south-west-going current which sweeps down off the coast of New South Wales. On the afternoon of December 8 I was wondering when I ought to drop the big genoa, when there was a loud resonant twang which made the boat vibrate. I got out as soon as I could to find out what had broken, but for a moment could see nothing wrong. Then I saw a topmast forestay snaking down instead of being taut and straight. I had not noticed it immediately because the genoa was still held up by the luff wire and the halliard. Both the heavy foretopmast stays were down, twisting about on the deck with one half in the water, but the two light stays were still standing. I dropped the genny and recovered it from the water without trouble, also the two wire stays. The tang at the masthead holding these topmast stays had given way at the weld. The question was, Had this fracture weakened the other two, lighter, stays? If they gave way, too, I should be deprived of headsails for driving the boat until I rigged a jury topmast stay, and even then the speed would be greatly reduced. I got out my low-power night glasses to look at the masthead, but the rain prevented my seeing anything. Those stays worried me until I made Sydney, but in fact the two remaining light ones held.

Next evening—the evening of December 9—a strange thing happened. I was at the stem, taking the starboard navigation light to pieces, when I suddenly felt that I was close to the water; that it was almost within reach, whereas the stem should be 5 feet above the water. I looked aft, and the boat seemed to have settled in the water. It must be sinking. I scurried aft, and went below to lift the hatch in the cabin above the bilge. I expected to find it full up with water coming in from some unknown hole with a tremendous rush; I was amazed to find no water at all in the bilge. There was nothing at all the matter. This must have been a *trompe l'oeil* or delusion like a mirage, but it gave me the sensation of having a boat founder under one's feet at sea. I hope I may never experience this in reality.

On the morning of the 10th, *Gipsy Moth* was becalmed, but in the afternoon a breeze came in from the north-east. I was headed again, but it was a fine sparkling day. I called up Sydney Radio and asked them to give Sheila a message that I had been becalmed since midnight, had only just begun to sail again, and had 102 miles to go.

In the afternoon a plane found me. I guess the pilot must have acted on the information I had just radioed, because I was at least 50 miles off the coast, and had given no position. He must have flown along the arc with a radius of 102 miles from Sydney. *Gipsy Moth* was creaming along, well heeled with a mainsail, a mizzen sail, a jib and a staysail set. After passing Gabo Island I set off on a long 80-mile tack out to sea, seeking peace from boats and aeroplanes. Unfortunately, the farther off-shore I sailed, the stronger the south-going current, and when I tacked inshore again on December 10 and sighted land in the dusk of the evening, I saw a bright light flashing ahead which I found to be Perpendicular Point, the north head of Jervis Bay. I ought to have been much further north. I felt sentimental at the sight of this light, because it was in this bay that I had pitched down in my Gipsy Moth seaplane in 1931, after completing the first solo crossing of the Tasman Sea from New Zealand to Australia. I had lost the top of my finger in that bay, through a piece of clumsiness on my part when I was hooking my Gipsy Moth to a crane to be lifted to the flight deck of the aircraft-carrier *Albatross*.

In spite of the warning on the chart that the south-going current flows up to 4 knots along this section of the Australian coast it was difficult to believe that this could be so, looking at the smooth regular sea. As well as the current, I had against me a NNE wind, dead in my eye looking towards Sydney. *Gipsy Moth*, hobbyhorsing in the chop, slowed down to 4½ knots, so that I ought not to have been surprised on Sunday (December 11), after completing a tack out to sea and back to Port Kembla, to find that I was actually further south at the end of it than when I started! I had a fit of despair, probably due to my feeling nearly exhausted; I felt that I might be out there tacking against the wind and the current for weeks.

I had reduced to storm sails in the fresh breeze in order to ease the pounding, but at midnight I decided that I must take a pull and set more sail, to make a big effort to reach Sydney the following day. It took me two hours in my exhausted condition to set the working jib and hoist the mainsail, then unreef the mizzen, and trim up the boat. I had to stop every few minutes for a rest and breath. After I had finished, *Gipsy Moth* was making only 4 knots to windward, the slamming stopping the boat nearly dead every minute or so. Now I could not get her to sail herself; either she pinched up too close to the wind, or paid off until beam on to it. At

05.40 in the morning I logged: "Been in the cockpit for 70 minutes trying to balance the rudder against tackle and shock cord. I fear *Gipsy Moth IV* is about as unbalanced or unstable a boat that there could be."*

At 08.30 I tried to start the motor, but the batteries were flat. I also tried to call up on the radio telephone but there was not enough current to make it work. Using navigation lights in the steamer lane the night before had finished off the remainder of the current in the batteries.

However, I plugged along, sailing as hard as I could. At least it was a lovely day. At 10.00 in the morning I tacked off Cape Baily at

---

* I learnt the hard way about *Gipsy Moth*'s sailing characteristics. I was much interested when I learned about the sailing model of *Gipsy Moth IV* which is being marketed by Hobbies Limited. It is the usual sailing model suitable for racing against other models on the Round Pond and suchlike places.

When Hobbies made their first prototype hull to scale, it had "all the appearance of static stability" when the first flotation tests were carried out. When the sails were set and sailing trials began it was found, however, that the keel was not heavy enough, and that the boat tended to heel over on its side, immersing the sails in the water. This is very similar to what occurred when *Gipsy Moth IV* underwent her first sailing trials. The keel was then redesigned by increasing the depth, the thickness and the weight of the ballast; also the keel was carried aft to the rudder post, just as Warwick Hood prescribed in Sydney. When the model was being tried out under radio control it was found that the rudder of the original design first resisted the control impetus and then went over with a "bang." Further sailing trials were then carried out on the model, and the performance was improved when the rudder area was reduced, and at the same time the rudder itself was increased in thickness, to line up with the modified keel.

It was then found that the mizzen sail "tended to tack over and veer the model off course," meaning that the mizzen sail was not balanced by the headsails, and consequently brought the model up into the wind. This same fault in *Gipsy Moth IV* itself was partly overcome in Sydney, when the topmast stays were moved further forward. This balanced the boat on most points of sailing. In the model, the designers reduced the mizzen sail area, which produced the same effect. If the model was rigged with a full-sized mainsail the sail stalled and flapped, thereby losing its drive. On the model the mainsail had to be reduced in size for the model to sail successfully. Finally, it was found that the speed and performance of the model were far beyond the makers' expectations. They thought that the hull design and rigging were now the best on the market, and when the model's performance was compared with full radio control racing yachts, it left those behind for both speed and controllability.

My comment on all this is: What a pity that the designers of *Gipsy Moth IV* did not have time to make a model to sail in the Round Pond before the boat was built! What a lot of trouble, worry and effort this would have saved me, by discovering *Gipsy Moth*'s vicious faults and curing them before the voyage!

the southern headland of Botany Bay. I had only 13½ miles to go to Sydney Heads. A smart blue police launch put out from Botany Bay, spoke to me, and gave me a welcome. I hoisted the White Ensign and the RYS burgee. Slowly I beat up the coast. As the land heated up, a sea breeze caused the wind to veer in direction, and I could nearly lay a course for Sydney, having to tack off-shore only for a mile or two every 5 miles. As I turned Sydney Heads, the wind was free at last, and it freshened up to a strong breeze. *Gipsy Moth* began showing her paces, and was romping along at times at 8 knots. I could not hold the tiller myself, but had to steer by means of the two tackles, one rigged each side from the tiller to the side of the cockpit. I could have eased the load on the tiller and rudder by paying off the mainsail, but I was now sailing fast with the wind aft of the beam, twisting amongst a fleet of boats of all sizes and kinds. I dared not risk having the boom squared off, for fear of a gybe resulting in a horrible foul-up of gear, followed by possible rammings or collisions. Through the loud hailer I asked the Royal Sydney Yacht Squadron launch to let me know when I could round up, and I asked the police launch to clear an area on my port side and astern, where I could round up and stop without being rammed by the big television launches and boats. This they did most efficiently. I rounded up, turned into the wind, and then paid off on the starboard tack, so that all the sails were aback. *Gipsy Moth* stopped almost dead, the launch came alongside, and the next minute Sheila and Giles were on board. It was a good reunion, and while we cracked a bottle of champagne on deck a police officer took the helm. As I could not start the motor without electricity, *Gipsy Moth* was taken in tow by the Sydney Yacht Squadron launch.

Gipsy Moth entered Sydney Heads at 4.30 P.M. on December 12 thus taking 107 days 5½ hours by the calendar or to be exact 106 days 20½ hours actual time after allowing for the change of longitude. The distance sailed was 14,100 miles. This was the total of the point to point noon to noon daily runs.

NINE

IN AUSTRALIA

THE CLIPPER route I had chosen to follow did not stop at Melbourne, which was the destination of most clippers, but went on to Sydney. This may require a little explanation, for Melbourne is a much easier landfall, it is 500 miles nearer Plymouth, and the passage to Sydney after passing Melbourne calls for tricky navigation through the Bass Strait, and then the need to keep inshore along the coast of New South Wales to avoid that fierce south-going current that I described in the last chapter. This is always liable to be hard going for a sailing ship, as it was for me, because of variable winds, and inshore currents, with the constant risk of being pushed into a bay, or of being becalmed and set on shore by a current.

Of course many sailing ships went to Sydney because their trade, mostly passengers or general cargo, took them there. As far as racing against the clipper times was concerned, I could have ended this first part of the voyage at Melbourne, and in some ways it would have been logical to do so. At noon on December 4, the ninety-ninth day of my passage, I was only 118 miles from Melbourne. I could have turned downwind and easily run into Melbourne within the 100 days from Plymouth. But I had personal reasons for feeling that I had to go to Sydney. Four times I have found my way to Sydney, each time on some exciting, romantic venture. I described this in *Along the Clipper Way*:

• • •

"On my first visit I steamed into the magnificent harbour from New Zealand; I was a blighted swain who had jumped on board the steamer in Wellington, New Zealand, because of an ice-blooded, heartless and haughty maiden travelling in the ship to Sydney. Though I had the usual profound belief that it was impossible, my bleeding heart survived this ordeal. My next visit was when I flew my Gipsy I Moth plane there to complete the second solo flight made from England to Australia. That was in

January 1930. I was escorted in by a flight of planes and was so agitated at the sight of all the crowds on Mascot Aerodrome that I landed like a rabbit lolloping over a rough meadow. It was all a great thrill—with the uproarious, friendly Sydney welcome—which must surely be unique.

"The third time I came to Sydney was from the east after I had made the first solo flight across the Tasman Sea from New Zealand to Australia. This was in my Gipsy I Moth seaplane and it was another thrilling experience to be alighting and taking off in that little seaplane in the great Sydney Harbour. The fourth visit was to start a flight from Sydney in a Puss Moth monoplane to Peking and then on to London: this was in 1936.

"And so I like to imagine sailing ships from England passing through Sydney Heads to drop anchor in the peaceful waters of Sydney Harbour after the 14,000 mile passage from Plymouth."

• • •

I was proud now to meet again that wonderful Sydney welcome, and felt that of all places in Australia this was where I should be.

Within ten minutes of stepping on shore, I was facing a press conference of, I was told, ninety-four different press outlets, including television and radio, the biggest, it seems, that had ever been held there. This was a change indeed after being alone for over three months, battling day and night without a break of more than a few hours at a time. I saw a film of this conference run through afterwards. I was interested to note how slowly at first an idea put to me in the form of a question penetrated my brain, and obtained a reactionary response. As the minutes passed, however, the film showed my receptiveness speeding up. A lot of the questions were tricky, metaphysical ones, which I thought rather stupid to fire at a man who had been alone for 100 days. After dealing for a long time with the basic facts of life, such as survival, one's values change completely as to what should, or should not, be taken seriously. To the question, "When were your spirits at their lowest ebb?" the obvious answer seemed to be, "When the gin gave out."

The Royal Sydney Yacht Squadron had invited me to tie up at their own dock, and I gratefully accepted. The mainspring of this delightful and excellent Yacht Club was Max Hinchliffe, ex-Captain of the Australian Navy. He had a tremendous boyish enthusiasm. Before I arrived, Sheila, when she first met him, had thought he was unresponsive, until she found that she had been talking to his deaf ear, the reason why he had retired from the Navy.

I don't think it would be possible anywhere to find a people more generously friendly than the Sydneyites, and particularly the Sydney Yacht Squadron. This club has its own boatyard, with shipwrights, joiners and engineers. All their facilities were offered to refit *Gipsy Moth* for her Cape Horn venture. Max was tireless in helping me. He immediately enlisted the help of Warwick Hood, the naval architect, who had designed the *Dame Pattie,* the 1967 challenger for the America's Cup. I already knew, and very much liked, Alan Payne, whom Sheila and I had met in Newport, Rhode Island, after my 1962 solo crossing of the North Atlantic; he was the designer of the Australian 12-metre *Gretel,* which competed against the Americans for the America's Cup in 1962. Alan had given up his private practice as a naval architect, and was designing craft for de Havilland's outside Sydney. He also offered to help and advise me, so straight away I had most wonderful help and advice from two of the naval architects I admire most in the world.

First, they tried to dissuade me from going on in *Gipsy Moth IV,* which they considered an unsuitable design for the job. I told Warwick how she had been built specially strong with a view to surviving a capsize and roll over. "Yes," he said one day, "but she might not come up again with that shape of hull." I said nothing. Alan expressed much the same views, and also tried to dissuade me from continuing. These men knew what they were talking about; capsizes occur in the wild Tasman Sea. I will not go into details of their views and our conversations.* When they found that I was going ahead with the voyage they brightened up visibly, and set about making *Gipsy Moth* as seaworthy as they possibly could. I told Warwick how *Gipsy Moth* broached to as easily as the flick of a cane. He put this down to the shape of the keel, and designed a steel extension to fill the gap between the lowest part of the keel and the heel

---

* I have been criticised for running down *Gipsy Moth IV.* "Don't forget," Sheila said to me, "that she has brought you further and faster than any other small boat has ever sailed on a passage." Let me say at once that I think she is a very handsome boat and if she is controlled she can go fast. Time after time she has reminded me of Lisette, the famous mare. Lisette belonged to General Marbot, ADC to Napoleon. Marbot was able to buy her because she had a bad habit of killing grooms. Marbot controlled this viciousness as far as he was concerned and she saved his life, once by her great speed, a second time by treading down and killing a Russian who was lunging at Marbot with a bayonet, and a third time by killing a Russian officer striking at Marbot with a sabre which wounded Lisette. I admire Lisette immensely, but I do not think I could ever have been fond of her.

of the rudder. He would have liked another extension of the keel forward, and I feel quite certain that he was right, but it was not practicable. I wanted the four topmast stays from the stem to the masthead reduced to two, and he agreed to that. I also wanted them footed as far forward as possible. He was somewhat reluctant to do this, but I was positive that the centre of the fore-triangle needed moving forward. This made the boat easier to tack and less difficult to balance. Warwick insisted on a totally different plan of stowage of all my gear and stores. Broadly speaking, the principle was to concentrate the weight amidships, and keep the ends light and buoyant. He would have liked to have a broad stern instead of the narrow pointed one, but I did not think that that change was practicable. Warwick did not just stick to theory, he spent hours up the mast, checking the rigging, and would tackle any troublesome job such as making the anemometer and the wind direction indicator work, which they had refused to do until he took a hand. He completely changed the loads on the mainmast shrouds, with a view to reducing the compression on the middle of the mast in the event of a capsize, when past experience has shown that the compression is apt to break the middle of the mast into several pieces which are shot out. (I may say that, except for two stays, I never adjusted any of Warwick's rigging afterwards.) Alan was in full agreement, and added one or two items for safety; for instance he made up two strongbacks, as he called them, to reinforce the forehatch which was heavy, weak, and generally of bad design. I remembered that its miserable little hinges had torn out of the woodwork the first day I sailed the boat on trials. The drawback to these strongbacks was that they bolted the hatch down permanently, so that sails could not be dropped down into the forecabin from the deck. Unfortunately, as will be related later, I did not fit these strongbacks soon enough after leaving Sydney.

Meanwhile the craftsmen in the Sydney Yacht Squadron yard were hard at work on *Gipsy Moth*. I had never seen faster and more efficient work done on a boat. The long Christmas holidays delayed the job, but Bob Williamson the engineer, for one, worked during his holidays to get forward with *Gipsy Moth*'s schedule. Jim Perry, the yard manager, who was an excellent shipwright and joiner, made great efforts to staunch the deck leaks. He fitted a quarter beading all round the doghouse, where it joined the deck, and stopped every leak there, except one. He made a big effort to staunch the leaks all along the edge of the deck by using a caulking of expanding rubber, which cut down the number of leaks considerably, but they were due to basic faults in the design or construction and it was an impossible task. He tackled the hatch over the companionway from the cockpit, which used to sluice me frequently if I was working at the galley when seas were sweeping the deck. He improved it greatly, but I still got a douche of sea water down my neck when a sea landed on top of the hatch.

The Lewmar winches had given me a lot of trouble and landed me in difficulties several times. I usually tack *Gipsy Moth* without needing a winch for the jib sheet. I start taking in the sheet as the boat comes head to wind, and have enough taken in with the sheet cleated up by the time the tack is completed. I do rely, however, on the winch spinning freely with the couple of turns of rope which I have passed round it. On several occasions the winch would not budge; it was seized up. By the time I got the sheet off the winch it was too late to cleat it up, and the tack was completely spoiled and useless. I would have either to head off the wind and wait until I had freed the winches, or wear the ship round back on to the other tack, and then proceed to free the winches. My cursing was unprintable, especially when this happened in the dark. I wrongly assumed that the jamming of the winches was due to salt water. On reaching Sydney we looked into this matter thoroughly and found that it was not the salt water at all, but the fact that three different metals had been used in the production of the winch and that the jamming was due to electrolytic action. I thought it incredible that a firm could offer such winches for off-shore sailing. An Australian firm making Barlow winches sportingly presented me with a set of these in Sydney. On the homeward passage, I never had to clean them, or even give them a spot of oil and they looked brand new at the end of it. What was so annoying was that I had specially asked the designer of *Gipsy Moth IV* to specify a different make of winch, and I even chose the model with him at the Boat Show. I wondered how this different make which had given me such tremendous trouble had been fitted.

As for the self-steering gear, Jim Mason took this in hand. He was the skipper and owner of *Cadence*, the yacht which had just won the Sydney to Hobart Race, one of the three most coveted prizes of off-shore racing, the other two being the Bermuda and Fastnet Races. Of these the Fastnet is likely to be the most difficult, the Sydney-Hobart the toughest, and Newport to Bermuda has had to limit the entry to 150 yachts. Jim Mason made two stainless steel plates for the steering oar to replace those which had snapped in half, and strengthened them. Unfortunately, they made the self-steering gear heavier still. Jim Perry repaired the wind vane itself, and as a result this also was heavier. To try to overcome the disadvantage which must result from the increased weight, namely that it would require more wind than before to move it, we fitted a heavier lead counterpoise. This, in turn, put more strain on the vane gear, and later in the voyage I removed it and replaced it with the old, lighter lead weight.

The sails went off to be repaired and various anti-chafe patches were sewn on. When we came to a trial sail, I was worried about the much heavier self-steering gear and asked for a special self-steering sail with a boom to be made. This sail was completed and delivered within twenty-four hours of ordering it from the sail makers.

All this time Sheila, Giles and I were leading a strenuous life. To start with we had a tremendous Sydney welcome to survive. There was an incessant pressure and temptation to enjoy ourselves. I wanted to reach the Horn before the end of February, which meant leaving Sydney by the middle of January, at latest. My Sydney friends felt that I had finished a voyage on reaching Sydney, and it was difficult for them to feel the urgency for me to get away, though they understood the reasoning which required it. I should not have got away for months if it had not been for Sheila and Giles. Sheila has an extraordinary flair for dealing with the public relations side of a project, and after I first arrived she took a lot of the pressure off me from press, radio and television demands. Giles, with some of his girl friends, unloaded *Gipsy Moth* so that work could be started on her, and acted on my behalf to start a dozen different operations in conjunction with Max. After settling the first flurry of paper work and discussions, Sheila started organising the revictualling and replenishing of stores. This was midsummer, and all the time the hot Sydney sun shone with a scorching heat for anyone fresh from England. The amount of work to be got through was tremendous. I had hoped my elder son George who had been living in Australia for twenty years and his wife Gay could help me. But they had been married only a year.

We had to press on with the work so I saw little of George and his wife after our first meeting. I was decidedly below par physically, and seemed unable to get enough rest to pick up condition. My leg was still bad enough to prevent my walking properly. I think that if I could have had the exercise that I am used to, I would quickly have got fitter. I started doing exercises every morning after I got up, but that was not enough. Swimming might have been a good thing if I could have found a secluded patch of smooth water, but since I had trouble with my lung I hate putting my head under water, and I could not face the wonderful surfing for which Sydney is famous. Colin Anderson, whose son Robert is the godson of Tony Dulverton's mother, is a dentist who served with the Australian Air Force during the War; he fixed up my broken tooth for me, but got very agitated about my lameness and persuaded me to go to a doctor (Warwick Stening) who astonished me by saying that from Colin's description he had thought at first that I had a tumour on my spine! I mention these things because they were all part of a steady pressure on me from many different quarters to discontinue my voyage.

Two photographs taken on my arrival caused me an immense amount of trouble. The first was of Giles giving me a hug when he leapt on board. He is much taller than I am, and pretty husky, and the photograph makes me look like an old man of a hundred weeping on his shoulder. (Perhaps if I had been a vegetarian from birth, like Giles, who has never eaten fish or meat in his life, I might have been as tall and husky as he is, and the trouble which arose from this photograph would not have happened.) The second photograph was taken, as I stepped ashore, looking down on me from above, which nearly always produces a disagreeable picture of someone; a police officer was holding one of my arms, and Giles, or someone, was supporting me by the other; and altogether I looked like the oldest inhabitant of Little Teapot by the Sea being helped out towards his one hundred and tenth birthday cake. These ghastly photographs were circulated in Britain, together with some of my outspoken criticisms of *Gipsy Moth IV*. As a result I had a telegram from Tony, the principal owner of the boat, saying that on no account must I continue the voyage. I replied telegraphing him to disregard newspaper reports, thanked him for giving me a chance to pull out if I wanted to without losing face, and ended the telegram: "Anyway I am sailing." In fact, the boat was on charter to me for a peppercorn rent for two years, and the charter expressly stated that it was intended that I should attempt this round-the-world voyage. I was told afterwards that another organisation which had contributed some money towards the cost of *Gipsy Moth* in return for the advertising value, had wanted to publish a statement disclaiming any responsibility if I came to grief on the second half of the voyage. Undoubtedly I was in very poor condition when I landed at Sydney. I had had little sleep for the previous two nights beating up against wind and current, criss-crossing the busy steamer lane. My left leg was still lame, and I could not balance on it, which is why I let someone help me ashore, and I was certainly undernourished, if not partially starved. I reckoned that I had lost 40 lb in weight, but my family declared this exaggerated nonsense. I regret I did not weigh myself until I had been ashore among the fleshpots of Sydney for ten days, but I was still 24 lb under my normal weight then. Captain Alan Villiers, who probably knows more about Cape Horn sailing conditions than anyone else, as far as square riggers are concerned, burst into print with the following letter in *The Guardian* of January 11:

"I see that the redoubtable Francis Chichester plans to sail homewards by way of the Horn, as one would expect. But I hope that this time he will not drive himself singlehanded against some record of 'average' made by some clipper ships. I would strongly suggest that he either ship some of those young fellows who abound in Sydney, used to the Tasman Sea (a nasty place) in rugged yachts, or heave-to by night or whenever he requires to rest, on the passage.

"In my opinion, no self-steering device can be really satisfactory over the 6,000 mile run from Sydney towards the Horn. Sailors learned long ago that the price of survival there is constant vigilance and expert helmsmanship, with equally constant attention to the set of the sails. The strong winds can and often do change suddenly and most violently through six or eight compass points, bringing up a vicious cross-sea in which the running ship staggers and lurches and rolls. She can be flung off course in a moment, and she is fortunate if she can get back again.

"The sea has an unbroken fetch right round the world down there: a ship runs within the ice line: she has to get down to south of 57° South.

"The master has to be looking, or adequate and experienced assistants must watch with clear eyes. It is a simple thing for the yacht to find herself lifted on some great sea boiling underneath her in its headlong rush towards the Horn, quite out of control in the cross-sea brought up by the shifting wind. And so she broaches-to, falls into the trough broadside-to, with the tremendous tumult of the ghastly breakers murderous and merciless around her. Such a vessel as the *Gipsy Moth IV* can then be rolled right over.

"The answer is to heave-to in time, yielding to the sea and not trying to run in it, with a rag of canvas in the after rigging to keep her head up, a drip of oil through the for'ard lavatory pipes to drift to wind'ard and make a slick there, in which the yielding vessel may live. Meantime, the west winds will continue to drive her towards the Horn; she will make it, probably.

"In the full-rigged ship *Joseph Conrad*, I had to heave-to five times between the Islands and the Horn, though she was a strong ship and I had three splendid watch-keeping officers. In the four-masted barque *Parma* we broached-to one night. She pooped a big sea. It washed the steering compasses away, and there she was flung athwart the maddened sea in a moment, rolling violently, swept fore-and-aft, the main deck a boiling of violent and turbulent waters like the bottom of Niagara Falls. We lived, by the grace of God and the strength of that well-built Scots ship. But a good many ships failed to survive such tests.

"I do not want to see Francis Chichester land back in England a wraith again, as he came to Sydney. I do want to see him land. We cannot spare him."

Captain Villiers expanded these warnings in an interview with John Seddon in the *Sun* of January 12, which I reproduce here:

" 'I beg Chichester not to attempt it. The outward trip he has made is simple compared with this one. That yacht may suddenly be lifted on boiling seas and rushed headlong towards the Horn.

" 'The winds shift as if they are being controlled by some demon.

" 'When I took the barque *Parma* round, she tossed in the maddened seas, rolled violently, swept fore and aft by the breakers and the main deck swamped with boiling turbulent waters which were like the bottom of Niagara.

" 'That voyage presents the lousiest, most incredible seas I ever came across in all my years at sea. The worst any man will ever meet.

" 'I don't know what drives this man to go on tempting the might of the seas.

" 'Chichester is magnificent, laudable. He is a wonderful fellow. Quiet, determined and capable.

" 'God has been very good to him, and very patient. But to handicap yourself with such a monstrously small yacht in those seas at the age of sixty-five and after a serious operation seems to me to be asking a little too much of God.'

"Captain Villiers, who gained fame when he sailed a replica of the *Mayflower* from Plymouth, England, to Plymouth, Massachusetts, in 1957, is one of the few men with first-hand knowledge of what Chichester and his 53-foot *Gipsy Moth* are facing.

"He remembers vividly the screaming tumult and the mur-derous strength of the breakers when he sailed the fully-rigged sailing ship *Joseph Conrad* round the Horn. He was mate of the *Parma*, which he sailed on the same vicious course.

"Chichester watched a film of the vindictive seas of his chosen homeward course on a visit to Captain Villiers's Oxford home before he sailed single-handed to Australia, said Villiers.

" 'It made him very thoughtful but I couldn't get him to change his mind.

" 'He knows that he has 6,000 miles of fearful sailing through the Roaring 40's and the Shrieking 50's of the Tas-man Sea which is open to the Antarctic, before he gets to the Horn.

" 'I faced them with a full, experienced crew and officers. I would not attempt it single-handed and I don't know any professional seaman who would. The risks are too great.

" 'I don't see how he can keep going by himself—he will be flung around miserably for about six weeks.

" 'Chichester has done enough. I've told him that he is an inspiration now, but he won't be if he is thrown into those savage seas. We need this man and this inspiration.

" 'He is a redoubtable man with abundant courage and we cannot spare him.' "

I have the greatest respect for Alan, and secretly I agreed with everything he said about the Horn, but I replied: "No matter what anyone says anywhere, I am sailing as soon as I can. I wish they would pipe down and let me get on with the job."

I had quite a big enough job, a man-size job I reckoned, to get the boat and gear in order soon enough to get away on time, to collect all the stores and gear required for a four months' non-stop passage, to get the radio links organised with New Zealand, Argentina and Britain, as well as to deal with a hundred other problems such as radio beacons, weather charts, ordinary charts. Max Hinchliffe gave me invaluable help; for example he wangled a corrected volume of radio beacon frequencies as a gift from the Captain of HMAS *Perth*, the Australian Navy's cruiser; and most important, he dug up the relevant pages from the Admiralty's *Ocean Passages of the World* giving details of the clipper route in the Atlantics for different months of the year. John Pleasants not only checked the radio links for the second half of the voyage, and checked over the radio telephone, but also discovered that one of the insulators on my starboard backstay aerial was cracked. A replacement was impossible, so he made up a fresh insulator himself. I came to realise that this backstay aerial was the better of the two, and ended up by relying on it entirely. I was immensely impressed by the efficiency of my Australian helpers. I had a lot of help, too, from the Chief Naval Officer at Canberra, Commander George, RN, who exchanged signals with HMS *Protector* patrolling in the Falkland Islands area. *Protector* sent me the wonderful news that there was no ice north of 60° S in Drake's Passage. All the time I was under a steady bombardment of press articles and letters from retired sailors who had been round the Horn, besides hundreds of letters from a few who had not the faintest notion what they were talking about, predicting my watery end if I persisted, or begging me not to go on with the venture.

The following appeared in a round up of clairvoyants expressing their views for the coming year in the *Sunday Express*, January 1, 1967:

> "Lone yachtsman Francis Chichester is doomed to failure in his attempt to sail around the world. This is the opinion of clairvoyant Marjorie Staves. 'But he will come home to one of the greatest welcomes in our history,' she told me. 'He will give up due to lack of physical strength. But any man who has such great mental strength as to make me feel it across thousands of miles is going to make a wonderful try.' "

All these negative wishings and willings on the part of different people use up valuable strength in resisting them, just as prayer and positive wellwishing give strength, and lend support. Just as Alan Villiers carried great weight with his opinions in England, Captain John Jagoe, a retired sea captain in Sydney, had great publicity in Australia when he said that I had only a fifty-fifty chance of survival, and that I must be "a glorious bloody fool" to attempt it. Incidentally, he said that it was nonsense to assess the average clipper passage as 100 days, and that Lubbock in his books had only quoted the fastest clipper passages of the year, and that the 100 days was the average of the fastest; that 127 days was the true average, which I had beaten handsomely. He sounded a great character and we enticed him to our hotel for tea and a talk.

At about this time I jumped off the stem of *Gipsy Moth* on to the jetty, my foot slipped on the edge of the planking, and I came down a purler, hitting the bone of my good leg on the edge of the wharf. This was seen by a reporter, and more articles appeared, asserting my unfitness, and that I should be stopped from proceeding. I tried to point out that, on the contrary, the fact that I had picked myself up and got on with my job ought to be a qualification for continuing the voyage, but I thought that this argument was received with undue glumness. Although all these things depressed me, I had found out about the hazards of the voyage, and had weighed them up three and a half years ago; and it was then that I had decided to attempt the voyage. There was no question now of whether I went on or not. Sometimes I got positive support which gave me strength; particularly, I remember with gratitude the strength I drew from Lady Casey, the Governor General's wife, whom I had known for many years because of being a fellow patron of Gertrude McKenzie's Flying Club outside Melbourne. Maie Casey, who is one of the outstanding women of the century, said, "Pouf! Take no notice what the papers say or anyone else says, go right ahead."

Some of the forecasts were amusing, if you can call a barbed arrow which sticks into your flesh amusing. One night Sheila and I were walking up to the Village for some dinner at a Chinese restaurant, when we passed a man haranguing or preaching to the crowd. When he saw me he stopped, came over, and thrust a pamphlet into my hand, saying, "You need this; you, more than anyone, should prepare to meet your doom."

I do not believe that there is any other woman in the world who could have stood up against this steady sniping from doom forecasters as Sheila did. I had an active role to play, and also I should be away once the passage started, whereas Sheila would be left with even worse attacks to repel. She not only had the endless questions: "Aren't you frightened that he will be drowned?" but also "How could you bear to let him go?" To make matters more difficult for her she sprained her ankle in Sydney. The Sunday before I left she got up suddenly from off her bed to answer the telephone, her ankle was "asleep," and when she put her weight on her foot the ankle doubled up under it. She tore three ligaments.

TEN

CAPSIZE IN THE TASMAN SEA

GILES HAD to return to Oxford, and I was sorry to see him go. I think both of us were thinking of the uncertainty of life. I badly missed his help, too. I was making every possible effort to get away, feeling that every week's delay could mean more unpleasantness at the Horn. At last the time came when I could give out that I was leaving at 11.00 hrs on Sunday, January 29. When the day came there was a tropical cyclone north-east of Sydney, and it would have been advisable to delay my leaving. But I hated to do this. I think I have always sailed when I said I would. Max Hinchliffe advised me to get south as much as I could because of the storm, but foolishly I disregarded this excellent advice.

There was no storm in Sydney itself that morning—it was a fine, sunny day. And so, at 11.00 precisely, *Gipsy Moth IV* slipped her moorings and stood out to sea. Lord Casey, the Governor General, had presented me with three miniature bales of wool to be carried by *Gipsy Moth* to London and I reckoned that they were travelling by the smallest wool clipper that ever left Australia! I had a crack crew, all friends, to sail the boat to Sydney Heads. In spite of her foot, Sheila took the helm, and the ship was worked by Alan Payne, Warwick Hood, Max Hinchliffe and Hugh Eaton. Hugh had been working for several days without a let-up helping to get *Gipsy Moth* ready for sea. At the Heads, my crew transferred by way of a rubber motor boat to Trygve Halvorsen's launch, which was standing by as a tender. Sheila and I parted as if for a day. She has an uncanny foresight in spiritual matters, and had no doubt but that we should meet again. I must confess that I wondered rather sadly if we would as I sailed away from the fleet.

I passed Sydney Heads at 12.15, and at 14.30 the last of the accompanying boats left me. I had trouble with the propeller shaft, which I couldn't stop rotating. The brake would not work, so I had to dive down under the cockpit, head first and feet up, to fix the

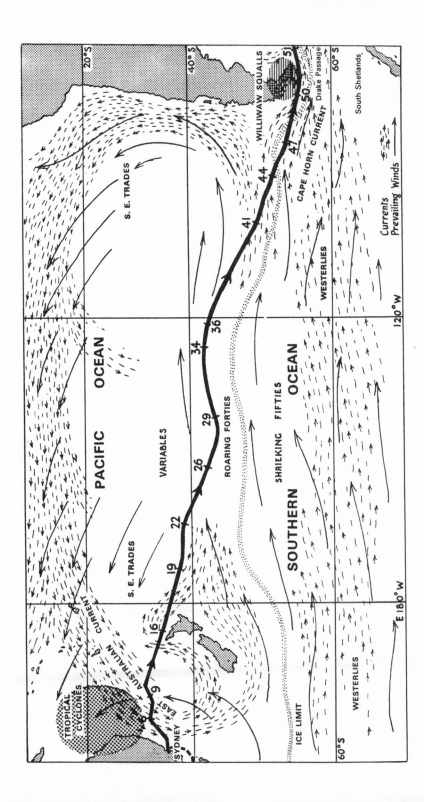

thing. I didn't enjoy these upside-down antics, and I felt horribly seasick. By 18.00 I was becalmed, but the calm didn't last long. There was a dense roll of clouds above the horizon, and wind began coming in from the south, at first lightly, but soon blowing up. By 19.00 it was coming at me in a series of savage bursts. At first I ran off northwards at 8 knots, then I took down all sail and lay ahull— that is, battened down, without sail, to give completely to the sea like a cork—in a great deluge of rain, reducing visibility to about 50 yards. Soon it got dark, and it was *very* dark—absolutely pitch dark. I was seasick and turned in but didn't get much rest. After about three quarters of an hour I heard the self-steering oar banging about, and went on deck to deal with it. The wind then was about 35 knots, and I thought that *Gipsy Moth* could stand a jib and get moving again. I set a working jib, but it was too much for her. So I replaced it with a storm jib. With this I left her to fight her way slowly east at about 2 knots and turned in again, determined to sleep all night.

I stayed in my bunk until just after 04.00, when the wind began coming still more strongly and I went up to drop the storm jib and lie ahull again. We stayed like this for most of the day; it was too rough for even a storm jib with the wind blowing at 50 knots or more. In the afternoon I did set a storm jib, reefed to only 60 square feet,* a mere rag of sail, chiefly to try to cut down thumping in the heavy seas. I hoped that the thumping was due to the self-steering gear, and not to the new false keel.

In spite of the storm, radio conditions were good, and at 8 A.M. I had a good radio talk with Sheila which cheered me up. I was still sick from time to time, but slowly began to feel better, and gave myself some brandy, sugar and lemon, which I managed to keep down. The weather forecasts were bad with renewed cyclone warnings. This was Tropical Cyclone Diana, which was reported to be moving SE at about 20 mph. I tried to work out where it was in relation to me, and I reckoned that the worst of it would pass some 270 miles to the east of my noon position. That was something, but the whole area of the Tasman Sea was violently disturbed with winds from 40 to 60 knots, gusting up to 80 knots in squalls. There was nothing I could do about it. I did not worry over much, but just tried to exist until the storm passed.

That Monday night was as foul and black a night as you could meet at sea. Although it was pitch dark, the white breakers showed in the blackness like monstrous beasts charging down on the yacht. They towered high in the sky, I wouldn't blame anyone for being

---

*I had had reefing points fitted to this sail in Sydney.

terrified at the sight. My crosstree light showed up the breaking water, white in the black darkness, and now and then a wave caught the hull and, breaking against it, sluiced over the decks. As I worked my way along the deck I thought: "Christ! What must it be like in a 120-knot wind!" I dropped the remaining storm sail, furled and tied it down. *Gipsy Moth* had been doing 8 knots with the little sail set, and I thought she would be less liable to damage lying ahull with no forward speed. As I worked my way aft again after finishing the job on the foredeck, I looked at the retaining net amidships, holding the two big genoas bagged up, and the 1,000 feet of warp in several coils. I knew that I ought to pass a couple of ropes over the net between the eye bolts at each side for storm lashings—I had always done this before on the passage out. But these ropes had not been re-rigged in Sydney and I was feeling ghastly, I thought due to seasickness. (From something which happened later I can only deduce that the chief cause of my trouble was the Australian champagne I had drunk. For some reason this acted like poison on me.) Whatever the cause of my trouble, I weakened, and decided to leave the extra lashing until the morning. When I got below and had stripped off my oilskins I rolled into my bunk and put all the lights out. This was about two hours after dark. The bunk was the only place where one could wait below, for it was difficult to stand up, and I should have been continually thrown off if I had sat on the settee. However, lying on my back in the bunk, I dropped into a fitful sleep after a while.

I think I was awake when the boat began to roll over. If not, I woke immediately she started to do so. Perhaps when the wave hit her I woke. It was pitch dark. As she started rolling I said to myself "Over she goes!" I was not frightened, but intensely alert and curious. Then a lot of crashing and banging started, and my head and shoulders were being bombarded with crockery and cutlery and bottles. I had an oppressive feeling of the boat being on top of me. I wondered if she would roll over completely, and what the damage would be; but she came up quietly the same side that she had gone down. I reached up and put my bunk light on. It worked, giving me a curious feeling of something normal in a world of utter chaos. I have only a confused idea of what I did for the next hour or so. I had an absolutely hopeless feeling when I looked at the pile of jumbled up food and gear all along the cabin. Anything that was in my way when I wanted to move I think I put back in its right place, though feeling as I did so that it was a waste of time as she would probably go over again. The cabin was 2 foot deep all along with a jumbled-up pile of hundreds of tins, bottles, tools, shackles, blocks, two sextants and oddments. Every settee locker, the whole starboard bunk, and the three starboard drop lockers had all emptied out when she was upside down. Water was swishing about on the cabin sole beside the chart table, but not much. I looked into the bilge which is 5 feet deep, but it was not quite full, for which I thought, "Thank God."

This made me get cracking with the radio, at forty-five minutes after midnight, and two and a quarter hours after the capsize. I was afraid that the radio telephone would go out of action through water percolating it, and that even if it didn't, if the boat went over again the mass of water in the bilge must inevitably flood the telephone and finish it. I had to try to get a message through to say that I was all right, so that if the telephone went dead people would not think that I had foundered because of that. I called up on the distress frequency 2182 and got Sydney Radio straight away. As usual they were most efficient and co-operative. I asked them to give my wife a message in the morning to say that I had capsized, but that I was all right and that if they got no more messages from me it would only be because the telephone had been swamped and packed up, and not because I had foundered. I asked particularly that they should not wake up Sheila in the middle of the night, but call her at seven o'clock in the morning. I said that I did not need any help.

I am not sure when I discovered that the water was pouring in through the forehatch. What had happened was that when the boat was nearly upside down, the heavy forehatch had swung open, and when the boat righted itself the hatch, instead of falling back in place, fell forward onto the deck, leaving the hatchway wide open to the seas. It may seem strange that my memory is so confused, but it was a really wild night, the movement was horrible and every step was difficult.

I must have got out on deck to pump the water below the level of the batteries. I found the holding net torn from its lashings. One of my 600-foot genoas had gone, a drogue, and 700 feet of inch-and-a-half plaited warp. The other big genoa was still there in its bag pressed against the leeward lifeline wires. I don't remember how I secured it. I found the forehatch open and closed that. A section of the cockpit coaming and a piece of the side of the cockpit had been torn away. I was extremely puzzled at the time to know how this could have happened. The important thing was that the masts were standing, and the rigging appeared undamaged. I think it was then that I said to myself, "To hell with everything," and decided to have a sleep. I emptied my bunk of plates, cutlery and bottles, etc. One serrated-edged cutting knife was embedded close to where my head had been, and I thought how lucky I was. I had only a slightly cut lip; I do not know what caused that.

My bunk was soaking wet, which was no wonder, considering that in the morning I could see daylight through where the side of the cockpit had been torn away just above the bunk. But I did not give a damn how wet it was, turned in, and was soon fast asleep. I slept soundly till daylight.

When I awoke the boat was still being thrown about. All that day it was blowing a gale between 40 and 55 knots. I was still queasy and unable to face eating anything. I had not had a proper meal since leaving Sydney. Now and then I had some honey and water, but even that was an ordeal, for I had not filled up my vacuum flasks with hot water before starting as I always intend to do before a voyage, so that I can have honey and water hot as soon as I feel queasy. And I was faced with this awful mess; it looked like a good week's work to clear up, sort and re-pack everything. I have rarely had less spirit in me. I longed to be back in Sydney Harbour, tied up to the jetty. I hated and dreaded the voyage ahead. Let's face it; I was frightened and had a sick feeling of fear gnawing inside me. If this was what could happen in an ordinary storm, how could a small boat possibly survive in a 100-knot greybearder?

After this I made another tour of inspection, surveying the damage. Some extraordinary things had happened. The long mahogany boathook which had been lashed down at the side of the deck was jammed between the shrouds about 6 feet up in the air. By a great stroke of luck the locker under one of the cockpit seats, which had a flap lid with no fastening at all, was still full of gear, including the reefing handles for the main boom and the mizzen boom. I suppose the jumble of ropes and stuff which filled this locker (so that it was practically impossible to find anything in it) had jammed so tightly when upside down that nothing had spilled out. On the other hand, sundry winch handles, which had been in open-topped boxes specially made for them in the cockpit, had all disappeared.

Down below some queer things had happened. To start with, there was that foul smell. I sniffed the bilges, but it did not come from there. I tried the batteries, but they fortunately had been clamped down securely in the bilge and were perfectly all right. At last I tracked it down to the vitamin pills, pink vitamin C. The bottle had shot across the boat from the cupboard above the galley sink, and had smashed to pieces on the doghouse above my head. The pills had spread all over the windows in the doghouse, where they partly dissolved in sea water. I tried to mop them up but the melting vitamin mixture smeared into the joint between the Perspex and wood of the windows and into every possible crack and cranny. For the time being I had to put up with the stink. The irony of it was that I never used a vitamin pill on the whole passage!

I worked at the pump intermittently, stopping for a rest after every 200 strokes (the water had to be "lifted" 10–11 feet) and doing some other job as a change from pumping. When at last I got to the bottom of the bilge I found an assortment of plates and crockery, and also I found plates beside the motor, and one right aft of the motor. I was much puzzled at the time to know how these plates had got into such extraordinary positions, but realised later what had happened. The motor had a wooden casing covering it in at its forward end in the cabin, and the top of this is a step which hinges upwards. This lid had flown open, so that the plates had shot through the gap and when the boat righted herself, the lid had closed down again. One of the strangest things happened at the forward end of the cabin, where I kept on finding minute particles of razor-sharp, coloured glass. It was a long time before I tracked down the origin of this, but one day I came across a cork stuck into about an inch of the neck of a bottle. This was a long time later, but I mention it here because it provided some valuable evidence. It was the cork and neck of a bottle of Irish whiskey, which Jack Tyrrell of Arklow, who built *Gipsy Moth III*, had sent me as a present at the start of this voyage. I knew exactly where this bottle had been standing, in a hole cut in a sheet of plywood to take the bottle in the wine locker on the starboard side of the cabin. This locker had a flap-down lid. So I knew exactly where the bottle had come from. I also knew exactly where it had gone to; it had hit a deck beam in the ceiling of the cabin, making a bruise a quarter of an inch deep in the wood. Here it had shattered into a thousand fragments, and it was not till even later in the voyage that I found out where most of these were. At the foot of Sheila's bunk on the port side of the cabin there was a shelf, of which half was boxed in with a flap-down lid. In this case also the lid had flown open when the boat went over, the pieces of glass had shot in, and the lid had closed down again. As I write this, the glass is still there. The last fragment of glass I found was one that had dropped onto the cabin floor from somewhere and lodged in the sole of my foot when I was going barefoot. The point about this glass is that it enabled me to measure the exact path of the bottle, which showed that the boat had turned through 131° when the bottle flew out of its niche; in other words, the mast would have then been 41° below the horizontal. I wondered if the shock of a wave hitting the boat had shot the bottle out of its locker, but there was other evidence which convinced me that this was not the case. On the roof of the doghouse the paintwork was spattered all over with particles of dirt up to a line just like a highwater mark on a beach. This dirt must have come from the floor of the cabin when the hatches above the bilge flew off. The particles were so small they would not have any momentum if a wave had hit the boat with a shock; they would have got on to the roof only by dropping there through gravity. What I have described and other little bits of evidence which I came across during the succeeding months convince me that the yacht rolled over until the mast was between 45 and 60° below the horizontal, and I don't believe it would have made much difference if she had come up the other side after completely rolling over.

But this detective work came later. I must return to the state of things at the time. There was butter everywhere and over everything, for 2 lb of butter had landed at the foot of my bunk, and splashed and spread. Coat hangers in the hanging locker were broken, and the basin was full of my clothes. Also in the basin was a Tupperware box containing my first aid equipment. Both cabin bunks had collapsed, spilling the contents of Tupperware containers on top of the contents of the drop lockers. Tins of food, fruit and milk were jumbled up on the cabin floor with shackles, sextants, biscuits and cushions. All the floor boards had taken to the air when *Gipsy Moth* went over, so everything that could find its way to the bilges had duly got there. My camera stand had broken in two, but the loose half was still lying on deck up to windward. The main halliard was tangled with the burgee halliard.

Gipsy Moth capsized on the night of Monday, January 30. My log notes briefly: "About 22.30. Capsize." Heavy weather continued throughout Tuesday, January 31, and I spent the day lying ahull, doing what I could to clear up. The electric bilge pump would not work, so I had to pump by hand, trying to repair the electric pump in the intervals of hand pumping. After I had cleaned the impeller the electric pump worked for a few minutes, but then sucked at an air lock. The bilge was still half-full, but gradually I got the water down. I streamed my remaining green warp in the hope that it would keep the yacht headed downwind, but without any sails up the warp seemed to have no effect. So I hauled it back inboard and coiled it. The socket for the vane shaft of the self-steering gear was nearly off, so that had to be repaired, a dirty job which put me under water now and again. Thank God the water was warm! As I dealt with these various jobs one after another, my spirits began to pick up. I had been unbelievably lucky. The masts and rigging were all intact, which I attributed largely to Warwick's rigging. I felt a sense of loss that one of the big genoas had gone overboard, but I could get on without it. I was upset at losing one of my drogues and the 700 feet of drogue warp that went with it, for I had intended to stream a drogue at the end of a long warp to slow down *Gipsy Moth* and to keep her stern to the seas in Cape Horner storms. Later, after I had pondered the details of my capsize for many hours, I completely discarded the warp and drogue idea. So the loss of those items was not as serious as I thought at the time.

As the day wore on I began to feel a little hungry, and I lunched on three slices of bread and butter and marmalade. The bread was pretty mouldy, but it was solid food, and went down well. My log for that day notes cheerfully: "18.20. Called Sydney Radio. Told Sheila the tale."

That radio talk with Sheila meant much to me. She was as calm and confident as always, and never for a moment questioned my decision to carry on. I said again that I did not want any help. She was distressed as I was about the mess in our beautifully tidy boat. I could tell her about everything, because she knew exactly where everything was. I remember telling her about the horrible smell like stale, spilled beer, from wet vitamin tablets sticking to the cabin roof. I told her that I had spares on board for most things, and that in time I should be able to tidy up. I drew strength from her.

ELEVEN

"I HAVE BEEN DAMNED LUCKY"

THE ADMIRALTY sailing instructions for square-rigged ships stated emphatically that ships leaving Sydney for the homeward voyage round Cape Horn should proceed south-east to pass south of New Zealand, no matter what the wind was after leaving Sydney. That was the Clipper Way, and the maps in my book *Along the Clipper Way* show the route passing south of New Zealand or, at the most northerly, going through Cook Strait between the North and South Islands of New Zealand. For me, in the situation in which I found myself after the capsize, other considerations were compelling. To have gone south would have meant thrashing into a head wind, and with the appalling mess on board still to be cleared up I did not want to do it. The cabin was still a chaos of tins and stores, and to clear a passage through it the yacht had to be kept upright. I had to head north-east to keep her sufficiently upright to make a start on clearing up, and then I kept going on the same heading while I did more clearing up. Finally, I decided to carry on and sail north-about round New Zealand, instead of south-about; the going, I reckoned, should be easier, and the weather milder and warmer. As well as all the clearing, sorting, repacking and relisting of stores for six months that had to be done below, I needed as smooth sailing as I could get to enable me to repair the damage to the cockpit, where the water was pouring off the deck into my berth. I was at a low ebb physically, partly from having eaten next to nothing since leaving Sydney, partly from having felt ill or queasy so much of the time. But I was getting better, and the sheer weight of work to be done, although depressing in some ways, helped me to recover my spirits.

The weather continued rough, but by Wednesday morning, February 1, I had the yacht sailing again, under a trysail and working jib. I refastened the foredeck net, rescued the broken pole-stand for my camera, and recovered the boathook from the rigging. There was still a full gale blowing, but the sun was out, and life began to seem more cheerful. But I worked slowly, and was often thrown off balance. I put this down to being weak from lack of food.

Towards noon I knocked off for breakfast, and had a splendid meal of coffee and toast and marmalade. I was also careless, and scalded myself rather badly by tipping a mug of newly made coffee over my arm and leg. It was my own fault for trying to cut toast on a swinging table with a mug of coffee standing there. I applied bicarbonate of soda at once and congratulated myself that things might have been much worse. After breakfast I had a snooze.

I awoke about 13.30 from a heavy sleep and a vivid dream that I was in Baghdad opening a shop. It was a most realistic dream, and for a few moments after waking up I thought that I was in Baghdad. But I soon came back to *Gipsy Moth*, got up, and got to work again. I treated four small cuts on my right hand and my scalded right arm, wondering while I did so why only my right hand and arm had suffered, and there was nothing on my left. I felt better for my sleep, and set to work on what I reckoned to be the worst of the many jobs in front of me, fixing the propeller shaft-brake, which had come adrift again, and the engine's exhaust cut-off, which had been jammed open. I reckoned that if water entered the engine through this open exhaust valve it could mean the end of battery-charging.

I disliked both jobs extremely. Dealing with the exhaust valve meant lying on my belly, with my arms stretched above my face. The shaft-brake meant similar contortions, head down, with my feet up beside the engine. The shaft was spinning fast while we were sailing. I had been warned before leaving England to prevent this spinning, and had thought much about the best way of tackling it. At first I had a go from the side of the engine beside my bunk, and managed to stop the shaft temporarily. But I needed to reach across to the other side of the engine and was afraid of stretching my body over the top of the shaft for fear of its spinning again and catching my clothes so that I would be held down there, unable to move. Finally, I crawled through to the starboard side of the motor from the after-hatch, and got the job done. Both the exhaust job and work on the shaft-brake were made easier for me by a 13-inch spanner and a universal grip tool that had been given to me in Sydney, but I was "down under" on the job for an hour and forty minutes.

The wind seemed to be dropping a little, though still blowing around 30–40 knots. I considered setting a bit more sail, but decided against it, and went on with clearing up. I should have been glad of a rest, but I felt that I must try to get things more ship-shape in case the weather worsened again. It was hard to know where to begin. Bottles, tins and bags of fruit had shot out of their lockers to where the cabin bunk had been before it collapsed. Seven large airtight containers, all full of food, had been stacked on top of the other bunk, and most of these had ended up on top of the port-side mess. They had burst open, and their contents had spilled around them. On the port side there had been sixteen loaded containers, and these, too, had burst open and crashed down on the vegetables and fruit below. I made a start to starboard, and worked for two and a half hours at tidying up and restowing things in the bunk, three drop lockers and three settee lockers. I came across half a dozen bad apples and lemons, which I was glad to find, to get them over the side before they contaminated anything else. All the bread was going mouldy, and I decided that it would have to be rebaked. But that was enough for one day, and I turned in.

A depressing sun sight next morning (February 2) put me only 124 miles from Sydney, which I felt must be a record for slow going. The weather forecast offered a promise of slowly moderating sea and south-east winds, which were at least better than winds dead on the nose. There was nothing for it but to get on with the job of clearing up. I tackled the mess on the port side of the cabin, which was harder than working to starboard, because the yacht was heeled to port at an angle of some 35°, and this made it difficult to lift or move things there. I had to move everything away first to get standing room before starting to stow. Some of the containers were pretty heavy—one had 15 lb of wholemeal flour in it. Working in that mess of food and stores was like engaging in a lucky dip, and the interest of finding things helped to keep me going. I came across my eggs, packed in plastic foam containers, and I was astonished to discover that only two were broken. The mess that those two eggs made was enough—I dreaded to think what it would have been if all the eggs had broken. Apart from the satisfactory reduction of mess, I was relieved to find my eggs intact, for eggs are among my most valuable sources of food, and I suffered much from the loss of my eggs on the way to Australia.

Twenty pumps cleared the bilge, which was a relief, but there was water in the forepeak; I had to siphon that out with a long pipe. The water there must have come from a deck leak.

I was delighted to find the bilge keeping so dry, because a full bilge would have been a serious menace to the radio. Odd things kept turning up—and not turning up. One strange disappearance was a vacuum flask, which *must* have been on board somewhere, but which had vanished. The plates and crockery in the bilge set a problem in recovery, for they were inaccessible except to the end of a 6-foot pole. I left them for the moment, deciding that I would have to think about this.

Next came the cockpit. This was an urgent job, for water poured into my bunk through the damaged cockpit when a sea came on board, but I needed better conditions on deck for working at repairs. My sleeping bag and blankets were soaked through. In the immediate excitement after my capsize I had scarcely noticed how wet they were, but I didn't fancy going on sleeping in wet things. So I managed a temporary repair to the cockpit with sealing compound and a plastic covering, and hoped that this might serve until I could think of something better.

As night fell this day I reckoned up my profit and loss account so far since leaving Sydney. The loss was severe. The boat was still in a dreadful mess, and I had sailed only 185 miles since starting. For four days I had been bumped about and thrown, twisted, accelerated and jerked as if in a tiny toy boat in a wild mountain stream, and I was sick of it all. But everything that mattered on *Gipsy Moth* was intact; she had capsized and righted herself. She had been through an experience which few yachts have survived intact and she could still sail. It continued rough, but at last the wind had eased, and even if it was only a lull, it was a relief to be free for a while of that tiring, menacing roar and the whining in the rigging. The Tasman Sea was now much as it was when I had flown it in 1931, on the first solo flight from New Zealand to Australia. There were the same blue-black clouds, and, before darkness came, the same occasional shafts of sunlight slanting from cloud base to the sea.

The fact was, I had been damned lucky. "Yet," I logged, "I could not be more depressed. Everything seems wrong about this voyage. I hate it and am frightened. Now I am going north-about New Zealand, whereas the Admiralty sailing directions say one should always go south-about no matter what the wind. That is a worry." In four days I seemed to have got nowhere. But if I had gone south, and attempted to plug into that wind, I should equally have got nowhere. At least I had cleared up nearly half the boat and made some things work again. I cut the mould off four loaves of bread, and rebaked them for 30 minutes. Then I turned in, hoping that my bedding would keep dry now.

I slept for ten hours, and when I awoke the sun was shining. I had breakfast, and went to sleep again, waking to feel a great deal better. The sea was moderating, and there was work to do on deck. I re-sheeted the genoa staysail, and unreefed the mizzen. The next job was to unravel the main halliard from its tangle with the burgee halliard—there is always trouble with burgee halliards.

There seemed a constant leak of water into the forepeak, so I tried a larger pipe for siphoning it out. I renewed a dressing of sealing compound to the broken cockpit side, fixing plastic sheet all over it with drawing pins, and adhesive tape along the edges. I doubted if it would stick for long, but it was better than nothing.

Saturday, February 4, found me only 100 miles from my beloved Lord Howe Island, nearly due south of it. This was where I rebuilt my Gipsy Moth seaplane after it was wrecked on my flight from New Zealand to Australia. I felt a great nostalgia for the friendly island, and wished that I could be going there. The sea was moderate, and I set the mainsail after reshaping a bent slide in a vice. After an overcast morning, the afternoon brought a fine hot day, with an azure sky all round. It seemed a good time to go fishing for my lost crockery in the bilge. I fastened a toy bucket to the end of the 6-foot burgee stick, and managed to rescue three bowls, one mug, and one broken jug. Then I got on with the task of tidying up the port side of the cabin—and what a job it all was. There were the contents of the fifteen big Tupperware containers to be restowed, and all listed so that I should know where to find them. I tied down one side of the bunk in four places with laid cord, doubled, and wished that I could lash down everything, though I decided that this was too long a job to tackle then. I collected fragments of glass from the cabin ceiling where the bottle had smashed. I was interested to find that by leaning over the side of the yacht I could watch Warwick Hood's added keel piece—I could see it cutting through the water like a red shark's fin.

In the evening of this Saturday I had a long talk on the radio with Sheila, who told me that the P and O liner *Himalaya*, when near Sydney, had been struck and damaged by a giant wave at 22.20 on the night of my capsize. No doubt it was the same wave that did me down.*

---

* Staff Captain Adie of the passenger liner *Himalaya*, 28,000 tons, was reported as saying, "Chichester can keep the bloody Tasman."

I was plugging into the Trade Winds, south-east by east in general direction, and I felt that my tactics in deciding to go north-about New Zealand were bad. But as the sea moderated after the cyclone the sun came out, and in spite of being on the wind most of the time, the yacht began to average 134 miles a day. There were still occasional big seas which I thumped into, and when this happened *Gipsy Moth* would be slowed to about 3 knots. But I kept remembering that in similar conditions on the way out to Sydney, before Warwick Hood doctored the boat, she would have stopped dead. I was a bit puzzled at seeing no flying fish. When I had flown over this sea in 1931, hordes of flying fish would leap from the water whenever I flew just above the surface, but now I saw not one.

At noon on Sunday, February 5, I was almost exactly half way between Sydney and Cape Maria Van Diemen, at the northwest tip of the North Island of New Zealand, 550 miles each way. A week out, only 550 miles sailed. My log notes:

• • •

"550 miles in a week is my record for slow going. Of that 550, I took four days to do 185 miles—an average of 46 miles per day! However, I am still alive and kicking, which is the chief thing, I suppose."

• • •

Throughout these days I was having trouble with the self-steering gear. It seemed unable to control the helm of the boat. I spent many hours trying to coax it to work. I know now that there were two quite different sources of trouble and that one of these was not the fault of the self-steering gear at all. On February 5 I logged:

• • •

"I found that the heading I wanted, namely about 47½° off the true wind while doing about 5¼ knots, was most critical; each time I got the sail trim balanced with the self-steering gear disconnected, if I left the boat to sail herself she either came up into wind and would have stopped in irons or else she paid off to 65° or more off the wind going quietly at a great lick but 30° off the direction in which I was trying to head."

• • •

Owing to the shape of the hull the *angle of heel* was the critical factor and *not* the heading of 47½° off the true wind as I thought. If the wind increased enough to heel the boat 2 or 3° more the forepart of the yacht slithered over the surface of the water until it pointed 30 or 40° downwind of the direction in which I was trying to head, whereupon the yacht gathered speed and tore off at a great lick in this wrong direction. If, however, the wind lessened enough to decrease the heel 2 or 3°, the hull shape was such that the boat at once started griping up to windward until finally it ended up pointing dead into wind and stopped dead. Later when I had at last understood this (second) tricky habit of *Gipsy Moth*'s, I found there was no way to overcome it except to trim the sails so that *Gipsy Moth* avoided the critical angle of heel; in other words, I had to sail her more upright than the critical angle or more heeled, but must at all costs avoid having her heeled exactly at the critical angle of heel.

The second trouble with the self-steering was due to the self-steering oar and its gear being top-heavy. Instead of the oar having a natural tendency to stay upright in the water, being top-heavy it would flop over to one side or the other. In light airs the wind vane had not got enough strength to overcome this flop-over tendency. I experimented with cords attached one each side to the steering oar, fastening these cords so as to keep the oar upright. With this arrangement if the vane wanted to change the heading of the boat it had first to overcome the pull of these cords to make the oar turn. Later I kept the oar upright by fastening four strands of shock cord on each side; these shock cord preventers were anchored one to each side of the pulpit at the stern.

At this time, however, I had not yet realised the causes of the trouble and I was trying one remedy after another without success. I thought that there might be too much weight on the counterpoise of the wind vane and tried making do with less. I oiled the worm gear which seemed to be sticking. I tried disconnecting the self-steering and balancing the sail trim before connecting up the self-steering again. (Since Warwick's improvements were made to the keel, *Gipsy Moth*'s sail trim could be balanced for a short while.) I would also get the self-steering oar balanced and would then connect the self-steering gear to the tiller; but immediately I did so the heading of the boat would change and either she would come up into the wind or pay off downwind. At the time I thought it would drive me barmy but I kept at it day after day trying every way I could think of to make it work. The self-steering performance slowly improved as time went by. I fixed the shock cord preventers to the top of the self-steering oar on February 20 which made it self-righting, as I described earlier. This meant, however, that the vane had to overcome the pull of the shock cord before it could twist the oar.

I was much better off when I finally discovered about the critical angle of heel. Before that discovery, whenever *Gipsy Moth*'s heading slipped off to leeward, I had blamed the self-steering gear for being unable to hold the boat to the required heading; whereas, of course, this sliding off to leeward was due to the shape of the hull, and was no fault at all of the self-steering gear.

Maybe I made a blunder navigationally by not going south of New Zealand, but as Sheila said to me in one of our radio talks, this did give me a chance to "rehabilitate" in warm weather and comparatively kindly seas. On the night of Monday, February 5, I had to say goodbye again to Sheila, when we had our last radio talk before she left Australia for Hong Kong on her way back to England. I was sad to part with her. I restored my morale next morning by having a shave. It was my first since leaving Sydney, and I was thankful to get rid of the irritation on my face from the beard growing there. It was tough shaving, and I had to stop and clean the razor six times when it clogged up and would not work. That shave, with the usual navigation, trimming the self-steering gear, siphoning out the forepeak, and breakfasting took up the whole morning. I spent the rest of the day making a better repair to the cockpit. It was a slow, frustrating job, with difficulties everywhere. I had to search the boat to find materials to make repairs, and it was a hard task to use tools at a big angle of heel. However, I kept at it, a little bit at a time for hour after hour.

Thursday, February 9, was a good day. The wind veered, and for the first time since leaving Sydney I enjoyed some perfect sailing. It was pleasant, warm weather, and I wore only shorts for working on the foredeck. I passed 135 miles south of Norfolk Island, which I had visited on my 1931 flight, and called up the island to say how sorry I was that I could not visit them again. The Administrator, Reginald Marsh, sent me a delightful message, saying, "We feel as if you belong a little to us, because the memory is with many Norfolk Islanders of how in 1931 you brought to them their first aircraft visitor."

I saw a Royal New Zealand Air Force plane, looking like a wartime Fortress; I noticed that it had US on its tailfin. Its fuel mixture seemed to be too rich, for there were four trails of black smoke from its engines. I wondered if it was all right, and I began to be a little worried about whether I could accommodate the whole crew on board if they pancaked into the sea. However, there was no trouble. The plane made half a dozen passes at *Gipsy Moth*, and then flew off. I thought it was a friendly gesture from New Zealand welcoming me.

Next day I passed North Cape, the north-west tip of New Zealand, about 90 miles off. I had come some 1,300 miles since leaving Sydney, and had 5,400 miles ahead of me to get to Cape Horn. *Gipsy Moth* was picking up speed and going well, though slowed up a little by the extra keel area. But due to leaving Australia later than I had planned, and the poor showing of the first week, I reckoned that I should be at least three weeks later in reaching Cape Horn than I had hoped. However, that could not be helped, and I went on with my chores; rebaked the last of my loaves from Sydney for the second time because they were mouldy again, painted the repair to the cockpit side, and searched the foredeck for leaks, applying sealing compound to a number of places. I sowed my first crop of cress to provide, I hoped, fresh greenstuff until I reached the Horn, and fixed four sheaves to the stern pulpit to make better leads for the control lines to the self-steering oar.

Auckland Radio broadcast a warning giving the latitude and longitude of a log of timber afloat, which I noted carefully. Logs and trees carried downwind by flood have always been a hazard round New Zealand. Collision with one could sink a yacht.

I had a small triumph on Sunday, my second Sunday out from Sydney—I found my missing vacuum flask! It came to light when I turned out my bedding for an airing on deck—it was underneath the mattress. Either I must sleep hard, or that mattress must be good and soft. The flask was smashed to bits inside. The opening through which it must have come as it was flung from the far side of the galley is only 16¾ inches wide, and my head on the pillow almost framed this opening. I was glad that it had missed me. I noticed a pronounced dent in the deck beam just above my head, and I think that the flask must have struck that.

To make sure that things that needed doing got done, and were not overlooked in the next crisis, I used to keep a list of jobs in hand from day to day. I called this my "agenda." It may be of some interest to give my agenda for this period of the voyage. Here it is:

Check water tank connections
Secure cockpit locker with hasp (actually I used cordage for this)
Fix preventer to galley drawers
Try self-steering vane without extra lead

Freshen nip of tiller lines to self-steering
Check engine water level
Stow burgee stick
Rig tiller tackle to cabin
Try more slack on self-steering oar
More solid cockpit repair to keep deck water out
Drylube tiller lines
Examine alternator belts
Dry out cockpit locker
Open counter ventilator on dry days
Devise hold-down for tins in settee lockers
Spray bolt cutters
Fix starboard foredeck net
Stop starboard deck ventilator
Main topping lift
Start mustard and cress
Rig tell-tale on self-steering
Clean Very pistol
Sort out pole uphauls, downhauls, outhauls and lifts
More hooks in "cloaks"
Deal with remains of deck net
Fix knotted warp for stern drag
Study camera light meter
Free Lewmar jammed main sheet slide stop
Fix lanyards to winch handles
Refill meths containers and bottle
Tauten leech in genoa stays'l
Free head of mains'l caught outboard in backstay
Check fruit and water
Sow wheat germ
Fix pendant for jib halliard
Fix lanyard for jib snap shackle
Dry out flying boat sextant box
Dry out bag of winter woollies
On calm day, up mast to dud crosstree light
Devise means of keeping pillow in heeled bunk
Dry out seat locker by my bunk
Fix lanyard for bilge pump handle
Spray e.l. capstan
Service blast horn
Fit rope end for pole outboard in place of shackle

Fix lanyard for reefing handles
Repair mizzen stays'l anti-chafe patch
Calm day—paint possible leaks over forepeak
Fit larger pendants to jib halliards
Chafe preventers on shrouds
Repair outhaul foot of mizzen
Put up more cup hooks
Remove flying cleats used for trysail tackles
Deal with leak at foot of my berth
Rig storm jib sheets
Renew pin and bolt in self-steering vane as soon as weather
    makes possible
Deal with twisted shackle, storm stays'l
Fix a waterproof torch
Consider fresh position for inspection lamp, foredeck
Examine crosstree leads at deck and fuse
Deal with stays'l halliard twisted round stays
Check off-course alarm
Strengthen inspection lamp
Fix tarred twine for anti-chafe tie backs
Inspect dead Harrier unit underwater
Drylube chafing ropes
Re-lash mizzen 3rd slide up
Check cabin compass
Repair bolt of the sheave in the fife rail, loose
Deck bolt of stern pulpit looks loose
Freshen nip of all signal halliards

This list is nowhere near a complete record of the work done on
Gipsy Moth—it is rather a list of merely extra jobs. It omits all sail
changing, radio work, adjustments to the self-steering gear, navigation, all regular work in the galley, and all the backbreaking tasks of
tidying up after the capsize. Some of the jobs listed—the cockpit
repair, for instance—took several days to get done. Nevertheless,
incomplete as it is, my agenda may give some idea of the human
effort needed for singlehanded ocean sailing.

On top of all this, over a period of two or three weeks from the
time I passed Norfolk Island, I worked hard at preparing for
another capsize. For instance, I fastened down the loose hatch lids
of all the cabin settee lockers so that the hundreds of tins, bottles
and tools in them could not all break out again as last time. I was

puzzled to know how to secure these lids without making them difficult to open when required. Finally I bored a lot of holes, so that I could anchor lengths of ¾-inch cord in the locker below, then pass cords through two holes at each end of the lid and secure the lid by tying the two ends together; I lashed a lanyard to each winch handle and reefing handle so that they would not be lost overboard. Altogether I went through the whole ship securing, where possible, everything that could cause damage or nuisance by breaking loose if the boat rolled over.

The settee locker with the most dangerous contents in the event of a capsize was the one with the heavy tools in it, such as a vice, big spanners, etc., also a 20-lb lead weight. I had to unload 130 tins from another locker before I could set to work on it. However, I logged: "The thought of all the contents of these lockers hitting the ceiling with a whang gives me the heebie-jeebies."

TWELVE

TWO THURSDAYS

I HAD now a vast stretch of the Pacific ahead of me, 5,000 miles of the lonely rim of the world. It took mankind almost the whole of human history to discover how vast the Pacific is—almost to the end of the eighteenth century geographers just couldn't believe that there is so much sea, and insisted on "balancing" the globe with a wholly imaginary Great Southern Continent. It was left to our own James Cook to disprove its existence, and even after he had sailed over what was supposed to be land, some people could not bring themselves to believe him. No one can sail in these seas without thinking of the great seamen in their often cranky sixteenth, seventeenth and eighteenth century ships who slowly displaced legend with geographical fact, and added to man's knowledge of the world—Magellan, Drake, Anson, Fernandez de Quiros, Dampier, Bougainville and, above all, Cook. We shared the same ocean and the same storms, but they faced one dreadful hazard that I was spared—scurvy. I read many accounts of scurvy when I was doing the research for my book, *Along the Clipper Way*, and all of them are horrifying. The worst I know is that in the account of Anson's voyage round the world, and it is worth setting out again if only to show that man has progressed at least in some directions. Here is an extract from that narrative:

> "Soon after our passing Streights Le Maire, the scurvy began to make its appearance amongst us, and our long continuance at sea, the fatigue we underwent, and the various disappointments we met with, had occasioned its spreading to such a degree that at the latter end of April [1741] there were but few on board who were not in some degree afflicted with it, and in that month no less than forty-three died of it on board the *Centurion*. But though we thought that the distemper had

then risen to an extraordinary height, and were willing to hope that as we advanced to the northward its malignity would abate, yet we found, on the contrary, that in the month of May we lost near double that number; and as we did not get to land till the middle of June, the mortality went on increasing, and the disease extended itself so prodigiously that, after the loss of above two hundred men, we could not at last muster more than six fore-mast men in a watch capable of duty.

"This disease, so frequently attending long voyages, and so particularly destructive to us, is surely the most singular and unaccountable of any that affects the human body. Its symptoms are inconstant and innumerable, and its progress and effects extremely irregular; for scarcely any two persons have complaints exactly resembling each other, and where there hath been found some conformity in the symptoms, the order of their appearance has been totally different. However, though it frequently puts on the form of many other diseases, and is therefore not to be described by any exclusive and infallible criterions, yet there are some symptoms which are more general than the rest, and, occurring the oftenest, deserve a more particular enumeration. These common appearances are large discoloured spots dispersed over the whole surface of the body, swelled legs, putrid gums, and, above all, an extraordinary lassitude of the whole body, especially after any exercise, however inconsiderable; and this lassitude at last degenerates into a proneness to swoon, and even die, on the least exertion of strength, or even on the least motion.

"This disease is likewise usually attended with a strange dejection of the spirits, and with shiverings, tremblings, and a disposition to be seized with the most dreadful terrors on the slightest accident. Indeed it was most remarkable, in all our reiterated experience of this malady, that whatever discouraged our people, or at any time damped their hopes, never failed to add new vigour to the distemper; for it usually killed those who were in the last stages of it, and confined those to their hammocks who were before capable of some kind of duty; so that it seemed as if alacrity of mind, and sanguine thoughts, were no contemptible preservatives from its fatal malignity."

My vegetarian diet, my cress and lemon juice, the knowledge painfully acquired by humanity from the sufferings of those old seamen, would guard me against this scourge. I had much to be thankful for.

Having sailed out of the Tasman Sea north of New Zealand I had to make southing once more towards the Forties. If I had made a mistake in going north-about New Zealand, I had the benefit of some lovely weather now, to set me up for the hard and harsh conditions that I knew I must meet soon.

An hour after midnight on February 13 I thought I saw a fish, but my powerful torch showed it to be a horrible kind of jellyfish like a translucent eel a yard long with a row of brown spots like buttons equally spaced along its back. It was able to move, twisting slowly, away and down. There were myriads of luminous things, visible in depth throughout the sea. They were points of light, which went out when I shone my torch on them.

Next morning I heard a noise like faint rifle fire and found hundreds of small porpoises leaping into the air. The noise was from their hitting the water, the surface of which was nearly calm. At noon I had made good only 180 miles in the past three days. I had been pinched up hard on the wind to light easterlies. I wondered if those light easterlies were due to my being too close off the northeast coast of New Zealand. At noon on the 14th I was only 100 miles from East Cape, New Zealand. According to the forecast the winds were westerly 60 miles to the south of me. This was tantalising and I tried to get south whenever there was an opportunity. On Wednesday, February 15, I had a laundry day, and washed out my shirt and shorts. I tried out a new idea of washing the clothes first in hot sea water, then rinsing them in sea water before giving them a final rinse in fresh water to get out the salt. It saved fresh water, and worked quite well.

As I approached the 180th meridian and the International Dateline I had a marvellous day's sailing, with a run of 217 miles. That was from noon on Wednesday, February 15, to noon on Thursday, February 16—my first Thursday, for crossing the dateline gave me another day which was also Thursday, February 16. With a fine, beam-on reaching wind, I knew that it was going to be a long run, so I took an extra sight to check things when I made my sun observations. I took four observations, and when the run came up so long, I took yet another sight for a still further check. Running the position lines up and back to noon, three met in a point, which was most satisfying. There may have been some error in my position the day before, but even so it was a wonderful run, and I think by far the longest day's run ever made by a singlehander. I gave myself a bottle of Veuve Clicquot to celebrate, though as usual champagne brought me no luck, and my second Thursday began with rain and a backing wind. To try to defeat the influence of the champagne I had two glasses of Whitbread's beer from the keg, which was excellent.

In the middle of the night between my two Thursdays I suddenly felt suspicious about the great 217-mile run of the previous day. Since leaving Australia the run between sun fixes each day had been on the average 12½ per cent greater than the dead reckoning run—i.e., the Harrier had been under-reading by that amount.* But the dead reckoning run the day before the 217-mile burst had actually been greater than the run between sun fixes and it was this which made me suspicious. When I came to rework the sun fix I found that I had made a silly blunder. My 217-mile run should have been only 189 miles while the run the day before should have been more—164 miles instead of 138. I logged: "Never mind, I enjoyed the champagne and I did cover 189 miles that day which is very good going."

My second Thursday gave me an extra day's sailing buckshee on the way to the Horn, but I should have to lose ten hours of it through having to put the clock forward an hour every 15° of longitude. Time, except dawn and nightfall, meant nothing to daily life in that immensity of sea, yet I had to take meticulous care to know the time accurately to within a second for navigation. The dateline has given mariners a headache since it was first invented. After crossing the dateline, the only way that I could avoid making mistakes over the time was to head every page of the log with my local date and day of the week, as well as the difference between my local time and Greenwich time. For example, *The Times* newspaper wanted a dispatch from me on Monday, February 27, I was then about 1,900 miles east of New Zealand. I had found that the best time to transmit was an hour or so after dark. Therefore I had to send my message at 9 P.M. ship's time on Sunday, February 26, which equalled 7 A.M. on Monday, February 27, Greenwich time.

---

* On 25 days when I had good fixes between February 7 and March 28, the speedometer under-read 560 miles or 16½ per cent.

I was worried by a spot on the chart marked "Breakers Reported, 1960." Such entries on Admiralty charts come from reports made by merchant ships, and they are marked as a precaution until there has been time to survey the area in detail. A report of "breakers" may mean anything, or nothing. It is easy enough for the sea to trick the eyesight of a man on watch, so that "breakers" are reported in all good faith, when really there is no more than some delusion of eye by waves and sunlight or moonlight on the surface of the sea. But there are still unknown reefs in the Pacific, and no mariner can ignore the possibility that a new reef has been sighted. This particular spot marked "breakers" hadn't been investigated, so I had to assume that it was dangerous though there was no proven hazard nearer than the Maria Theresa Reef some 500 miles to the north. It seemed to lie almost directly on my course.

That sign "breakers" on the chart gave me a strange feeling. There was no one within 700 miles if the boat should run on a reef. Perhaps I was jittery on Saturday the 18th when I wondered if I was near another reef. A biggish sea began running for a light breeze. It was a tumbly, breaking sea heaping up to points and pyramids. It set me scanning all round to see if there was a reef in sight. I even turned on the echo sounder; it indicated that the depth was more than 50 fathoms, but it would not register a depth within a few feet of a coral reef which has vertical sides.

On Sunday, February 19, the unknown reef—if it was a reef—was some 200 miles ahead of me. I wanted to change course either north-east or south-east to give it a wide clearance, but every time I tried to change course the wind blocked me, and seemed to want to head me back towards the reef. To make things worse, the sky was overcast so I could not get a sight to give me an accurate fix of my position. I dreaded the hazard of this possible reef. It was not a lump of land which one could see—in a low boat like *Gipsy Moth* you would be lucky to spot a reef awash a mile away; or less at night. And I could not keep watch all the time. At intervals I switched on my echo sounder to see if there was any indication of the sea's shallowing, but always it reported "no bottom"—that is, the bed of the ocean was below its reach of 50 fathoms.

I kept my sextant handy in the cockpit all the time to snatch a sight if there was a momentary chance of one, and just before sunset on February 20 I did manage to get a hazy sight. This gave me my longitude and showed that I was 6 miles west of the meridian through the breakers; but I could not tell if I was headed straight for them or to the north of them. My dead reckoning said I was headed 20 miles to the north of them but it was unreliable with no fix for 190 miles. I scanned the horizon with binoculars every fifteen minutes, until it became too dark to see at all. By that time I had sailed another 9 miles and by then must have been east of the reported position of the reef; so I felt reasonably safe. Is there a reef there? I still do not know, but the only safe course is to assume there is.

I was troubled at this time by a return of the cramps I had suffered from on the way to Sydney. Then I got at least temporary relief from drinking a half-glassful of sea water. I had got some salt tablets in Sydney to take instead of sea water, but I tried three times to take one, and every time it made me sick. So I went back to my sea water, and again it seemed to do good.

I was now in the Forties again, and I noticed a creeping lethargy which I think must be connected with air, wind and weather in the Southern Ocean. I noticed it in the Forties when I first entered them in the Atlantic on the way out to Australia. When it was blowing, I felt reluctant to do anything unless I had to, and when it was fine, I just wanted to do nothing. I was even quite glad at having to turn out at night to make a sail change, because I felt that it justified my having a long lie-in in the morning. I suffered from a severe headache at times, which I think must have been a form of migraine, and sometimes I felt quite ill when I had to go on the foredeck. On Wednesday, February 22, I was lucky to escape injury in a nasty fall. I was setting the mainsail, and as I pulled on the halliard a slide stuck in the mainsail track. I pulled harder, to try to free it, and the slide suddenly gave way. The halliard came to me with a run, and I fell flat on my back. It was a bad fall, but I was thankful that I didn't hit my head on anything as I went down. Usually I have one firm handhold when I am doing anything on deck, but this time, I suppose, one hand must have been fiddling with the slide, and I was so intent on watching it that when it freed suddenly I was caught off balance. The only damage from my fall was to my right elbow, which became very sore. From then on that elbow seemed to get blow after blow.

There were good moments, though, when I would sit in the sun in the cockpit, drinking mugs of Whitbread. It amused me every time I drew off a half-pint from the keg in the bilge, and I would think, "What a place to be sitting drinking beer, in glorious sunshine, with a deep blue sea and light blue sky." It was never too hot, because of the southerly breeze coming up from the Antarctic.

Once when I was sitting in the cockpit like this I tried to calculate whereabouts was the nearest human being to me. There might have been a ship somewhere in the vicinity, but unless there was, which was unlikely, the nearest living person would have been in the Chatham Islands, some 885 miles away. Out of the sun it began to be chilly, so I fit my cabin heater and found it a great comfort. I had one bad shock, which is duly timed and entered in the log, as befits its seriousness.

• • •

"Wednesday, February 22. 19.25. I have just realised I have only four bottles of gin left, enough for four weeks. My favourite hard drink on this voyage. I reckon I have been pretty stupid not to have brought plenty. I'll just have to ration it, and no hard drinks at lunch. It might be worse—I might have none."

• • •

February 24 was Sheila's and my thirtieth wedding anniversary. The day began in England at 14.00 my time, and I took a few photographs from the cabin companion when I reckoned that our wedding day really started. It was not exactly a good place for wedding photographs for a gale was getting up, and Gipsy Moth was rolling in a rough sea. I logged:

• • •

"I got a brace of shaky sun shots through a gap in the murk overhead but it takes ages to see the sun and then get a horizon among the tumult of waves. Also it is bad for the sextant with spray on the mirrors etc., but it does make the day less dreary to have a position. It was very difficult to stand in the cabin and I was thrown on to the Primus stove at breakfast, not that I minded much but it was bad for the stove, bending the frame. Fortunately I had just moved away the cup of coffee made with boiling water which had been standing on the stove."

• • •

No matter how rough the movement I could always keep a glass or cup full of liquid on top of the Primus stove. This was due to the Primus framework having been made specially with a tray underneath the stove. The whole thing was free to swing and the tray made a good pendulum; it was not only heavily made itself but usually had also a pot of marmalade and a pot of honey standing on it as well as the flat toaster and often a heavy frying pan. Sitting in my swinging chair I could reach all the articles on this tray as well as lift off saucepans or kettles from the top of the stove without moving from my seat. The swinging seat and the swinging table were very well placed; I could also reach the beer tap without moving from the seat, and take books from the shelf to my left hand under the shelf which carried the growing mustard and cress. I also had a bundle of newspapers within reach. Now I come to think of it there were other important things within reach too; a bottle of gin and a bottle of brandy in the cupboard under the Primus; salt, pepper, bitters, methylated spirits and matches were all in a shelf outboard of the swinging stove. As I could sit upright in this chair no matter what the heel of the boat it was one of the most successful pieces of equipment on the boat. It was designed by John Jurd, the foreman joiner of Campers and by myself. At the time I was speaking of when I fell on the stove, the heel inclinometer was recording 55° of roll one way and 30° the other way. I wrote in my log:

• • •

"I wish I was at home with my darling and feel sad to be away from her, but that is how life goes. I have only just finished break-fast, and will drink her health later. The day in London spread from 2 o'clock P.M. here today until the same time tomorrow. If this gale continues, I may wait until tomorrow for my celebration party."

• • •

I didn't wait. I decided that there was too much gale to get into my smoking jacket, but I had my wedding day celebration that evening, and wrote:

• • •

"I am drinking a toast to Sheila in the delicious Montrachet she brought out from England, and left on board for me. A long life, health and happiness, with grateful thanks for our happy thirty years together. A very remarkable, exceptional woman is Sheila. I did what is supposed to be un-British, shed a tear. Life seems such a slender thread in these circumstances here, and they make one see the true values in life, mostly things (or whatever you may call them) which one disregards, or brushes aside when with people. I must not get too sentimental. I will return to the Montrachet."

• • •

I enjoyed that wine. I can't say that I enjoyed the gale, but it must be admitted that gales save a lot of effort in a small boat at sea—with a gale of wind established, there is little sail changing until it ends. I ended my wedding day by going on deck to tidy up.

I adjusted the leech line of the genoa staysail to stop the leech from flapping like a flag in the wind, and adjusted its sheet lead. I passed a line among the spinnaker poles with their topping lifts, uphauls, downhauls and outhauls to stop their noisy drumming in the wind. I refurled the mainsail, hoisted the trysail a foot or two higher, downhauled its luff, fitted the short boom crutch in the deck and dropped the main boom into it. Then I headed a little more off wind for a bit more speed. I was then at 43° S, and did not want to go below 45° S before I changed heading for the Horn.

That gale lasted off and on—mostly on—for seven days. It was fast going, but rough. From time to time the speedometer needle stuck at its limit of 10 knots for what seemed like long periods, though it was probably only a few seconds. When a steep swell started under-running the ordinary rough sea, *Gipsy Moth* started surfing. Down below I could often tell when there was a big surfing breaker on the way. First there would be a low, quiet roar, and then the wind would increase suddenly by 10–15 knots. Next, the boat would heel sharply to windward, then whip across to the leeward heel, with white water boiling along the lee deck. There was always a biggish swell. The sea was much the same as when *Gipsy Moth* broached to south of Australia. The sun was shining brightly then, and in this equally lonely part of the Southern Ocean there was often sunshine too, giving a brilliant sparkle to the white wave crests, and making the rough sea seem almost unreal. But the roar of the wind, the roll and whiplash heel were reality enough. I was puzzled by the violent roll to windward before the boat went over to leeward, and wondered what caused it. I think a wave must push the bottom of the keel before it affects the top, and then, when the surface caught the top, over she would go in the way one would expect.

Gipsy Moth behaved well, and did not broach to. On the way to Australia I used to wait anxiously for her to broach in these conditions, but after the work done on her in Sydney, she seemed much more stable, and to run more truly. I never ceased to be surprised that Warwick Hood's addition to the keel could make so much difference. All the same, I didn't want to take risks, and I knew I ought to drop the mainsail when the wind reached over 30 knots. I often tried to get photographs of rough seas from the cockpit, but as soon as I was ready with the camera there would be nothing worth snapping and I hated waiting around. As usual, there would be a succession of impressive seas just after I got below.

It was a worrying business as the wind became marginally stronger to decide whether to drop the mainsail or to leave it up. I wanted speed, but these decisions were hard on the nerves, like waiting and wondering in an ocean race if the spinnaker is going to blow out, or if you dare carry it a little longer. Only here the mainsail was much more serious, with the masts at risk if it should go. When I decided to hand the mainsail and got below after doing so it would feel as if the yacht had stopped, but in fact speed did not drop much, from 7½ to 6 knots, perhaps. And I would be relieved to jog along in comparative peace.

Noon on February 25 finished my fourth week at sea. With a week's run of 1,058 miles *Gipsy Moth* was beginning to make a proper speed at last. I had sailed 3,350 miles from Sydney and by midnight was half way to the Horn.

The night of February 26 was a particularly dirty one, with freshes or squalls up to 40 knots. I sailed under a reduced rig of staysail genoa and working jib, which seemed to meet the circumstances, although the going was rugged at times with heeling. But it was not bumpy, thank God. There was a lull in the early morning, and I set the trysail, wondering as I did so whether it ought to have been the main. However, I distrusted the lull, and decided to bide a while before hoisting the main, for time after time when I had set the main I would have done better to keep to the trysail. It was cold on deck, and below, and I dug out my winter woollies.

This was a grey day, with only a few vistas of pale blue sky, and a watery sun occasionally. It was as well that I had kept to the trysail, for the wind freshened as the day wore on, and by afternoon a storm was getting up fast, with a rapidly falling barometer. I dropped the jib and the trysail, leaving the genoa staysail, but wondering if I ought to change that down while the light was good and before the gale grew worse.

I had to turn out in the night. *Gipsy Moth* was making heavy weather of it, with the genoa staysail up and the wind going up to the limit of 60 knots on the recorder; with a sailing speed of 6 knots downwind, this meant a wind of at least 66 knots. I dropped the genoa staysail. In doing so I lost grip of the halliard tail which blew out to leeward, and it stayed out like a stick in the air. I could only hope that it would suitably jam when the wind dropped so that I could recover it.

I made two mistakes over this operation. Firstly, I should never have left the fore-triangle without a sail. I ought to have set the spitfire (reefed storm jib) when it showed signs of blowing up in the afternoon. I thought that the way on the yacht would keep her sailing downwind under bare poles, but as soon as I dropped the staysail, she broached to, and lay ahull. Secondly, if I did leave the yacht bald-headed I ought first to disconnect the self-steering vane so that it would not be forced when the yacht broached to and the heading suddenly changed by 90° in a wind of more than 60 knots.

I was very hungry when I got below after my struggle in the night, and gave myself some baked beans on toast, with a mug of chocolate. I was still hungry after that, but didn't fancy any of the available foods. A wave washed over the deck and fairly deluged the galley floor through the closed hatch. I caught some of it at the Primus, but luckily not much. It's odd how relative things are! While I was mopping up in the galley I thought that it had suddenly fallen flat calm—the wind had certainly decreased momentarily, but it was still blowing at 35 knots! It was soon gusting at 55 knots again, but in the lulls (relative lulls, that is) there was almost silence. It was very queer.

In the morning I recovered the staysail halliard. The end of the rope tail had caught between the foretopmast stay, the spitfire luff, and a hank, and by standing on the pulpit I could just reach it. Relieved at recovering the halliard, I considered more sail, but decided that another sail was not needed if I could unreef the spitfire. I dropped it low enough for me to pull the reefing points undone, then hoisted it—and found that I had blundered. I had not resheeted to the bottom clew, so the part which had been reefed was now flapping. I gybed before the next move, which was to lower the storm jib again, and fasten the staysail sheets to the bottom clew. All this took time, and there was no let-up in the wind, which was still blowing around Force 9 and, if anything, increasing. So I refurled the storm staysail which I had been preparing to hoist. Then I pumped the bilge, clearing it with 73 strokes, which was not bad considering all the seas which had come on board. Next I examined the self-steering gear. The bolt and the pin attaching the vane to the shaft were wearing big holes in the wood. I decided that I must renew the bolt and pin, but feared that the woodwork would eventually give way, and could not see how to prevent this. I hoped it would last out somehow. The seas were big and rough, looking like the Cape Horners I had seen on Alan Villiers's and John Guzzwell's films.

This took up the whole morning. After a brief rest for lunch, I put on all my deck clothes again and went forward to set the storm staysail. But along came a burst of 45 knots, and I cancelled the project. At five o'clock in the afternoon I dressed up again to set the sail, but again decided against it as soon as I got into the cockpit. Although it seemed calm at times in the cabin, there was still a lot of wind, with a very big swell running. The troughs looked like deep valleys, and the rolling was fierce. I should have liked to get up more sail before dark, for the glass was rising, and I felt that there must be an end to the squalls soon. But it was still rugged weather. Since two o'clock that afternoon I had averaged 5.8 knots with only the storm jib (107 square feet) set.

By seven o'clock it was almost dark. In such weather there was nothing to do at dark, except to turn in and read in my bunk. I didn't seem to get hungry for dinner, or any evening meal, and it was not comfortable sitting in the cabin. I could afford only one light, for if I lit the cabin brightly it used too much current, and one small light was gloomy to sit by. I could not tackle any joinery or chores because the movement was too violent. It was a big physical effort to keep one's body in position, and one had to concentrate so much on not being thrown about that no mental effort was left for anything that required care and concentration. Those whip rolls of anything up to 60° one way and about 30° the other demanded great strength in holding on, or balancing on one's legs. There were some monstrous waves rolling up. I looked out through the cabin hatch above the washboards in the companion, saw a big wave coming, and was so interested in watching it that I did not duck in time, and got a bucketful on my padded coat and head.

I had been having trouble with my paraffin stove, for the outlet pipe was being backwinded by the gale. I cured this temporarily by moving the cowl for the pipe outboard of the hood over the companion, and the stove seemed to be working all right. That was a great comfort.

While I was entering up my log at 08.45 on February 28 a big wave forced the self-steering vane to slip, and the boat came up aback on to north. I hauled on the control line which I had led into the cabin so that I could help out the steering oar, but I could not get the boat back on to its course. Later I found that this cord was twisted round a rod on the deck. I dressed as fast as possible and put the boat back on course, but closer to downwind than before. The seas were running bigger than I had yet seen, monstrous things, and

Gipsy Moth needed to run nearly straight downwind. The self-steering gear seemed undamaged; how it survived an hour in those conditions I could not understand. I considered what best to do, and finally went forward and lowered the storm jib sufficiently to reef it by tying the row of reef points. The heading was not so good but I was concerned only with survival without damage. The second crosstree light had failed, which was a blow, because it left me without deck lighting from aloft. I did not have a good waterproof torch; the two I had were both duds, and I could not get any other kind in Sydney.

Two hours later the sea was just as rough. I kept on wondering if it would be safe to turn 20° off downwind to give a better heading, but told myself that I must remember that an hour or two of a better heading was relatively unimportant; the thing was to arrive. Twice the self-steering vane slipped when the boat was slewed round in a wave, and each time I put the boat back on to its correct heading. I logged:

• • •

"I don't want to put any more strain on the self-steering than I have to. It will be a messy job trying to repair it over the stern in these conditions."

• • •

That evening I wrote:

• • •

"My fair weather has not shown up: there is a big swell running like hills rolling down on the boat, but fortunately the slopes are not too steep. There is still a turbulent sea on top of it and Gipsy Moth is knocked half over every now and then. With the last one I thought the dishes would fly out of their niches, etc. I should like to point up to a better heading, but it might be wiser to wait. If a real rogue of a wave arrives it is better to be headed downwind even if it is off-course."

• • •

I was sailing 30° off downwind. I should like to have come up another 30° closer to the wind, but dared not go across those waves.

THIRTEEN

TO THE HORN

THE GALES of those seven days carried me across 1,115 miles of ocean, and left me with some 3,000 miles to Cape Horn. I began to wonder what I should do if the gale now blew from the opposite quarter as happened to Drake when he ran for three weeks before north-easters after leaving Magellan Strait. What an appalling thought! At one in the morning of March 1 I increased my sail area by 300 per cent. The week of gales had ended. I had finished it with only the little spitfire sail of 60 square feet set. The strongest wind I recorded was 67 knots. The seas were always different. The worst, which rolled up with the last fierce squall, were like steep banks moving on to the boat with a rough turbulent sea on top of them. No wonder the clipper captains ordered their helmsmen not to look astern. Sometimes the seas made me think of valleys; at other times of moving hills. *Gipsy Moth* behaved well, and did not broach. I accepted her flick heeling up to 60° but did not like it. I once thought the crockery would fly out of the vertical holders, but only the gash bucket shot a horrid mess of eggshells, potato skins and tea leaves over the cabin floor. I was using the bucket at the time, and had its locker door open.

I was now convinced that *Gipsy Moth* could do nothing else but run before the wind in very bad seas. There just must not be land ahead! I understood now why the clippers aimed to reach the latitude of the Horn 300 miles west of it.

Dawn that day brought me a fine sky, with a few fair-weather clouds. The sea was still lumpy, with a big swell running, and it was difficult to stand on deck. But I managed to sort out sundry sheets and halliards and after resheeting the genoa staysail, I hoisted it. With only that and the little 60-foot spitfire up, *Gipsy Moth* was doing 5½ knots on course. I felt that she could do with more sail, but was still distrustful about whether the squalls had really packed up, and decided to bide a while. But I could not bear to think of good wind being wasted, and an hour or so later dressed up again and hoisted the mizzen. I noticed that the lower pin holding the self-steering vane to the shaft had slipped out, so I replaced it. There was no wear in the pin itself, but only in the woodwork holding it.

That was a busy day, for improvement in the weather always means a lot of deckwork. Also, I wanted to take the chance of baking some more bread. I put the yeast to rise, and just as I had done so went to take a noon sun shot. When I got back to the yeast, it might not have been there! I kneaded the dough just the same and set the loaves to rise, but nothing happened, so I dumped the lot in the ocean and started afresh. That was the first failure in bread-making that I can recall. My second batch, baked from some Australian wholemeal, was delicious.

Some notes from my log:

. . .

"01.30. Back from a field day on the foredeck. 1. The inspection lamp, carried forward to the main mast is excellent to work with. 2. Dropped the working jib; the tail I added to the existing halliard tail has made that job easier. 3. Changed twisted shackle on spitfire. 4. Changed over jib sheets. 5. Hoisted spitfire. On return to the cockpit I decided there would certainly be too much sail set in an hour or so's time, and, in fact, there was nearly too much now, so I returned with the lamp and dropped the genoa staysail. *Gipsy Moth* seems to be going nearly as fast and the difference in comfort is amazing. Down below at 6 knots it seems almost as if she is not moving. The extra speed was attractive but reserve of power and everything else should be the motto on this passage. My one-piece suit is a work of art; but it is wetter inside than out. I think a cupful of water condensed inside it. Also my jersey was wet at the sleeves and, of course, my scarf and shirt wet at the neck. Now for some supper.

"07.50. Dropped the trysail and raised the main. I have a much easier drill for this now when downwind; not such a Herculean labour, but still as good as a run in Hyde Park any morning before breakfast.

"19.10. It is misty, drizzly weather, nearly fog like the North Atlantic. I have been a busy bee since five o'clock. I had a go at the leak into the foot of my bunk. Then was hard at it with one sail change after another, furling or bagging sails and coaxing the self-steering gear to work. What next with the wind? I hope it does not keep on backing and end up in the east, right in my eye.

"22.10. Good R/T contact. Got all messages through. Hard work, though.

"22.30. A dark night, black. Nearly becalmed. Wind reads 5 knots, but I expect the true wind is about 2½ knots.

"March 4, 11.55. Took advantage of light airs to slap paint on possible leaks above foot of my bunk and on the deck above the forepeak. Looks horrible with my bad painting, but the leak is the thing. I got plenty of paint on my coat but took it off with paraffin. I reckon that if only I could *find* these leaks, I should be able to staunch them with enough sloshes of paint on them.

"14.13. An albatross is flying up to within 10 feet of the stern; I fed it some gash which it seemed to relish. I have finished my fresh butter. So far my sewing repair of the mizzen stays'l is standing up to usage. Nice sailing with a pretty flat sea and enough breeze. Long may it last.

"19.07. Took advantage of light airs to have a field day below deck. Item, inspected batteries and topped up with water (very little needed). Batteries fully charged. Inspected freshwater tank in motor (O.K.). Prepared steering Monitor ready for action. Transferred speedometer battery cells to a Tupper to keep them dry. I nearly got to the galley drawers which have been on my list since February 7!

"20.40. I keep on trying to coax the self-steering to take control. The mizzen stays'l makes this very difficult in light airs, and this wind is fluky all the time, with freshes and near-calms.

"March 5, 00.45. The off-course alarm works well, but is pretty alarming when trying to sleep! Its *raison d'etre* of course! Quandary now, what's to do? At present pointing 155° (SSE, i.e., 40° off course) with wind nearly abeam. Not enough wind to work the steering gear if I head downwind. Shall I down the miz. stays'l? I think so, then the self-steering might hold her pointing nearly downwind. Speed must be forgotten.

"01.30. I will see if the other gybe would be better. An important factor is that the boat continues to move without going aback with the wind nearly abeam, whereas she is likely to go aback if I try to steer downwind in this near-calm. I'll go see, anyway.

"02.25. I dropped and bagged the miz. stays'l and would like to set it on the other gybe, but there is not enough wind yet to make the anemometer vane indicate a wind direction. Better bide a while, I fancy, until the wind declares its intentions. Quite a balmy night, black except for a lightening in the sky low in the SE. Gybed, did I say it?

"03.50. A good thing I did not hoist the miz. stays'l again. We have now come slightly on the wind, and it would not set. Raining.

"06.00. For the second time this night the off-course alarm had me out of sleep when the heading was 45° off, due to the wind veering. Wind now about north-east and has freshened to 15 knots. Raining.

"10.55. I got my sleep in pieces last night; ended up with a last and most welcome drop-off from 08.30 to 09.40. I woke to a Force 6 north-easter. Then, out and about, first dropping the main and housing the boom in its crutch. Still had too much sail for on the wind, so dropped the genoa stays'l and hoisted the storm stays'l in place. Light rain or drizzle on grey morning. Poor visibility, 10/10 overcast. Wind from north-east. I *hope* it has started to back towards north again.

"11.00. Time for some breakfast, though I had baked beans and toast with hot chocolate at 3 o'clock.

"12.30. Still raining hard but the sky looks much brighter, as if the sun is above only a thin layer of overcast. There seems less water in the forepeak after my painting spree yesterday in spite of the rain and the spray due to being on the wind. There was not enough to siphon out. The white paint also helps by high-lighting any unfilled crannies, and I shall go over it all again looking for cracks or crannies.

"16.10. Wind dropped. Must set mains'l unless wind change is about to happen. Drat! transmitting due in 50 minutes, and I want some lunch.

"16.38. Mains'l up and set.

"17.23. No luck with R/T to Buenos Aires or the British Antarctic Survey. Too early, I think. (I cannot spend hours at the radio telephone trying to make contact, as would a full-time operator.)

"March 6, 01.25. Tried to soften the terrible banging and cracking of blocks and ropes, due, I think, to the swell underpassing. Each swell crest robs the sails of all wind as well as heeling the boat.

"07.40. The off-course alarm woke me, and I assumed we had been headed 45° off course to the south-east, so I snoozed on as there was nothing much to be done about it when nearly becalmed. But when later I cast a sleepy eye at the tell-tale compass above me I found we had been headed off downwind to *north-east*! I hopped out then and trimmed the sails, but there is not enough wind to turn the wind vane. No speed records today, I guess.

"14.30. After a morning becalmed for three hours, we are now plugging into a Force 6 easterly. We were galloping down to the South Pole, so I tacked, assuming this weather layout will have a veering wind, as did that easterly a day or so ago. I would say the wind has veered 10° since I tacked. I feel out of gear today, though better since an hour's sleep at noon. I can't get on without my sleep ration. I'll be a devil and have a drink, and then some lunch.

"16.45. What's wrong with me today? I was in the middle of lunch when *Gipsy Moth* went aback. I went out in the long oilskin coat and wore her round on to course again. Trousers and cabin boots pretty wet in heavy rain. Then blowing up and already 30 knots, so I dropped the genoa staysail. Then the boat would not go with only a jib and mizzen, so I dressed up and set the storm staysail. Now the wind has dropped to near calm, and *Gipsy Moth* is hobbyhorsing, doing half a knot. She wants all that sail back, of course. However, I'll have another go at finishing my lunch first. I think we are in the eye of a tiny local depression.

"17.20. After a calm *Gipsy Moth* is now sailing herself—with the self-steering disconnected—on a heading of due *west*, at 3 knots. Can you beat it? However, I have finished my spaghetti, and will into the fray yet again.

"18.45. This day, or the weather, is playing tricks on me. Just now I hoisted the genny stays'l again in place of the storm stays'l. I was expecting another fresh of wind like this afternoon, but instead, the wind suddenly backed from east to north-west. The boat seemed stuck so I hoisted the main, too. While I was doing so the wind veered 40° before I got back to the cockpit, so now we are sailing beam-on to a north wind (roughly speaking). I seem to have been mucking about with sails all day, and got nowhere at all. Fog and drizzle. Visibility 500 yards. I feel like another drink now, but nothing brings on a shemozzle more surely than my enjoying a drink, and I have had a bellyful of dashing out into the wet for emergencies today. Oh, well, what drink shall I have?"

• • •

The one big want I had then was a quiet night and a good sleep, so I turned in at 8 P.M. and was soon asleep. But the brandy hot must have done it—I was woken up at 9 P.M. by a gale squall, and had to reduce sail quickly. So I dressed again and took care over the oilies, because it was raining heavily—the deck was running rain like a stream. I had quite a job. First, I dropped the mainsail, then the mizzen, then the working jib. After that I hoisted the spitfire and left it with the genny staysail. Then I turned in again to try for some more sleep, but judging by the wave which then hit the boat with a roar of wind in advance of it I thought I was in for a noisy night.

• • •

"March 7, 03.35. I am debating whether to drop the genny stays'l and/or turn downwind. We are not going very fast at 5.4 knots. It is the waves striking from abeam which concern me, but surely they should not be knockdown size yet?

"07.25. I was out in my judgement; the wind has dropped from 35 to 25 knots; now we need more sail up, and would have been poorly placed if I had dropped the genny staysail at 03.30. The barometer is still dropping steadily at $3/8$ millibar per hour—there is big wind about, I guess. What to hoist? I had a good sleep last time but need more so will hoist the trysail and not the main.

"08.30. I housed the main boom in its crutch and hoisted the trysail. No difficulty except for ropes and wires catching up in things (as usual). The trysail is just the right sail. *Gipsy Moth* seemed to spring to life. She seems to me to be doing considerably more than recorded, I would say $6\frac{3}{4}$ k. against $5\frac{1}{4}$ k. on the dial. A sudden thought, I tried the batteries of the Harris, and they are nearly flat. Therefore the speedometer would be under-reading, though I believe the correct mileage is still registered. No fix for three days; just one sun position line yesterday. If I had been a bit quicker off the mark I could have shot the sun again and got a fix, but by the time I got my gear to the cockpit, the sun was back behind the overcast. I have set a reefed mizzen, which improved the speed and enabled me to improve the heading. I don't want to gallop off south-east for the Horn yet.

"15.00. Hurrah, the sun is out! How bright the future seems for a moment! The fog we have emerged from looks like a great bank of white smoke drifting from a fire along the west horizon. I changed the spitfire to the working jib. This is a delightful point of sailing, with the wind on the quarter, but not so fast as with a beam wind.

"19.20. After three days without a fix the error in my estimated position was 21½ miles too far north.

"22.20. Dropped both the mizzen and the working jib. When the wind lulls, we are under-canvassed. But I think the only thing to do with this boat is to shorten sail as soon as there is a squall. It means turbulent air, which is likely to continue and perhaps get worse. In this case there was a sudden shift of wind of 40° and there were big waves, I think three, with the first of the new wind. The first hurled the boat well over 65° I would say, and she stayed there so long I wondered if for some reason she could not get up—long enough for me to wait for her to come upright and then, when she stayed down, long enough for me to struggle out of my swinging chair and start for the cockpit to see what was happening. I will now have another shot at finishing my mine-strone soup. I dumped the remainder in a vacuum flask.

"March 8. Gybed at about 04.15. Daybreak about 04.30. Sea more kindly on this gybe, and nearly astern, whereas before it was often nearly abeam. (Later) I was woken up at about 7 o'clock by some big rollings, or rather hurlings, in waves which were near to being dangerous. Most reluctantly I got up and dressed to see if there was anything I should do. But that lot of bad waves seemed to be in a patch, and since I got up we have been in the usual Southern Ocean rough sea that goes with a 35-knot wind. There seems to be a succession of rain squalls, each building up a few big dirty seas. The speed of the boat varies from 4 to 8 knots, and sometimes it is so quiet in the cabin that I look up to see if we have stopped. I seized the opportunity of the sun's coming out bright for a while to get a sun observation. I took 6 shots, but do not feel sure of them because there are big waves only giving occasional glimpses of the distant horizon for perhaps a second or two, which entails snap shooting. I will plot the shots on graph paper which shows pretty clearly how much they are likely to be in error; also shows clearly any 'rogue' shots. Ate my last apple last night and found the first bad grapefruit. I fear the eggs are not going to keep. My beloved wind tell-tale (a thin ribbon of light chiffon) which streams in the wind from the bottom of a monometal rod dangling from the wind vane has carried away. This is a loss because I look at this tell-tale many times in a day. I can look at it from the cabin without having to go into the cockpit and it not only gives me the strength and direction of the wind near the sea surface, but also, if it is not streaming in the same direction as the wind vane itself, it indicates how much load there is on the self-steering gear.

"21.30. I felt it was useless turning in early, and thought of leaving all my clothes on. Sure enough, a fresh of wind, 30 knots, with some fairly hefty waves. Too much for Gipsy Moth with that sail area. She heels over to 35°, and when a big breaker strikes abeam, it bashes her too far over. One big wave came along while I was in the cockpit, and I noticed that the wind definitely roared and speeded up before the wave arrived. It must be the displacement of air by the mass of water. I'll be the death of a can of soup and then for some sleep (I hope!)."

• • •

In changing winds I had to get my sleep in snatches. I had an off-course alarm, which four apprentices at the Kelvin Hughes works rigged up for me. It made a hideous noise above my bunk if the wind changed 45°. The previous night, for instance, it had me jump out of my sleep three times, and each time I had to dress in oilskins and change sail or retrim. The pitch dark night and the grey dawn with misty drizzle reminded me of the North Atlantic.

• • •

"March 9, 11.40. Interrupted breakfast to reduce sail, because the lee deck was too often under water, rushing water, indeed, and there was unnecessary strain on the boat. So dropped genny stays'l and jib and hoisted spitfire in place, leaving only trysail and spitfire set. Bright sunny day but strong breeze up to 40 k. and some fierce waves. I turned 20° downwind, which eased things a lot.

"12.45. Still eating breakfast, which I last interrupted to get a noon sun observation. Maybe it was a good thing I did so, because the sky is totally overcast now a few minutes later.

"Day's run 179 miles. This is my 40th day at sea. I have sailed 5,083 miles and have 1,604 to go to the Horn. For the past 6 days I have been headed direct for the Horn and am now at latitude 47° 08′ S which is 311 miles nearer the South Pole. I put on my winter woollies this morning: wool shirt, long underfugs and thick socks, but it has turned out warm in the sun and with oilies keeping all air out I was parboiled on the foredeck. I shall need a pint of sea water tonight to keep the cramps away.

"March 10, 05.00. I cannot recall Gipsy Moth ever sailing so well, so quietly and smoothly, nearly upright, and with a good average speed of 7.4 k. for 8 hours (which is as much as she will do in comfort). Further, I have not been in the cockpit during this period. Long may it last! (Later) I got a sun sight at about 08.15, but it was difficult with grey cloud scudding over the sun, big waves hiding the horizon and spray on the sextant and my spectacles. It took me 17 minutes to get six shots. I plotted them on graph paper afterwards, because they seemed so uncertain, but the biggest difference of any from a guessed line of average was only 4′ (the equivalent of 4 miles).

"14.12. Motor trouble. It had become increasingly hard to start the motor. Today after about 12 attempts the motor fired, but did not pick up. Finally it laboured on at 400 revs. It took 14 minutes at full throttle before these revs increased. It sounds like fuel pump trouble. I must study the handbook, but feel that engineering will be difficult in these seas now the wind has started howling again.

"15.30. When the wind begins to howl in these seas, and the anemometer reads up to 40 knots, it is time to shorten sail and prepare for a blow. I interrupted the lunch I had started and dropped the trysail."

• • •

I was getting used to the wild wind systems of the Southern Ocean. I could forecast with fair accuracy what the wind was going to do next. For example, on March 11 a log entry reads:

• • •

"I have gambled on the wind continuing to veer. I trimmed the sails and the self-steering gear to head 36° to the north of the heading for Cape Horn. I then turned in and had a remarkable sleep till 7 A.M. without having to stir from my bunk. My hunch paid off handsomely and the boat is now headed within 10° of the direction of the Horn after averaging 7.1 knots all night."

• • •

When I worked out my position on March 10 I found that I was 175 miles short of the spot where Brigadier Miles Smeeton, his wife Beryl and John Guzzwell somersaulted in *Tzu Hang* on February 14, 1957. It is interesting to note that this is still some 1,200 miles short of Cape Horn itself; all this Southern Ocean is formidable, not just near the Horn. If you look at a globe, you will see why these seas are like no other ocean anywhere: there is no land to break their force as they sweep endlessly round and round the spinning globe. That makes for tremendous swell, even on a calm day. There is nothing to break the force of the wind, either.

The extracts from my log give a fair idea of daily life on *Gipsy Moth IV*, endless jobs to be done to keep her sailing at her best, endless action to forestall the hazards of wind and sea, to help the yacht in her struggle across this formidable, lonely ocean. I had luck sometimes; I felt that Providence was on my side over that motor. Thinking over what might be causing trouble, I concluded that air must have got into the fuel system when I used the motor for charging my batteries with the boat bouncing about in a rough sea. I decided that I should have to bleed the whole fuel system to get rid of any air lock—and this meant that I should have to get at the fuel pump, priming pump, filter, etc. Here Providence stepped in, to give me an unexpectedly calm day. Even so, it was a long job. I found that the priming pump was on the inaccessible side of the motor, visible only in a mirror after crawling from beside my bunk, behind the motor, and under the cockpit. There, lying on my side, I could feel the priming pump, but could see it only by using a mirror. It was claustrophobic work, with my head lower than my feet. I worked at it for a whole morning, and eventually had the satisfaction of seeing fuel oil squirt out of the pipes that feed the atomizers. Then I knew that the fuel system was working properly—but still the motor wouldn't run well. Suddenly I realised that now there could only be one cause of the trouble, that the throttle was not working. The throttle, or cut-off, which stops the motor should open automatically, but it was jamming closed. Through seawater corrosion, the spring which should open it could not do so. As soon as I opened the cut-off by hand, the motor started like a bird whirring off. I worked on to take advantage of the calm conditions, and had nothing to eat that day until the afternoon, but then I had the great satisfaction of having located the trouble and fixed it—a most excellent appetiser. I took further advantage of that same calm to bake some more bread, which I had thought I might not be able to do until well past the Horn. Although it was a remarkably calm day, *Gipsy Moth* averaged 7⅞ knots for 3 hours to 5 P.M.

I had a charming, unexpected visitor on my way to the Horn. I was on the side deck with the inspection lamp one night when something soft and warm, not cold like ropes and gear are, fluttered in my face, startling me. It was a Mother Carey's Chick, dazzled by the light. I picked it up and put it in a safe place in the cockpit, and after I had finished my job I put it on the after deck, from which it could hop into the air or sea as it might like best when I put the lights out. A Mother Carey's Chick is the most wild creature I know, yet it is both soft and delicate, and with most charming manners. It will not attack, and stays cosy and warm in one's hand. It is so small that one's hand easily closes round it.

I was sad next morning to find the Mother Carey's Chick in the cockpit again, dead. It must have got back into the cockpit from the after deck after I had turned in. I fear that it had been injured in some way, and hoped that it had not got under my foot at any time. I don't think it had been hurt by me—I feel sure that I should have known about it if I had trodden on, or struck, it.

With Cape Horn seas in mind, I took the precaution of fitting wooden strongbacks to the forehatch. Alan Payne had made them up for me in Sydney—I reckon he felt as I did, that a big heavy hatch with light fastenings was a potential danger in trouble.

On Monday, March 13, I had a big day's run. This time it was between good positive sun fixes at each end of the run. Unfortunately I made it a short day of twenty-three hours, that is, I advanced the clocks an hour to compensate for running down the easting through 15° of longitude. The run came out at 191½ miles for the twenty-three hours. This was an average speed of 8.326 knots, and at this speed the day's run of twenty-four hours would have amounted to 199.826 miles. So that even if I had not made it a short day I would still have been nearly one-fifth of a mile short of the 200 miles I was always hoping for. That elusive 200 miles!

I was now left with 937 miles to the Horn. Five more days like that last one would do the trick! I was excited.

The note in the wind, a fierce driving noise, foretold a dirty night, and I had to face a north-east gale blowing up to 45 knots. At 03.00 I logged that I had had "a fairly serious beam sea just now." I could expect no relief from the bashing that the boat was getting, unless I turned and ran south. I reckoned that I could run for about 150 miles south before reaching the iceberg area. The wind had shifted, veering 30° during the past fifteen hours. If it shifted a further 30° in the next fifteen hours I could, in an emergency, if driven too far south, gybe and head away from the ice area, even if it meant sailing away from the Horn. In other words, I could avoid driving into a trap. Having worked this out, I dropped the staysail and turned downwind running off to the south.

• • •

"It seems as quiet as in a meadow by comparison," I logged, "unfortunately the heading is now 5° west of south but I hope it won't be for long. I had one souser in the cockpit, but my excellent deckwear which I had bought in Sydney kept me dry. I remembered in time to drop my arm: I have got a bad habit of holding on to the mizzen mast with one hand at the level of my head, and of course a sea hitting me in this position just runs straight down my arm there. It's an ill wind . . . etc.—the wet oilskins and the water that comes through the hatch give the cabin floor a good swill and a clean which it might not otherwise get."

. . .

I did not have to run south for long; at 08.00 the sea and wind both abated, and I was able to point 60° off downwind. It was still raining, and the visibility was poor. Everything below was either dripping or running wet. I was still pointing too far south, but I could keep going for another thirty hours at that gait before reaching my southern limit. My hands were nearly numb, and I had a rum hot with lemon.

At 17.00 that afternoon I hoisted the mainsail. I counted up that I had hoisted or dropped twelve sails in the past twenty-four hours. It already seemed ages ago that I had been worrying about being carried among the icebergs due to being forced to run before the seas, though, in fact, it was only fourteen hours before. By midnight that night I was becalmed and in a thick fog, thick enough to see it drifting in the cockpit. The latitude was now 54° S and the distance from the Horn 750 miles. It seemed an odd place to be short of wind!

I was restlessly impatient, hoping to be able to get past the Horn without a storm, hoping that the fair weather system I was in on March 15 with only 700 miles to go would last out. I took every possible advantage of it, securing everything I could think of, doing everything I could on deck. It seemed too good to be true. As things turned out, it was.

On Thursday, March 16, I at last got a fix, the first for 3 days and 390 miles of sailing.

. . .

"I was like a duck with two tails," I logged, "when I found the error of my surmised position was only three miles out in distance and two and a half miles out in direction. I only hope I can get as good a result if I get stuck in Drake's Passage for three days without a sight, but of course the currents are fierce there."

. . .

That evening I got through to Buenos Aires on the radio telephone at last. Robert Lindley, the *Sunday Times* correspondent, took my dispatch. The British Antarctic Survey in the Falklands was also picking up my radio, so Robert told me, but I was unable to contact them. I logged:

. . .

"I am rather exhausted but very pleased that I got a message through. Strange that they can hear me clearly at Buenos Aires and the Falkland Islands and I cannot hear them at all well. I cannot get a fifth of what they say. I understood British Antarctic Survey to say that there was no ice north of 67° south. I suppose this only applies to the neighbourhood of the Horn and not where I am now, but even so it is grand news."

. . .

On March 17 I wrote in my log:

. . .

"If only the Horn would keep this up: smooth sea, delightful sailing, definitely bracing air, sun shining, and I don't think I ever enjoyed a breakfast more than that one—grapefruit, potatoes fried in butter and eggs scrambled with a pinch of herbs, followed by two rounds of *Gipsy Moth*'s best wholemeal bread, with marmalade and butter. Coffee hot, and at the right end of the feast."

. . .

It might seem Mediterranean weather, but this was still the Southern Ocean. I had a reminder of the need for constant vigilance about an hour after I wrote about that splendid breakfast, when I saw a blackhearted squall to windward in an otherwise bluish sky and blue sea. Fortunately, it did not hit me.

I felt an increasing impatience, and kept on plotting my track. This was a gentlemanly gait. I could have sailed faster by setting up a bigger jib, but that meant lugging it from the forecabin, through the cabin and heads (lavatory) to the cockpit, and back along the deck, because the forehatch was now bolted down with Alan Payne's strongbacks. I did not relish this—and so far in that Southern Ocean there had always been a strong wind pretty soon after a spell of near calm or light airs in easterly weather. I decided to make do with the sails I had out.

For weeks now I had been having a private race with the sun to see whether I could round the Horn before the sun crossed the line going north. When I was still 442 miles from the Horn, the sun was 1° 21′ south of the line, that is, 81′, equivalent to 81 miles (sea miles) on earth, and moving north at 1′ (1 mile) an hour. I was sailing at

5½ miles an hour, and I reckoned that if I could keep up that pace I should win by about 3½ miles.

Albatrosses, magnificent, majestic birds, like everything I had imagined about albatrosses, and not like the smaller variety I had seen on the way to Australia, were always interesting. One particularly hugely winged bird used to come for scraps from the yacht. I kept them for him and he would snap them up in a moment, and then keep circling the boat closely, as if asking for more. I felt that my vegetarian leavings must be a great disappointment to him. As I neared the Horn some whale birds, or prions, showed up. I had not seen any for ages. They are lovely creatures, and a thrill to watch, as graceful as swifts, and wheeling like swallows. Work went on. My log notes:

• • •

"I suppose I make a proper Charley of myself by mucking about with the mizzen staysail. It is only one better than a spinnaker for giving trouble, that sail. It does help enormously on some headings with speed, but sometimes seems bent on making a fool of me. I had a memorable tussle with it, going on for two hours, in my impatience to keep going now. First, I hoisted it, and it would not set, because the wind headed the boat as soon as the sail was up. So I hauled it down, bagged it, and dumped the bag in the afterhold. While I was doing this, my back bent on the job, there was a wind shift, and when I straightened up, the conditions were ideal—for what? A mizzen staysail! I felt a bit glum, then decided to have another go, hauled out the bag, and went all over the business again. The sail did some good for a bit, but the fluky wind made conditions very difficult for it. The self-steering gear just would not keep the boat anywhere near a fixed heading."

• • •

At 22.25 that night (March 17) just before I turned in, I wrote the requiem to that day in the log:

• • •

"Back to Square One. I have been trying for 5 hours to control the boat with the mizzen staysail set, but could not succeed. It's a matter of balance, I think; if she was all right for a 5-knot breeze she went off course up to 90° for a 12-knot one. Anyway, I have given up at last because I want some sleep, and have dropped the damn thing. Now we seem pretty steady on course. Good *night*."

• • •

That night was memorable in another way as well—I slept out of my day clothes.

Next day, Saturday, March 18, I was as excited as a schoolboy at the end of term, waiting for the time to leave school. In spite of the fluky wind and all my troubles with the mizzen staysail, we had not had a bad run the day before, 163 miles, which left me some 302 miles to the old Ogre. I reckoned that I was only 100 miles from Noir Island, outside the Cockburn Channel, where Joshua Slocum had his big adventure with the Milky Way.* The Diego Ramirez Islands, which I was aiming at, were 249 miles ahead. I badly wanted a sun shot to check my position, but the sky was overcast, and there was not much chance of one, though I kept my sextant ready in the cockpit just in case. In the afternoon I tried to pick up Ushaia or Punta Arenas radio beacons, which seemed the only ones possible for me to use, but couldn't. I tried again just after seven o'clock in the evening, and I did get a bearing of Punta Arenas, but I hoped that it was not right, because it put me in the western end of Magellan Strait! Another shot was worse, putting me east of the Horn! However, I had now found the frequency for the Punta Arenas beacon, which was quite different from that given in the Admiralty Manual, and I could have another go in the morning. My log for that day closes:

• • •

"I have set the off-course alarm to sound off if the heading changes 45° from 080°. I had better try for as much sleep as possible tonight, because I don't suppose I'll get much tomorrow, with all those islands around."

• • •

---

*The Milky Way is the name given to a mass of rocks and rocky islets off Tierra del Fuego, north-west of Cape Horn. In March 1896, Joshua Slocum, making the first singlehanded voyage round the world in his sloop *Spray*, was driven back towards Cape Horn by a furious gale, after reaching the Pacific through the Magellan Strait. He spent an appalling night among the rocks and breakers of the Milky Way. Describing it in his book, *Sailing Alone Round the World*, he wrote, "This was the greatest sea adventure of my life. God knows how my vessel escaped." He added, "The great naturalist Darwin looked over this seascape from the deck of the *Beagle*, and wrote in his journal, 'Any landsman seeing the Milky Way would have nightmares for a week.' He might have added, 'or seaman as well'."

FOURTEEN

ROUNDING CAPE HORN

WHEN I was researching in records and old logs in preparation for my voyage it was soon apparent that the seas around Cape Horn had a reputation unique among all the oceans of the world; more, they have had this reputation for as long as man has known them, ever since Drake deduced that there was the passage that bears his name between Cape Horn and the South Shetland Islands off Antarctica—Drake Strait.

Cape Horn is an island, or rather the tip of an island, a massive cliff some 1,400 feet high that stands where the Pacific and Atlantic oceans meet, at the southerly end of the South American continent. Why has it such an evil reputation? I tried to answer this question in my book *Along the Clipper Way*.

"The prevailing winds in the Forties and Fifties, between 40° S. and 60° S., are westerly and pretty fresh on the average. For instance, off the Horn there are gales of Force 8 or more on one day in four in the spring and one day in eight in the summer. Winds have a lazy nature in that they refuse to climb over a mountain range if they can sweep past the end of it. South America has one of the greatest mountain ranges of the world, the Andes, which blocks the westerlies along a front of 1,200 miles from 35° S. right down to Cape Horn. All this powerful wind is crowding through Drake's Strait between Cape Horn and the South Shetland Islands, 500 miles to the south. The normal westerlies pouring through this gap are interfered with by the turbulent, vicious little cyclones rolling off the Andes. The same process occurs in reverse with the easterly winds which, though more rare than the westerlies, blow when a depression is passing north of the Horn.

"As for the waves, the prevailing westerlies set up a current flowing eastwards round the world at a mean rate of 10 to 20

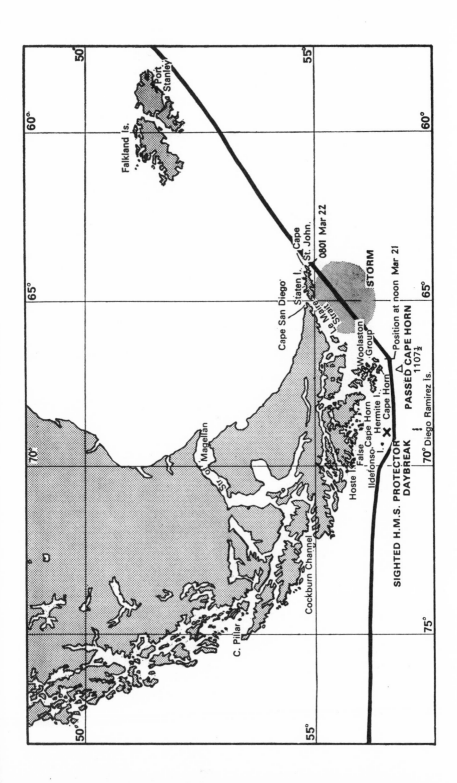

miles per day. This current flows in all directions at times due to the passing storms, but the result of all the different currents is this 10 to 20 miles per day flowing eastwards. As the easterly may check this current or even reverse it for a while, the prevailing stream flowing eastwards may sometimes amount to as much as 50 miles a day. As with the winds, this great ocean river is forced to pass between South America and the South Shetland Islands. This in itself tends to make the stream turbulent.

"But there is another factor which greatly increases the turbulence. The bottom of the ocean shelves between the Horn and the Shetland Islands and this induces the huge seas to break. It is like a sea breaking on the beach at Bournemouth in a gale, except that the waves, instead of being 4 feet high, are likely to be 60 feet high.

"There is yet another factor to make things worse. Anyone who has sailed out past the Needles from the Solent when the outgoing tide is opposing a Force 6 wind knows what a hateful short steep sea can result. A yacht will seem to be alternately standing on its stem and its stern with a lot of water coming inboard. The same thing happens at the Horn on a gigantic scale if there is an easterly gale blowing against the current flowing past the Horn.

"What size are these notorious waves? No one yet has measured them accurately in the Southern Ocean, but the oceanographers have been measuring waves in the North Atlantic for some years. The British Institute of Oceanography have invented a wave measuring instrument which they use at the weather ships stationed in the Atlantic. Recently one instrument with a 60-foot scale recorded a wave of which the trace went off the scale. This wave was estimated at 69 feet in height, higher than our five storey house in London. An American steamship in the South Pacific is said to have encountered a wave 112 feet high. Brian Grundy who used to sail with me in *Gipsy Moth II* told me that when he was in the Southern Ocean in a big whaling steamer he reckoned that one wave was 120 feet high. L. Draper of the Institute of Oceanography says that, according to *Statistics of a Stationary Random Process*, if a sea of average height 30 feet is running, then one wave out of every 300,000 can be expected to be four times that height, i.e. 120 feet."

I do not think that Drake himself ever saw Cape Horn. We have two accounts of his passage, one by his chaplain in the *Golden Hind*, Francis Fletcher, the other by a Portuguese pilot, Nuno da Silva, whom Drake had captured with a ship he took off the Cape Verde Islands earlier in his voyage. Apparently da Silva accompanied Drake quite willingly for the sheer interest of adventuring into the unknown South Sea, for when Drake freed his other captives da Silva stayed with him. Piecing together Fletcher's and da Silva's accounts, and deducing Drake's navigation from them, I am convinced that Drake never rounded Cape Horn. He was driven west-south-west for 14 or 21 days (the accounts are indefinite about the length of time), he then sailed back over his track for 7 days as soon as the north-east gale had blown out. He fetched up at the Diego Ramirez Islands, where he anchored in 20 fathoms at the range of a big gun from the land. According to the *Admiralty Pilot* there is an anchorage close eastward of the middle of one island in a depth of 16 fathoms with a sandy bottom. I am convinced that Drake never saw Cape Horn, but discovered the Diego Ramirez Islands and correctly deduced, because of the big swell that rolled in from the Atlantic when the north-easterly gale was blowing, that there was a passage between the Atlantic and Pacific Oceans there.

I aimed to pass between the Diego Ramirez group and the Ildefonso islands, and to round Cape Horn between 40 and 50 miles south of it. I wanted to give the Horn a good clearance, because it is a bit like Portland Bill in the English Channel—the closer to the Bill you pass, the more turbulent the sea, especially with wind against tide. The water diverted by the Bill has to accelerate to get past it, and, in addition, the bottom shelves, so that the current is accelerated again because of the same amount of water having to get through where there is only half the depth. It is exactly the same case with the Horn, only the rough water extends 40 miles south of it instead of 6 miles and where a 40-knot wind would bring a turbulent, 6-foot sea by the Bill, it will be an 80-knot wind with a 60-foot sea off the Horn.

At midnight on Saturday–Sunday, March 18–19, I was approaching land. I was 134 miles from the Ildefonso Islands and 157 miles from the Diego Ramirez Islands. The nearest land was at the entrance to the Cockburn Channel, which Joshua Slocum had made famous. That was only 75 miles to the NE by N. The barometer had been dropping steadily for forty hours now. I got up and went into the cockpit, to find out what chance I might have of sighting land ahead. It was raining steadily. The big breaking seas showed up dazzling white with phosphorescence, I would say up to 100 yards away. The falling-off, seething bow waves were brilliant white. The keel was leaving a weaving tail like a comet 50–100 feet long, and under the surface. I thought that one would be lucky to sight land 300 yards ahead. This would pose a nutty problem for me next night if I didn't sight any land during the day. If the weather continued I should be lucky to get a fix, and with the strong currents known to be there, my fix of the day before would not reassure me much. I was uneasy about fixes with no checks since Sydney Heads: suppose I had been making a systematic error in my sights . . . But it was no good thinking like that. I realised that I must trust my navigation as I had done before.

I was lucky, and I got a sun fix at 09.22 next morning. That put me about 40 miles south-west of the nearest rocks off Tierra del Fuego. I was 77 miles due west of the Ildefonso Islands, and 148½ miles from Cape Horn.

There was a massive bank of cloud, nearly black at the bottom, away to the north, and I supposed that it was lying on the Darwin Mountains of Tierra del Fuego. There was no land in sight, although the nearest land was only 50 miles off. I now had a big problem to solve—where should I head? My then heading of 78° would lead me to Duff Bay and Morton Island, 15 miles north of the Ildefonsos. But I could gybe at any time, because the wind had backed to west by north. My main problem was this: if I kept headed for the Ildefonso Islands and Cape Horn, which was nearly in line with them, I should reach the islands in eleven hours' time, i.e., at 22.00 that night, which was three and a half hours after dark. This was too risky, because if it rained or snowed I should be unable to see the islands close to. The trouble was that if I bore away from the Ildefonsos, I should then have to cope with the Diego Ramirez Group. The bearing of that batch of rocky islets was only 22° (2 points) to starboard of the Ildefonsos. These islands have no lights, and are inhabited only for part of the year.

It was clear that I should not reach the islands until after dark. The currents were strong here in the neighbourhood of the Horn, running up to 22 miles per day in any direction in fine weather, and up to 50 miles a day in stormy weather. My fix of 09.30 that morning seemed a good one, but at the back of my mind was still the gnawing doubt about my sun navigation, with no check since Sydney Heads, 6,575 miles back. (It was unfortunate that I had made that blunder in my sun fix earlier, on the day before I appeared to have made the big 217 miles day's run.) I could avoid both groups of islands by gybing and heading south-east till dawn; that was safe tactics, but it meant quite a big detour, which I resented. I tried to puzzle out a dog's leg route which would take me between the islands in safety.

At noon the wind shifted, veering suddenly, which put me on a heading of north-east, so I gybed. Then the sun showed through the heavy clouds, and I got a sextant sight. This checked my latitude, for which I was very grateful. I had just finished plotting the result, and had decided on my best heading, when the wind backed in a few seconds from north-west to south. In a matter of minutes it was blowing up to a strong gale, Force 9. I dropped the mainsail, the jib and the genny staysail in turn. I set the spitfire, and found that was enough sail. "I wish," I logged, "that this famous visibility following a wind shift would prove itself! I should just love to get a glimpse of those islands." Until then I had been heading straight for the Ildefonso Islands, and now I decided that the time had come to change course and head midway between the two groups of islands. This put the wind slightly forward of the beam, so I hoisted a storm staysail with the spitfire jib. The barometer had suddenly risen 6½ millibars in the past hour or two. I hoped that the wind would not go on backing into the south-east, which would make it very awkward for me. By 21.00 that night the wind had eased to 15 knots at times, but with periodic bursts of up to 36 knots. I hoisted a bigger staysail, but with only the two headsails set the speed was down to 4 knots between the squalls. I decided to put up with this until I had got away from the proximity of that rugged land, so notorious for williwaws.

By midnight the barometer had risen 9½ millibars in the past 7 hours. It was a little less dark out: I could tell the difference between sea and sky.

If my navigation was all right, I should be now passing 18 miles south of the Ildefonso Islands, and at dawn I should be passing 12 miles north of the Diego Ramirez group. It was so dark that I did not think it worth keeping a watch, so I set the off-course alarm to warn me if there was a big wind shift, and I also set an alarm clock to wake me at daybreak. Then I put my trust in my navigation and turned in for a sleep. For a while I lay in the dark with the boat rushing into black night. I used to think I would be better off going head first into danger (in *Gipsy Moth III* I lay feet forward); but I still had the same fear. What would it be like if she hit? Would she crack with a stunning shock and start smashing against the rocks in the breakers? If I could reach the life-raft amidships could I get it untied in the dark, then find the cylinder to inflate it? In the end I slept, and soundly too.

Daybreak was at 05.00. It was a cold, grey morning. The wind had veered right round again to west by south, and the barometer was steady. There was nothing in sight anywhere, which was as it should be. The sea was pretty calm, so I decided to head directly for Cape Horn, instead of passing 40 miles to the south of it as I had planned earlier, in order to avoid the turbulent seas to be expected if closer to the Horn, and if a gale blew up. I decided to hoist the trysail and went on up to do so. I was excited about changing course to east by north after setting the trysail, because changing course northwards there meant changing course for home. I was then 40 miles from the Horn.

When I stepped into the cockpit I was astounded to see a ship near by, about a half-mile off. I had a feeling that if there was one place in the world where I would not see a ship it was off Cape Horn. As soon as I recovered from the shock I realised that because of its drab overall colour it must be a warship, and therefore was likely to be HMS *Protector*. On first sighting it, it had seemed like magic, but on thinking it over I realised that if they had picked up my radio message to Buenos Aires of the night before relating how I was aiming to pass midway between the two groups of islands sailing blind during the night, the warship had only to place herself half-way between the two groups, and if my navigation was correct I should sail straight up to her. I went below and called up HMS *Protector* on 2,182 kcs. She answered immediately. I said I would speak to her again as soon as I had set my trysail.

After setting the trysail I went down below for quite a while. I talked to *Protector*, and that used more time than it should have done, because I had great difficulty in hearing what her operator was saying. This was tantalising because I could clearly hear some land stations up to 7,000 miles away if I wanted to. After that I had my breakfast, and did not hurry over it, then wrote up the log, studied the chart and decided on my tactics, etc. While I was breakfasting a big wave swept over the boat and filled the cockpit half full. It took more than fifteen minutes to drain. By the time I had finished breakfast the wind had risen to 40 knots. At 09.00 I went on deck, and dropped both the trysail and the genoa staysail, leaving only the spitfire set. As I was finishing the deckwork a big wave took *Gipsy Moth* and slewed her round broadside on; in other words she broached to. It was lucky that I was on deck to free the self-steering gear, and to bring her round on to course again. I stood on the cockpit seat to do this so as to keep my legs out of the water in the cockpit. I looked round and there was the Horn, quite plain to see. It stood up out of the sea like a black ice-cream cone. Hermite Island, north-west of it, was grey and outlined against the sky.

At 10.43 I logged:

• • •

"I reckon I am east of Old Horn, but I can't get a bearing without going into the cockpit. Perhaps I had better, as I have kept all my oilskins on. Still gusting over 50 knots."

• • •

At 11.15 I took a bearing of the Horn and was then definitely past it. As I had made good 39 miles in the past five and a quarter hours, a speed of 7.4 knots, I must have passed the Horn at 11.07½ o'clock. I had no time or inclination at that moment, however, for such niceties of navigation. Before I reached the Horn the familiar quiet roar of wind was beginning; it was blowing up, and the sea was roughing up fast. I dare say that a lot of this was due to being only 7½ miles south of the Horn when I passed it. I was beginning to feel seasick, and had the usual lethargic reluctance to do anything. I just wanted to be left alone, by things and especially by people. I cursed the *Protector* for hanging about, especially as I noted that she looked steady enough to play a game of billiards on her deck.*

Just then I'm damned if an aircraft didn't buzz into sight. I cursed it. If there was one place in the world where I expected to be alone it was off Cape Horn; besides which this aircraft made me

---

* Apparently it was not as smooth aboard her as it appeared. A Reuter staff man, Michael Hayes, was aboard and recorded the following (published in a special issue of *Football Monthly*). "As I stood on the pitching and tossing deck of the Royal Navy Ice Patrol ship H.M.S. *Protector* 400 yards off, the sight was awesome. The translucent, bottle-green seas were moving mountains and valleys of water, rearing, rolling and subsiding with a fearful brute force. The 50-mile an hour wind slashed at the waves, slicing off foaming white crests and sending icy spume flying. Lead-grey clouds, blotting out the weak sun on the horizon, rolled across the sky, so low that it seemed I could reach up and touch them. The thermometer said the temperature was 43° F, but the numbing wind cut through my lined, Antarctic clothing like a knife, and salt spray swelled up and crashed against the face with stinging fury."

apprehensive. I couldn't say exactly why, but I think that an old flier has a perception which amounts almost to instinct about an aeroplane in flight. I thought this one would come down and crash into the water. How the devil was I going to attempt the rescue of its occupants in that sea? I tried to figure out a drill for rescue. Queasiness made it hard to think, and I was greatly relieved when it finally cleared off.*

Ten minutes after noon I logged: "I tried to be too clever (as so often, I regret). I went out to try to coax *Gipsy Moth* to sail more across the wind; the motive being to get north into the lee of land." I thought that if only I could make some northing, I would get protection in the lee of Horn Island, and the islands to the north of it. However, the seas did not like it when I started sailing across them,

---

* This was the aircraft, a Piper Apache, in which Murray Sayle of the *Sunday Times*, Clifford Luton and Peter Beggin of the BBC came out to look for *Gipsy Moth*. It was piloted by Captain Rodolfo Fuenzalida, formerly of the Chilean Air Force. Murray Sayle wrote in *The Times* of March 21:

"The flight out to find and photograph him at the most dangerous point of his voyage was a magnificent and terrifying experience. I flew from Puerto Williams, the tiny Chilean naval base which is the southernmost inhabited spot in the Americas.

"As my aircraft rose to find a cleft in the mountains of Hoste Island, the biggest of the Horn group, I was confronted with a superb sight. Green glaciers tumbling from the high snow-blanketed Darwin ranges into the Southern Ocean. As I flew by Cape Horn Island, its grey pyramid could be seen lashed by heavy seas and rimmed by breaking seas which appeared from time to time through the driving rain.

"South of the Horn the waves were driving eastward in long ridges of white and grey-green. Overhead were black driving clouds driven by the gale and a mile or two ahead the clouds were joined to the sea by rain in a black, impenetrable barrier towards the south and the pole.

"I picked up H.M.S. *Protector* first, wallowing in the heavy seas as she kept company with the yacht. Then I picked out the salt grimed hull of *Gipsy Moth* lurching forward as the seas passed under her. My Chilean pilot, Captain Rodolfo Fuenzalida, gamely took us down to 60 ft where spume torn from the seas lashed across the aircraft's windscreen. But I had time to pick out Chichester in his cockpit, apparently nonchalantly preparing for his change of course and the long voyage home.

"When my pilot waggled his wings in salute we were rewarded by a wave of greeting. 'Muy hombre,' said the pilot, which I freely translate as 'What a man.'

"On the flight home we had severe turbulence as we threaded our way back through the mountains, and we lost an engine over the Strait of Magellan. It was a flight I am not too anxious to repeat, but the sight of *Gipsy Moth* ploughing bravely through this wilderness of rain and sea was well worth it."

and a souser filled the cockpit half full when I was in it. As a result, I had to change all my clothes, and also put *Gipsy Moth* back on to her original heading. That kept me just on the edge of the wind shadow from Cape Horn, and that might have made for more turbulence.

However, the wind was backing slowly, so that I steadily approached the heading I wanted to Staten Island. Unfortunately, with the wind shifting into the south-west, I got no protection whatever from the land, and after *Protector* left (one and a half hours after noon) the seas built up to some of the most vicious I had experienced on the voyage.

When *Protector* forged ahead, turned round ahead of *Gipsy Moth* and went away, she left me with a forlorn, empty feeling of desolation. I think it is a far greater strain to have a brief sight of a ship full of people in such conditions than it is to be quite alone: it emphasises the isolation, because it makes one realise the impossibility of being helped should one require help. The odd thing was that I had not only no feeling of achievement whatever at having passed the Horn, but I had no more feeling about it than if I had been passing landmarks all the way from Australia.

It had certainly been a rough sea before *Protector* left; the cockpit had been filled five times up to then. It was an extraordinary sight to see the gear lever throttle control, and instruments of the motor which were placed half-way up the side of the cockpit, all under water. But that sea was kid's stuff compared to what was running three hours later. The biggest wind registered by the anemometer that I noticed was 55 knots. I was doubtful of the accuracy of this instrument in high winds, but even if it was only 55 knots that, added to the 8 knots of speed which *Gipsy Moth* was making, totted up to a 63-knot wind—Force 11. The seas were far more vicious than I should have expected from such a wind and they were frightening.

The self-steering gear seemed unable to control the heading so I went aft to inspect the gear. I found that the connection between the wind vane and the steering oar had come out of its socket again. I tried to replace its proper pin, but could not get it in by hand, so I fetched an ordinary split pin and used that.

I think that this particularly turbulent sea was due to being on the edge of soundings; a few miles to port the depth was only 50 fathoms, and a few miles to starboard it was 2,300 fathoms.

By 16.30, however, there had been one or two lulls, which cheered me enormously. I had been thinking that I should have to stay all night holding the self-steering control lines in my hands. These were the emergency lines which I had led into the cabin, so that I could help out the self-steering gear when it was unable to cope with a broaching of the boat.

At 17.37 I logged:

• • •

"A definite lull, with wind not roaring or screaming, and wind speeds down to 25–30 knots. Long may it last! The trouble with these gales is that I lose my appetite just when plenty of food is needed, I am sure. There were some wonderful pictures of big seas this afternoon after *Protector* left, but I just cannot face photographing them. Photography seems so paltry beside the tremendous display of force by nature."

• • •

I was headed north-east for the east point of Staten Island. *Gipsy Moth* was travelling fast, although she had only the storm jib set, and that was reefed so that the total area was only 60 square feet, which is not much for an 18-ton boat. The wind had swung round to south-west and I heard later that someone aboard *Protector* had said the wind was 100 miles an hour when she left *Gipsy Moth*. I think that was a misquote, but six hours later I was in an angry storm, as if the Horn was letting me know what it could do if it tried. The anemometer only reads to 60 knots which, with the boat speed of 6 knots, amounted to at least 66 knots, but I would say it was gusting up to 75 knots and perhaps occasionally 85 knots or 100 mph. Powerful seas roared past, and breaking tops came rolling down on to me from the stern. I thanked God that I could run before it. My only fear was that the wind would continue to back, and make the land a lee shore. There was far more power in this sea than in the one that had capsized *Gipsy Moth* off Australia, and if I had had to stop running and lie ahull—well, it couldn't have been done. The worst time was at nightfall. In the increasing darkness the seas were just terrific. I admit I was frightened for a while.*

---

* Clements, in *A Gipsy of the Horn*, writes: "A winter's gale on a lee shore is a nerve-racking experience. Not so a Cape Horn sea. One merely triumphs in the exhibition of such stupendous power and sublimity. Death itself would be a small thing in such surroundings." I think that things like this must be written in peace and security, weeks after actually experiencing Cape Horn seas.

However, fear does not last. I turned in and went to sleep. I slept for about two hours, until an hour after midnight. I found that the speedometer batteries had run down and I changed them. Unfortunately I did not allow for the distance run being under-registered. This might have had serious consequences. I logged:

• • •

"The rolling is frightful. It is very difficult to stand in the cabin. The wind is pretty strong still, 23–33 knots in the quieter periods."

• • •

The barometer had steadied. I ought to have realised that there was something wrong with the mileometer, because it registered only 8.8 miles run in three hours. All the morning I had been making good about 8 miles in one hour. I had run up the dead reckoning position at 22.00 using the distance recorded by the mileometer. I was on a heading of NE by E to pass close east of Staten Island. There seemed a good open space before me on the chart, with the east cape of Staten Island 85 miles ahead by the dead reckoning. The navigation looked so easy that I did not pay much attention to it.

At 04.40 in the morning I gybed, because *Gipsy Moth* had been forced up to a heading of NNE by the backing wind. I logged: "My hands are numb and I have difficulty in hanging up my coat or in writing." There was a strong wind still blowing, over 60 knots. I found that the long-suffering wind vane was catching up in the mizzen backstay, and I used a length of cord to prevent the backstay from fouling it. No wonder the self-steering gear had been eccentric in the gale! I had a hot rum to warm me up and wrote in the log:

• • •

"I now feel as tight as a coot, though I don't know how a coot could be tight. It was very good rum though. When we are going dead before the wind it seems as quiet as a church at times when the boat is not rolling. I think I am short of food—I have had only two square meals in two days, supplemented by snacks, mostly liquid like chocolate or honey and lemon. I am not sure that the paraffin stove is not upsetting me with carbon monoxide. Big wash-outs on the deck send a spurt of salt water down the stove pipe and the flames burn yellow instead of blue for a while. I have had a nagging headache for a day and have been wondering if the stove causes it. It is difficult to make the cowl work because of eddies from the gale blowing on to it from astern. The fumes are pushed back into the cabin."

• • •

There was nothing in sight at 05.30 and I had seen nothing while working for quite a while on the stern at daybreak. I felt hungry and started preparing breakfast. I chanced to look out of the window in the doghouse on the port side and I felt as if the roots of my hair all over my body had turned red. I was startled to the bone, when, on looking out of the hatch, I saw a vast craggy bulk of land less than 10 miles away, and we had nearly passed it. I expected Staten Island to be still 35 miles ahead. Had I been pushed in by the tide to close Tierra del Fuego in the night? If so I must be bearing down on Staten Island ahead as a lee shore in winds up to 40 knots. I took three bearings of a cape that *Gipsy Moth* was passing, from which I reckoned that we were 7 miles off it, and that the ground speed was 8.8 knots. As soon as I had sighted the land I had prised myself up in the companion and peered over the top of the hood above it. I was headed to pass a headland, leaving it 5 miles to port. I must establish my position. My breakfast, of course, had gone for a burton. Fortunately, the sun had risen nearly dead ahead; a sun observation would give me a position line which would decide how far up the coast I was. I hurriedly fished out the sextant and set to work. Meanwhile, the headland was rushing up fast. The hilly land rising to mountainous country behind it was moving up as fast as if I was passing in a train. I think I have seldom taken and worked out a sight quicker. At the same time I was taking it steadily, set on not making a mistake. I plotted the resultant position line. I was passing the East Cape of Staten Island. I could hardly believe it. I checked my working again—there was no mistake.

Although I could hardly believe it at the time, when I came to look at the chart and study the dead reckoning navigation, it all became simple. From my noon position near Cape Horn I had worked out the heading which would take me 5 miles past the easternmost cape of Staten Island. In fact, I passed 7 miles off it. The distance was 140 miles, and if I had worked out the time at the morning's ground speed of 7.4 knots my estimated time of arrival at the Cape would have been nineteen hours after leaving the noon position, i.e., at 07.00 on the Tuesday morning. In fact, I arrived there at one and a half minutes past 8. It took me longer, because the wind eased during the night, and *Gipsy Moth*, still with only the 60-foot spitfire set, slowed down. What I had forgotten to take into account was the fact that the speedometer batteries had run down, and had undoubtedly been under-registering; therefore I thought I was going much slower than in fact I was. That I overlooked this is understandable to myself; I got agitated and disturbed by the presence of the warship, and having to talk to her, and also by the arrival of the aircraft, and being anxious that she was going to ditch. I felt tired, strained and extremely lonely when they all cleared off. On top of that I was seasick, and later in a Cape Horn grey-bearder storm, and so I neglected to take account of the mileometer underreading.

Now Staten Island had rushed past, and already it was disappearing in the haze. At last I felt I had rounded the Horn properly, and was headed into the middle of the wide waters of the South Atlantic. As I left Staten Island, I had an immense feeling of relief. It was the same feeling as the clipper sailors record, of feeling that they were home when they rounded the Horn. Gradually this fades and vanishes, and is forgotten as the 8,000-mile voyage up the Atlantic proceeds. Those oceans turn out to be no lily ponds, as they seem to be after turning the Horn.

My log takes up the tale:

• • •

"March 21, 11.56. There is still a very rough sea. Thank God we are going downwind. When the boat is slewed round broadside to the seas, she gets a pounding straight away. The problem now is whether to change course to the north to pass west of the Falkland Islands, or head north-east as at present to pass east of the Falkland Isles. Considering the wind is sure to swing to the west after this, and that north-east is the downwind course we are on at present, the eastward passage is the obvious one. If I keep to this heading I can relax till tomorrow morning, when I must start cocking an eye for Beauchene Island. Meanwhile, what I must do is tighten up the wind vane, which now slips every time a good-sized wave hits the stern. I feel tired to the bone; this gale stuff goes on and on. The noise, the incessant effort to hold on, or balance, and avoid being thrown, the nervous strain of waiting for a socker wave, loss of appetite due to the movement, disturbed sleep. Put clocks forward one hour.

"14.20. I found that the bolt holding the wind vane to its shaft had sheared. With difficulty I replaced it with a new bolt without losing the vane in the Force 6 wind. I expect that one end of this bolt had sheared through some time ago, which is why I was so worried about the vane's erratic behaviour during the night. I think it is a miracle that it survived a big blow and rough seas. I got a sun sight. I hoisted the storm staysail and set the spitfire higher up its stay by using the tack pennant. We are jogging along quietly at 5 knots with those two sails only, and I think I will leave it so till the sea, which is still very rough by normal standards, goes down. I started the motor for charging. I used the heat starter which I seldom have to do normally. Now here is another seeming miracle—that the motor starts right away. After watching the instrument panel, the throttle and gear lever all under sea water for nearly a quarter of an hour, and considering that they have had several similar submersions, it is just like a miracle that it starts with no trouble. Now for some lunch.

"18.05. That blow is over: it is fine mild weather. It makes me feel I have rounded the Horn at last, and in a few minutes I am going to crack a bottle of champagne to celebrate. After that I want a big sleep. The boat is undercanvassed but that must wait. By the way, as I passed the Horn at 16.07½ GMT March 20 I won my race with the sun; but only just—by 15.275 miles, the distance which the sun was still south of the Line.

"March 22, 01.20. Another proper piece of Charleyism: I went off into a deep sleep at 7 P.M., and woke just before midnight to find we were headed *south* and going well! The wind had veered and I wondered when? I hope I woke when it happened, but doubt it, I was so tired. At least it was taking me away from danger, the Falkland group. If only I had set the off-course alarm! I must plot the DR from Staten Island. To show how I feel, I have not plotted the DR up from the Horn yet, or totted up the day's run. [It was 160½ miles noon to noon all under the spitfire only.] Meanwhile, I will run the DR up to the present and work out two positions, according to whether the ship changed heading when I started to sleep, or when I finished sleeping. Anyway I gybed as soon as I woke and so got close to the right heading. I avoided any blunders on deck, though still thick-headed with drowsiness. I tried to finish the job without a safety-belt on, but had forgotten the levered shrouds. So I had to don harness in the middle of the gybe to go forward and handle the shrouds. How I would relish 12 hours' solid sleep. I was thinking it was that warship and all the telephoning which fagged me. After 50 days plodding across the Southern Ocean alone, I needed the Horn to myself, somehow. This must sound daft, but 50 days' solitude is strong medicine."

• • •

Having written that, which, I think, truly reflected my feelings in the early hours of that morning, I decided to leave the yacht as she was going for the moment and go back to sleep. I stayed in my bunk until nine o'clock, when I got up and unreefed the spitfire jib, thinking that a scrap more sail would steady the boat. It did, and also increased her speed a little. Then I thought about breakfast, and was annoyed to find that I couldn't have any wholemeal toast because I had run out of bread. I breakfasted instead on Ryvita and butter and marmalade, which I enjoyed, but I like my wholemeal bread, so after breakfast I baked another batch. I had to give the albatrosses the rest of Lorna's cake (a splendid cake, given to me by Lorna Anderson in Sydney). I had spun it out too long, and the fat in it had turned rancid. There were seven albatrosses following *Gipsy Moth*, and they certainly did love that cake. They kept swooping close to the boat, only 20–30 feet away, obviously asking for more, but I had no more to give them.

It rained pretty consistently, with visibility down to a mile or so, and with no chance of a sight to check direction. But I reckoned that I was giving Beauchene Island a wide enough berth. That afternoon I figured that I must have passed over the edge of the Burdwood Bank (minimum depth 25 fathoms). The yacht had a rough time of it, with several waves breaking on her, and big, sweeping troughs with the waves. After this rough patch, the sea was comparatively smooth, with no considerable troughs. Later, after studying my dead reckoning I figured that we must have been on the edge of the bank around noon, and then sailed along the edge until we left it. That would tally exactly with the sea's suddenly becoming flatter and milder.

I was now headed out into the South Atlantic on a northeasterly course. My track was roughly parallel with the coast of South America and about 850 miles off it. Abeam to starboard was the island of South Georgia, 500 miles away. After that there was a big wide open space ahead in the South Atlantic for 1,600 miles, when I was due to pass Ilha da Trinidade, leaving it 500 miles to port. It was a great relief not to have to worry about running on to lee coasts in stormy weather; also I had a feeling of peace on getting away from the Horn area which had seemed decidedly overcrowded. I could relax.

I turned in early, and spent seven and a half hours in my bunk— a good sleep, but bad for navigation. I was awakened by that irresistible arouser, cramp, and got up just before 5 A.M. The barometer kept on falling and I logged that I wished I were well to the north in case it meant a big storm. The US Pilot Chart showed that there was not a considerable drop in gale percentage until I was north of 45° S. Between 50 and 45° S, 12 per cent of the winds recorded there were gales compared with 9 per cent in the lee of the Falklands and 26 per cent off the Horn. I reckoned, however, that I must be getting some protection from the Falklands, about 80 miles to windward.

Instead of a storm, the weather cleared up during the morning (March 23), and I had all plain sail set again, for the first time for ages. The wind had become a gentle breeze of about 14 knots, the sun shone, the sea was blue, and the barometer began to rise. I was heartened to go on deck to set the mizzen without adding any deck clothes, but this was a mistake, for that gentle wind was biting cold, even through my thick woollen sweater.

That day ended with a lovely starry night, a nearly full moon, and not a cloud in the sky. I turned in trying to think when I last saw such a sky, and couldn't remember one on the whole of this passage. Alas, my joyous looking forward to a sunny, quiet sail went awry. I went to sleep pondering about bringing out my big genoa to keep the yacht going in light airs, and woke to a northwesterly gale. I had to strip all sail off the yacht, except the working jib. The sun was shining, though, which was heartening. But it was bitterly cold, and my hands got so cold that I had difficulty in writing up my log.

On coming below after taking in sail I hung my deck trousers, soaked with spray, just inside the companion, where I thought that the water running off them would make less mess than in the cabin. Unfortunately, a souser wave overran the boat, and the bit that came through the hatch emptied straight into my trousers. You just can't do right in rough weather.

The sea that day (March 24) gave me a good pounding but it was not a high, or steep sea. Nor did the barometer drop a great deal. I figured that I was on the north-east quarter of a depression going through. By afternoon the wind had lost that roaring whistle which tells you that it is too strong for peace of mind, and changed to a sort of low, moaning roar. The sea remained very rough, and I waited until evening before setting the genoa staysail. I had a good supper of two Caroni rums, hot, two onions fried with a tin of baked beans, and a tin of pineapple. After supper I felt that more sail was needed, and my conscience told me that I ought to set the main. But I was reluctant to tackle it after my good supper, and wondered if the mizzen would do until dawn. Setting that would be only a tenth of the effort of hoisting the main. In the end, the mizzen seemed the job, and it changed the yacht's tempo at once. She began scuttling instead of lurching. After the gale it was a lovely moonlit night, and it was thrilling to be on deck in the moonlight with the lively sea, and the boat going well.

I put my thoughts into a radio message that night:

"At last," I reported, "I feel as though I am waking from a nightmare of sailing through that Southern Ocean. There is something nightmarishly frightening about those big breaking seas and screaming wind. They give a feeling of helplessness before their irresistible, remorseless power rolling down on top of one, and it all has ten times the impact when alone. Till yesterday I still felt I was in the wind shadow of the Horn. It was still wet, cold and grey and the wind still blowing hard. The seas were not so threatening but I shall be glad to get north of 50° S. without another big blow."

The off-course alarm shook me out of a heavy sleep at six o'clock next morning. I turned it off but cramp made me get up. It was a fine dawn, but very cold. I altered course downwind. Really I could have done with a poled-out jib, but the wind as I was going was near gybing point, so I left things as they were and waited for the gybe.

Doing my navigation that morning (March 25) I found that I had crossed the parallel of 50° S about midnight. The clipper captains, especially of the California clippers, considered this point very important, and always compared their times round the Horn from 50° S to 50° S. I crossed the 50th parallel west of the Horn in the Pacific at zero hours on March 12, and crossed it in the Atlantic at zero hours on March 25. That made thirteen days.

My mileage tally for the week that saw me round the Horn was 1,106½, an average of 158 miles a day, or 6.58 knots. This was the fifth week in succession that *Gipsy Moth* had sailed over 1,000 miles in the week; 5,230½ miles in 35 days, an average of 149.4 miles per day. These distances, of course, are run over straight lines between noon positions, and do not include tacks or digressions.

FIFTEEN

INTO THE BROAD ATLANTIC

I WAS now clear of the Falkland Islands, and sailing along the Clipper Way into the middle of the broad South Atlantic. Nothing can have changed much there for millions of years, and there was a strange, stirring attraction in being alone with the primeval life of the earth.

On Sunday, March 26, I logged: "Hot news! At noon today I passed half way!" I had sailed 7,673 miles from Sydney, and the distance along the Clipper Way to Plymouth was 7,634 miles by my measurement. I started plotting the different sailing routes up the two Atlantics recommended by the Admiralty's *Ocean Passages of the World* for March, April and May.

My son Giles, who is a bit of a wag, sent me a message through Buenos Aires radio: "Well done, but don't relax." I also got some questions from a girl reporter working for the *Sunday Times*, such as: "What did you eat on your first meal after rounding the Horn?" To this I replied by radio:

"Strongly urge you stop questioning and interviewing me which poisons the romantic attraction of this voyage. I am beginning to dread transmitting nights, and I fear losing my enthusiasm for worthwhile dispatches. Maybe this is because I have been alone for 58 days; I do not feel the same as I would if leading an office life. I have my hands full driving this boat efficiently and maintaining the gear in good order. Difficult radio communication is a great strain anyway. Interviewing makes it intolerable. I do not want to hurt your feelings but hope you can sympathise with my state of mind."

I was in a patch of light airs and badly needed my big genoa, which was still locked up in the forecabin by the strongbacks I had put on the forehatch. At daybreak on Monday, March 27, there

(continued on page 188)

TOP: *A verbal encounter off Victoria. Note the barnacles on the hull.* (THE *AGE*/MELBOURNE, CHICHESTER ARCHIVE) BOTTOM: *Sheila speaks on the radio-telephone off Sydney.* (SUNDAY TIMES/CHICHESTER ARCHIVE)

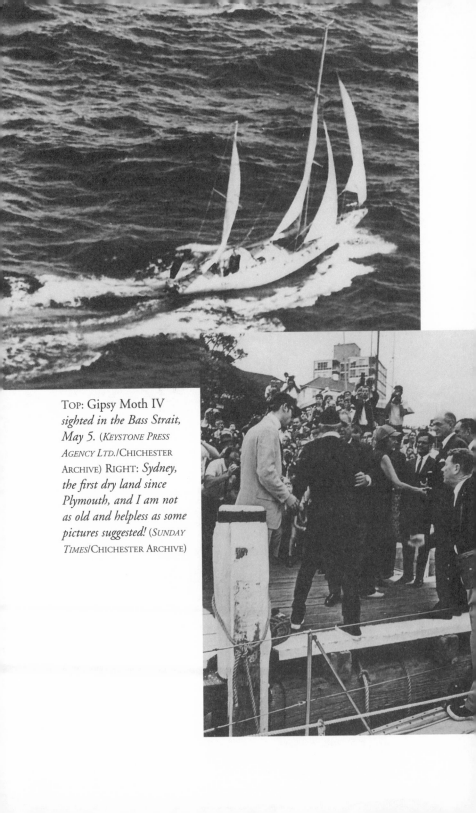

TOP: Gipsy Moth IV *sighted in the Bass Strait, May 5.* (KEYSTONE PRESS AGENCY LTD./CHICHESTER ARCHIVE) RIGHT: *Sydney, the first dry land since Plymouth, and I am not as old and helpless as some pictures suggested!* (SUNDAY TIMES/CHICHESTER ARCHIVE)

TOP: *The Press Conference, thirty minutes after I stepped ashore after three and a half months of solitude.* (AUSTRALIAN CONSOLIDATED PRESS/CHICHESTER ARCHIVE) BOTTOM: *Sheila and Giles check the stores for the return passage.* (SUNDAY TIMES/CHICHESTER ARCHIVE)

TOP: *The Press Conference before leaving after seven weeks in Sydney.*
(*AUSTRALIAN CONSOLIDATED PRESS*/CHICHESTER ARCHIVE) BOTTOM: *Leaving
Sydney with an enthusiastic escort against a backdrop of the new Opera
House and the famous bridge.* (*SYDNEY MORNING HERALD*/CHICHESTER ARCHIVE)

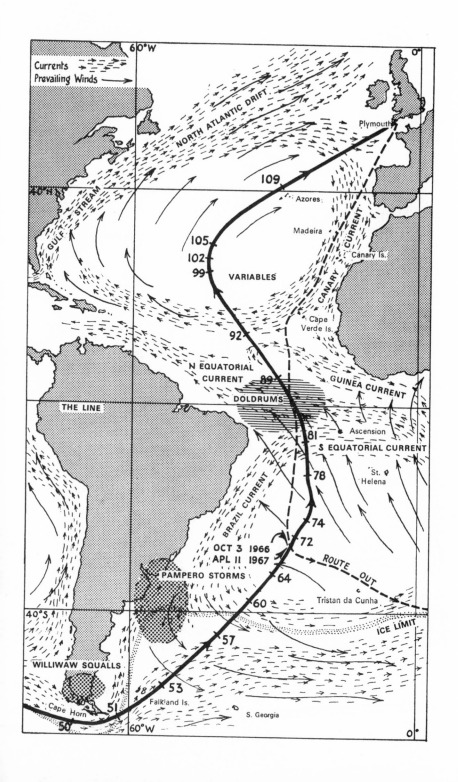

Currents ⇢⇢⇢
Prevailing Winds ⟶

60°W

0°

NORTH ATLANTIC DRIFT

Plymouth

40°N

109

GULF STREAM

Azores

Madeira

Canary Is.

105
102
99

VARIABLES

CANARY CURRENT

92

Cape Verde Is.

N EQUATORIAL CURRENT

89

GUINEA CURRENT

THE LINE

DOLDRUMS

Ascension

81

S EQUATORIAL CURRENT

78

St. Helena

BRAZIL CURRENT

74

72

OCT 3 1966
APL 11 1967

PAMPERO STORMS

64

ROUTE OUT

60

Tristan da Cunha

40°S

57

ICE LIMIT

WILLIWAW SQUALLS

53

Falkland Is.

S. Georgia

51

Cape Horn

50

60°W

0°

(continued from page 186)

seemed a chance of a breeze, so I decided to tackle the job of dragging the big sail right through the boat and getting it on deck. No sooner had I done this than the breeze freshened to 15 knots, and came ahead, so somewhat reluctantly I halted the genoa operation and had breakfast instead. But in the middle of breakfast I could bear it no longer. The breeze was light again, the morning fine, with a smooth sea, so I interrupted breakfast, went back on deck and finished setting the big sail. And what a difference it made! I kept it up all day, but at nightfall the breeze quickened, and I dropped it. On the wind, in any strength of breeze, *Gipsy Moth* did better without it.

I had a busy time sorting out charts for the Atlantic, and was sorry to find that I had no Pilot Chart for the North Atlantic.* Besides giving the average winds and weather for each route, these charts are crammed with interesting information. I missed the Pilot Chart, but it is difficult at the start of a long voyage not to forget something. Although I should be sailing mostly in April, I decided to follow the March sailing route up the South Atlantic recommended in *Ocean Passages of the World*. It would take me 700 miles farther to the east than the April route, but I judged it more suitable for a small boat.

On Tuesday morning, March 28, I started getting out of my bunk at 03.00 but fell asleep again for two hours. It was a trying day. *Gipsy Moth* jibbed at sailing a certain heading on the wind, and it happened to be a most valuable heading for windward work. I spent hours trying to induce her to keep to it. This was *Gipsy Moth*'s No. 2 vice making itself painfully felt. When a degree or more of heel made her ride off to leeward, as soon as she got into the attitude of sailing on her leeward bilge, she shot off like a salmon, and went suddenly quiet with it. In the end I gave up trying to coax her to sail close to the wind, and after she had slid off to leeward once again I left her there, and just enjoyed the speed and quietness.

To make up for these frustrations, I stood myself a notable lunch—I think it was the one I had enjoyed most on the passage. Here is the menu:

A clove of garlic, with a hunk of Gruyère cheese and a glass of Whitbread; a tin of Australian peas, a tin of salmon, and three potatoes in their jackets with plenty of butter; a tin of pears.

---

* Later I found a British Admiralty version of this Pilot Chart which was excellent in spite of being for the wrong month, June.

Hundreds of prions skimmed and flirted round the boat while I lunched, and when I dumped my bucket of scraps every one of them dropped out of the sky to see what he could get.

There was a thin layer of fog that night, with the moon looking fuzzy through it, but dawn brought a marvellous day. There was a light blue sky with very little cloud; the sea smooth and sparkling in the sun, and a straight horizon. I had not seen a day like it for a long time. I took advantage of it to check the index mirror of the sextant. That index mirror was deteriorating fast, where the quicksilver was peeling off at the back due to months of seawater sousings. I took advantage, too, of the stable boat to check the steering compass with a sun azimuth. I saw some well-defined "mare's tails" (high, filmy cirrus clouds), which are said to forecast a big wind.

By the afternoon I was headed by a Force 6 north-easter. As the sea got rougher, *Gipsy Moth* pounded and slammed badly. She bucked a large bottle of coffee powder into the air; it landed on the galley where the bottle smashed. I did not notice it for a time among the medley of crashes, and the fine coffee powder made a beastly mess. Wind and sea were increasing fast, and I kept on stripping off one sail after the other, until I had only the storm jib and storm staysail set. At 17.00 I turned across wind on to NW by W to ease the pounding. It steadily got worse, until at 20.20 I reckoned I must spare the boat, so turned downwind and ran before the gale. I felt seasick, and maybe this made it easier for me to turn downwind, but it was most disheartening to be sliding backwards towards the Horn at 6 knots. My hope was that the NE gale would veer to the south and thus finally bring me back on to my right heading. This was what always happened in the South Pacific with the small lows passing through.

I got an uneasy sleep for about an hour and a half, then found to my astonishment that the wind had *backed* to north *instead* of veering! This turned my previously bad heading of south-west into a shocker of south-south-west. So I dressed, and gybed on to east by south, and kept to that heading, which slowly improved as the wind backed to north-west, until by morning my heading was east-north-east. I was then able to set some more sail. However, the boat still got a drastic thrashing. I got a sea down my neck after I had finished all the sail changes and was still dry. I was trying to adjust the cowl of the Aladdin stove chimney, so that it would exhaust the fumes instead of letting them blow into the cabin. I was making a long arm over the top of the companionway with no oilskins on when a broadsider caught me fair and square. Twice *Gipsy Moth* dropped off the crest of a wave coming from abeam, and landed with a terrific crash.

Next morning (March 30) I felt as feeble again as on the passage out. I thought it must be connected with the gale, the movement, being shut in, lying down too long, and nervous strain, but later I wondered if it was due to the fumes from the stove being driven in by the gale.

It was grim out there. I had hoped to be clear of the Forties, but I seemed stuck, although the borderline was only 111 miles north. At 09.00 that day (Thursday) I was within sight of the spot I left at noon on Wednesday. I had sailed 115 miles, but my dead reckoning plot showed I had closed a complete circle. I thought of Slocum running before a gale for three days off Tierra de Fuego—in that time I should be half way back to the Horn.

Perhaps the Forties were giving me a farewell souvenir, grim, with a lumpy, confused swell from the north-west, and a breaking sea overriding it. Periodically a breaker on top of a swell peak picked up *Gipsy Moth* and dropped her in the trough on her side, with a terrific crash. I was on deck once when this happened, and the boat seemed to be in the air before she dropped. The din and rattle of things below when the boat hit the water made one wonder how the hull could survive such treatment.

March 30 was my shortest day's run, 15½ miles noon to noon.

That evening I had a really bad fall. I was standing on the weather deck, and, due to the heel of the boat, well up above the waterline. I was reaching up as high as I could to attach the aerial lead-in from the terminal through the cabin top to the backstay, when a sudden gust of wind hit my body such a blow that my grasp of the backstay was torn away, and I was flung in a heap to the bottom of the far side of the cockpit. I stayed motionless where I landed, wondering if my leg was broken. I relaxed everything while I wondered. For about a minute I made no movement at all, and then slowly uncurled myself. To my astonishment—and infinite relief—nothing seemed broken. I think it was absolutely providential that I had broken no bone.

Picking myself up and collecting my wits, I carried on with my radio work, and had a bad contact with Buenos Aires. When at last I finished the radio session I found that *Gipsy Moth* was 40° off course: the port side tiller line of 1¼-inch braided Terylene had snapped. I tied the two ends together, and felt lucky that nothing worse had happened. (In Sydney, it was reckoned that the load on these tiller lines before the keel was modified was up to 4 tons.)

Gipsy Moth was now on a broad reach, and I hoped for some sleep. My ribs and ankle hurt from the fall, and I felt utterly fagged out. I wrote in my log: "I must go easily until I have recovered from yesterday's gale and feel full of life again. To arrive is the big objective; to sail fast is much less important, but of course one wants to do it."

How quickly things change at sea—for the better as well as for the worse. March 31 brought a lovely morning, sun, and a sparkling sea, full of playful porpoises. It was quite warm. I left off my long woollen underfugs, but it was still hot working the sails. I was immensely happy and relieved to find that all my aches had gone by the time I got up. During the night I had had some difficulty in moving my ribs and ankle, and feared a bad stiffening. In the afternoon I was able to sit on the foredeck to sew up a seam of the genoa staysail, which had given way.

I sailed out of the Forties that evening. They may not roar in the lee of South America as they do on the other side of it, but it was a great event to get away from them. I had been sailing in or near the Forties nearly round the globe, for I was now only 2,400 miles from South Africa where I first entered them. To be candid, I think that anyone who sails a yacht in the Forties is a fool—but I knew that before I started. On the other hand, it was one of life's great experiences, and I would feel unsatisfied if I had not done it. I tried to celebrate the event with a bottle of Veuve Cliquot, but it was a flop drinking by myself.

After that everything seemed to change, as if the 40th parallel had been a magic wand. I forgot that I had ever needed heat in the cabin, and looked for light clothes. The night was wonderful, with a cloudless sky, and the stars so bright that I thought half of them were planets. I could read my steering compass by the half moon. (But I still felt that the stars were upside down—I was so used to looking at them in the northern hemisphere.)

Things were looking up in the climate line. I saw something like a transparent, iridescent ribbon reflecting light, right at the end of the counter. It was a fish, the first flying fish of the South Atlantic, about 7 inches long. I went to the cabin to get a cloth to hold it, but when I got back it had slipped through the scupper and gone.

I was now in the 1,200-mile-wide belt of variable winds, lying between the westerlies south of the 40th parallel, and the SE Trade Winds north of the 20th parallel. The wind was variable not only in direction, but in speed, and I was constantly setting or taking in sail. *Gipsy Moth* needed precisely the exact area of sail, no more and no less, for every set of conditions, and she wanted a different suit of sails for every strength and direction of the wind. It was trying work. By April 7 I was about half way through the variables, but they gave me a rough time. For three days I was headed by a gale, and twice I had to run south or south-west because of rough seas. I crossed the 30th parallel one day, and found myself south of it again the next. Between gales the wind never stopped varying, and I was tired out with trimming and changing sails. There were rain squalls, too, and some of these squalls had a fierce gale blast in them, which struck without warning, and laid the sails nearly flat before I could get out of my bunk. I fixed up some gear which I could work from my bunk to turn the boat downwind in an emergency.

At one time I seemed to be sailing through a flock of little cyclones. The wind would work right round the compass from south through east to north-west. It usually jumped round from NW to south, and if I was below it would put all the sails aback, with the wind on the wrong side of them, before I could reach the cockpit. Then I would have to wear the ship round tediously the other way until the sails picked up the wind again on the right side. A lot of squalls discharged such heavy rain that it seemed they must have emptied everything they had. I rigged my rain collector, because I had only 4 gallons left in my 40-gallon tank. The water came in so fast that I did not notice that the tank was full, and was happily filling the boat as well! The first water off the sail was brackish to taste, but I did not want to waste it, so washed four shirts and a pair of pyjamas. I soon regretted my enthusiasm because there was no hope of drying them.

At midnight on April 7 I found myself running back towards the Horn at 8 knots. Yet there was nothing else I could do, for it was the very devil if I turned *Gipsy Moth* across the wind. I did my best to be philosophical, and went to sleep, feeling the better for it when I woke. The wind was still blowing at Force 7–8, but there was some blue showing in the high, clouded sky, and I felt that the sea should ease soon. I was surprised at the heat, and felt like taking off my shirt at breakfast. The water was lukewarm, too. This was better than being cold. I logged: "Decidedly this is not too bad a situation. I think I am playing the spoilt child at not being able to sail fast."

In the middle of the next night (April 8) I went out into the cockpit to adjust the tiller with nothing on—I mean bare skinned, to save putting on oilskins. I did not feel cold in the wind, which shows how hot it was. Later that morning, I searched the foredeck optimistically for flying fish for breakfast, which was silly, because the big seas coming aboard would wash off anything. A lovely snowy white tropical bird with a long white tail like a single plume flew over and round above the boat.

I made up my salad beds that day. These "beds" were most valuable in giving me fresh greenstuff, but I had to resow them often. I began by sowing on flannel, but I found that soft paper did very well, and this was a good discovery, because combing out the old roots from the flannel to use it again was quite a chore.

The next job was to empty the forepeak of water, a task which I tackled at midnight on April 8–9, when I could not get to sleep. The watertight bulkhead there, of course, was a comforting safeguard, but—equally of course—it kept *in* any water which happened to leak in until it could be siphoned out. I led a long pipe, about 8 feet long, into the forepeak, and then bent down with my head on the cabin floor and sucked the end of the pipe until the water began to run through. As soon as I stopped sucking, the water stopped running. I worked for over an hour trying to get the water running freely, but it wouldn't respond. I concluded that there must be something wrong with the pipe, either something stuck in it, or a small leak. So I rigged an entirely fresh pipe and immediately it worked well. There was a lot of water in the forepeak and I was glad to get rid of it. I was rewarded for these midnight efforts by two small flying fish for breakfast.

April 11 was Sheila's birthday, and because of this I had made arrangements on my last radio contact with Buenos Aires to call direct to GCN4 in London, hoping that I should be able to get through with a message for her. London was 4,700 miles away, on a direct Great Circle bearing. That was an immense distance for the 75-watt transmitter of my Marconi Kestrel, but I could hear the London operator loud and clear, and got my own message through. I took a message from Sheila, that she was thinking of me on her birthday, and telling me that she and Giles were dining with Edward and Belinda Montagu that night (their wedding anniversary being on the same day). I was delighted to re-establish R/T contact with London, and logged: "This is a credit to the GPO and Marconi." I would have sent a longer message, but *Gipsy Moth* went aback in the middle of things, and as I didn't like to leave the self-steering gear locked to the tiller in such conditions, I signed off.

Another memorable event on Sheila's birthday was that I completed my circumnavigation of the globe, crossing my outward bound track at 21.45. This was a great thrill, because I had tried to go round the world in my seaplane in 1931, and failed. When outward bound, I was at the spot where the tracks crossed at 08.14 on October 3, so that the circumnavigation had taken me 190 days 13½ hours, or 6 months, 8 days, 13½ hours. This was just over *half* the time (5 days more than half-time) taken by Vito Dumas in the previous record time for a singlehanded circumnavigation—one year and seven days. In each case, of course, the elapsed time included time spent at ports on the way. Vito Dumas, in setting up his record, took just about half the time of any former singlehanded voyage round the world. So in halving his time, I could feel an honest satisfaction.*

But oh, those Horse Latitudes!† My log is full of exasperated jottings:

---

*I must point out, however, that I had a great advantage over Vito Dumas through being equipped with a self-steering device. When mine broke up, my speed on the wind dropped, and on the last 2,758 miles to Sydney without the self-steering gear I averaged 102 miles per day compared with 142 miles per day before that. His *Lehg II* was much smaller than *Gipsy Moth IV*, but, in my opinion, there was not much advantage to me in this because I think that, whereas his boat was too small, mine was too large. I am sure *Gipsy Moth* and I were better fitted out; on the other hand some people might think he had an advantage in being younger (as he was born a year before I was, he must have been 42 when he circumnavigated). I am not sure this was all advantage. The saying is that comparisons are odious. I must say that I think Dumas was a great sailor, and that I find his book, *Alone through the Roaring Forties*, just as delightful to read now as it was before I started this voyage.

†The name is a grim reminder of the old days of sailing ships. Passages through these variables were liable to take so long that horses (and other animals) carried as cargo used frequently to perish from running short of food or water.

• • •

"One could easily go barmy in these Horse Latitudes. As soon as I get below to log a retrim, the wind has changed the heading completely, say by 60°, and I have to start again."

"Is there a plan by the genie of the Horse Latitudes to keep me short of sleep? I have only to get into my bunk and drop off, for something to happen which requires urgent attention. Now *Gipsy Moth* is aback again. How in Hades does she do it?"

"One needs a rubber brain. The cockpit wind direction indicator reads 2° higher than the one at my bunk on the port tack."

• • •

I had been plugging into the wind for the best part of 1,000 miles, and I longed to pick up the SE Trades. Still, it was wonderful to sit in the sun and the spray on the foredeck, and I even tried to sing! It seemed roasting hot to go below after being on deck.

According to the US Pilot Chart, on April 12 I was 300 miles south of the limit of the SE Trade Wind belt. But the Admiralty Chart (No. 2202 A) was more encouraging, putting the average southern limit of the SE Trades as only 60 miles from where I was. I felt, "It should not be long now," and stood myself a drink. It was a greatly satisfying feeling to be driving north at last, but Lord, it was uncomfortable! With a 30° heel the bashing and the rocking were indescribable, and the moment *Gipsy Moth* heeled a little more she would suddenly develop lee helm, and gallop off at 8 knots, 40° farther off the wind. Whenever she did that she took some getting back, and often it would mean starting the whole battle of sail trim all over again.

The night of April 12 was truly lovely, bringing a bright Venus in the arc of a sickle moon lying on its back. All the stars in heaven seemed to be out. The bright stars made paths of reflected light on the smooth sea. Never before have I seen paths of reflected light on the sea from *stars*; from *planets*, yes, but not from stars. Later, as an extra treat, the wind backed enough for me to free the heading 10°. It was amazing what a difference that made to comfort, but my worry always was that if I gave *Gipsy Moth* 10° she was liable to take 40°.

April 13 was a big day, with a haircut and shave (though I feared that my Bond Street haircutter would not have been impressed). I was becalmed again, but I had now passed the average southern limit (according to the Admiralty) of the SE Trades, and I was excited by the hope that the next wind would *be* the South-East Trade Wind. Apart from the wind, conditions were perfect.

The sun on my skin at dawn was delightful, and there was no need of any clothes for sail changing at night—I wore only shoes, a cap and a lifeline. I took advantage of the easy sailing to sort out stores and to clean up mildew.

At 21.15 that night I logged:

• • •

"Here she comes, I reckon. I gybed, and presently some bubbles could be seen moving on the glassy surface. We were moving to a SE wind! Now the speedometer is reading—I think we are off! This calls for a celebration; I suppose one of those Australian champagnes—may I survive it!"

• • •

Alas, next noon I had to record: "My SE Trade has been a proper fizzle out. Most of the movement this morning has been due to a north-west or west wind." I had a visitor that morning, a 6-foot shark which swam around near the boat. It had very widespanning lateral fins, and I wondered if it might have been a big dogfish. I was so hot that I poured buckets of water over myself on deck. I had a job of work to do in repairing the compass light—the electrical connections and plugs were eaten away in several places. It surprises me that builders do not supply fittings to stand up to sea water; it does not seem anything like as difficult as making a camera to work under water, and that has been successfully done.

Gipsy Moth was in a contrary mood, and every time I left her alone for a while she headed off *west* and started sailing well. If she couldn't get there by bearing away, she did it by going aback. She was like a naughty puppy, heading off westwards whenever I looked the other way.

I gave up trying to mend the compass light. I had no soldering iron or blowlamp, and with the boat jigging about I could not fix the wire to the bulb holder of the lamp. I decided that it would be more sensible to hang an inspection lamp above the compass when I wanted to use it.

On April 15 it looked as if I was in the Trade Wind at last, after several disappointing false starts. That night I saw the Plough constellation for the first time on the voyage home, and it gave me a thrill.

Next day *Gipsy Moth* passed the 10,000-mile mark from Sydney.
I wrote:

• • •

"I ought to be cock-a-hoop, but instead I feel a little desperate,
apprehensive and homesick. I still have 5,200 miles to go [5,500
had I known it], so I have only done two-thirds of the passage.
Such hundreds of things can go wrong in such a distance. I seem
to have been a long time away from home, and home seems a
long time away. This is only weakness, of course. Between whiles
I am having a thrilling sail. The crescent moon is dead ahead
looking in through the cabin window at me."

• • •

On April 18 I wrote:

• • •

"I feel just damned lazy, and enjoying the sail. Also enjoying a
rest and leisure. What bliss to be in the cockpit with the sun and
warm breeze on one's skin, just watching the sea, and the sky, and
the sails, and meditating! There are stacks of things waiting to be
done, but I don't want to do anything until I am forced to. A
quarter moon is staring at me through the cabin skylight. I am
sorry that I am half way through the South-East Trades in three
days: I could do with a fortnight of this life. I used two lots of
young soya bean shoots for salad today, and cooked the remainder
which had grown to 6 inches. I am sorry to say that, cooked, they
were too tough to eat."

• • •

Putting my laziness into writing must have shamed me, for three
hours later I added to the log:

• • •

"Since my last entry I have fixed the camera shutter which
was not working; fixed the freshwater pump which was jamming;
filled five bottles with paraffin; filled the Primus filler tins with
meths from a new tin; made up a new graph sheet for the chro-
nometer and watch corrections; retrimmed for near calm three
times; and drunk two very welcome pink gins."

• • •

I had a wonderful four-course breakfast next morning. The sea
gave me a flying fish, and I added to the menu grapefruit, fried
potatoes and scrambled eggs, and three slices of wholemeal bread

with honey and marmalade. That day was my idea of blissful sailing. I did not wish to leave the cockpit, but felt that I could stay there for hours, musing on the past and the future while the warm air flowed over my skin and the sun filled it with life. *Gipsy Moth* sailed at a good speed, and there were no major shemozzles. Sure, it was hot in the noon sun, but a few bucketfuls of the ocean were delightful. In the afternoon I started clearing out the fruit and vegetable lockers. Surprisingly, there were few bad pieces; so far only one or two grapefruit, oranges and lemons. There was only one bad potato, but what a mess and stink it made! I was astonished that the potatoes in contact with it had not gone rotten too. These really were first-class potatoes, such as one never seems able to buy in England nowadays.

Going barefooted that afternoon I got a piece of glass stuck into my heel. It was a fragment from *Gipsy Moth*'s big knockdown in the Tasman Sea. It must have worked loose from clothes or woodwork high up, and fallen on the cabin floor. I was constantly coming across bits lodged in strange places.

On April 21 I lost the South-East Trades and entered the Doldrums. I was in a west-going current, flowing due west at between ½ and 2 knots. This current splits on the north-east bulge of South America, half flowing down the coast to Buenos Aires, and half flowing up the coast to the West Indies.

It was disappointing to have only had five good days' sailing out of the South-East Trades. But *Gipsy Moth* reeled off 818 miles in those five days, a daily average of 163½ miles.

In the evening I listened again to Giles's selection of music on the recorder. That was the first time I had done so on the passage—the last time I played it was when I reached the Roaring Forties on the way out. Then it made me so sad and homesick that I never played it again until now. Homeward bound, it was quite a different thing.

My second day's run in the Doldrums was only 83 miles—for two days I had been only ghosting along for most of the time. Those two miserable runs spoilt my chance of a good week's tally. I had been hoping for 1,150 miles, but instead made only 1,004.

On Sunday, April 23, I wanted to bake some bread, but there was a huge blue-black monster of a rain squall ahead. I waited to see what the brute would do. It seemed to pass from north, to north-west, to west, to south, and then came down on me from the south.

Rain started, just as I had the yeast to rise. The squall had circled *Gipsy Moth* to the west until it was due south again, when I thought it was safe and popped the bread in the oven. Immediately, the squall moved north, and seemed to pounce on *Gipsy Moth* like a cat on a mouse. It brought wind, and the skies emptied. I was forced to close the hatch and the companion to keep out the deluge. The heat, with the Primus going full blast, was terrific. It had been 87° in the coolest part of the cabin before I even lit the stove. However, I got my bread.

SIXTEEN

TRADE WINDS AND DOLDRUMS

I CROSSED the Equator at 03.30 on Monday morning, April 24, but it was too early in the day to celebrate. The Line was succeeded by Doldrums, long periods of calm, and then light airs coming from all round the compass. There was heavy rain between whiles.

By noon I was 21½ miles north of the Line. It was scorchingly hot, and I emptied bucketfuls of ocean over me every few hours. The cockpit floor was hot enough to burn my feet, and I had to cool it first with buckets of water.

I then celebrated crossing the Line with a pint of ale from the keg in the keel to toast Father Neptune. I hoped it would bring me luck—one can do with all the luck one can get. The ship's barber had another go at cutting my hair for the occasion.

One odd feature of my passage through the Trade Wind belt was that I kept on sighting land, which gave me a mental jolt every time, though I knew that there was no land nearer than Fernando Noronha Island, 350 miles due west, except for the St Peter and St Paul Rocks, 200 miles on my port beam. I believe this was due to unusual visibility, so that I would be looking at tops of clouds below and far beyond the horizon, and those were imitating every kind of land.

I kept jogging along northwards. Every mile of northing in the Doldrums is worth five anywhere else. Rain came at intervals in tropical downpours, like having a hose turned on to the top of the cabin. The endless windshifts were very trying, and I find an entry in the log for the night of April 25: "To hell with the whole outfit! I am going to try for a sleep." However, by noon that day I had made a good day's run of 142½ miles, which I thought a fine piece of luck in the Doldrums. I found that I had used 20 gallons of fresh water in nineteen days from the 40-gallon tank, so decided to fill up while still in Rain Squall Alley.

I could not see the sun clearly in the desilvered mirror of my big sextant, so I brought out the little flying boat sextant which Maria Blewitt* gave me after the 1945 war. It is a very handy instrument to use in the cramped quarters of a small yacht, and I was delighted with it. It has only one fault, that it is difficult to read off the altitude on the scale, and I dare say Maria found this a troublesome defect.

I missed the Pilot Chart for the North Atlantic which I had forgotten to bring with me, but the Admiralty Chart put me already inside the March (spring) boundary of the North-East Trade Wind belt, although still 660 miles south of the August (summer) boundary. It was exciting waiting for the North-East Trades to turn up.

In the next rain squall I connected the boom to my No. 2 tank. The rain was so heavy that the pipe in the boom couldn't take all the water, and it overflowed from the boom-end on to the deck with loud splashing.

In some 24,000 miles of sailing up to April 26, I had seen only one fish apart from flying fish. On this day I saw hundreds and thousands of small tunny. They were making every kind of leap out of the water, from high vertical jumps to long low curves. I saw two pass each other in the air, going in opposite directions. About twenty birds, dove grey with pointed wings and tail, and flying like doves, were screaming and diving into the water within 10 feet of the boat. This went on for about six hours from 11.00. The gathering of fish and birds must have been due to *Gipsy Moth* in some way because, although it was happening on both sides, and ahead, of the boat, I could not see fish or birds anywhere else during the six hours. Maybe they were all feeding on tiny fish which were swarming round *Gipsy Moth*, thinking that she was a whale.

I was always needing to conjure up some new idea, such as how to do the job of gear that failed, or how to keep out of trouble in a crisis. And there were countless other little things. For example, I always read when eating, but for a long time could not think of any way of propping up a magazine on my swinging table in front of my swinging chair. The flat surface of this table is only 12½ × 17½ inches. Suddenly the idea came to me—I pulled a magazine apart,

---

* Maria Blewitt has navigated yachts in the Fastnet and many other ocean races. She is the author of several manuals of navigation for yachtsmen.

and propped up a page at a time. This opened up a new field of interest and pleasure, by enabling me to read the coloured Sunday newspaper supplements which I had collected before I left Sydney. Incidentally, I am sure that to read a page continuously moving on a swinging table must be the best possible eye exercise.

Sometimes I saw strange things. Just before crossing the Line the boat appeared to be sailing up a gently sloping sea surface, in other words, uphill. At the time I was a little worried, but when I was 240 miles north of the Line I noticed the same thing again. This time the sea appeared uphill in every direction, as if I were sailing in a shallow saucer.

I flitted through the Doldrums as if I had a reserved passage. On the evening of April 26 the breeze veered to NNE and by noon next day I was sure of having reached the North-East Trade Wind. It began as a nice gentle breeze making for delightful sailing, even if slow. I pulled out the underwater speedometer unit on the east side of the boat, because I expected not to change heel for 1,400 miles. Father Neptune must have approved of my toast to him when I crossed the Line, so I drew some more ale from the keg and drank his health again, hoping for more luck.

I was not so successful in the galley. I cooked a golden sponge pudding which I had been looking forward to, but as I turned it out on a plate I felt seasick, and did not want it. Then I started baking bread. This was a stupid thing to do at nightfall, because I promptly felt so sleepy that I could not keep my eyes open, but I was stuck with the damn bread for an hour. I couldn't understand why the bottom loaf in the oven at my previous baking was quite uncooked inside: it was the first time this had happened. The odd thing was that the top loaf was well done, yet it was the top loaf that I always worried about in case it did not get enough heat in the tin oven. I believe the truth on this occasion was that the oven was *too* hot; that it rapidly cooked the *outside* of the bottom loaf, and hardened it up so much that the inside could not cook properly.

At this time I had almost a craving for fresh fish. On April 28 I found two more flying fish on deck, caught up under the furled sail on the foredeck. I decided that probably lots more fish had wanted to come aboard, but had been washed off again. To help them to stay with me, I rigged a length of small-meshed net along the leeward side of the foredeck. This proved a success, because next morning there were two flying fish there, which certainly would have gone or been washed overboard but for the net. They were not big—about 7–8 inches—but they made a nice meal for me. I think these flying fish had some important food in them which is lacking in tinned fish.

On April 29 I finished the fresh (ahem!) eggs, and I ate my last grapefruit, leaving only one orange and one lemon. I thought it amazing that the fruit had lasted so well, in such bad conditions of damp, violent movement and heat. In one way, I was not sorry to see the last of the eggs for I had grown nervous towards the end whenever I opened one. Some had been cracked in the capsize off Sydney, and nearly all had black mould patches outside, due to the wet lockers, though this did not always affect the inside of the egg.

My remaining cheeses had to go, too. There was an increasingly horrible smell in the cabin, which at first I attributed to rotting fruit or vegetables. But after I had checked all these, the aroma steadily became more nauseating every time I passed through the cabin. Then I found that it was due to five cheeses which had been shut in a plastic box. A roll of charts had fallen on to the box and pressed open the lid, thereby letting out the evil genie of the box. Those cheeses were not crawling or humming, they were swimming. It was an ordeal to get them into the sea. I had wrapped another cheese in some pages of the *Illustrated London News* and that one tasted all right though smelling pretty high. After the giant hum of the others I could not face it, and it also went off to the flying fish.

I was running short of diesel oil—I must have been crazy not to bring more fuel oil in jerrycans. At dark I wanted to rig up a light because of crossing the New York–Cape Town steamer route, and to save current, I rigged up a cheap hurricane paraffin lamp made by an American firm in Hong Kong. The flame flickered madly in the breeze when I hung it to the backstay, and it looked as if it would not last for 30 seconds; in fact, I never knew it blown out.

That night I logged:

• • •

"Big news! I have seen the Pole Star for the first time. Theoretically, of course, it was visible from the Equator, but cloud and the hazy atmosphere have prevented my seeing it so low down until now. *Gipsy Moth* is skittling along; I had to stop plotting on a chart because I could not hold a pair of dividers still enough."

• • •

This elation was followed by renewed trouble from my right elbow. It was very painful, and I feared that I must have damaged the bone. I hoped for the best, and put on tincture of arnica frequently.

The pain kept me awake, and I found that I could ease it only by holding the elbow above my head. Unfortunately, as soon as I dropped off to sleep, the arm dropped on to my face, and woke me up.

Later I found that my arm did not hurt if I *pulled* with that hand, or held on to something with it, which seemed miraculous to me. But it was most painful if I *pushed* as much as one finger with it. I wound a four-yard crêpe bandage round the elbow, which eased the pain.

When one thinks what a broken bone could entail, one's imagination can turn anything into a break. This was a grim day for me. Besides the trouble with my arm, I felt as if I had been poisoned. I moved unsteadily, was light-headed and had a mild roaring in my ears. After each essential job I flopped back in my bunk. However, I managed to do everything necessary, though with much cursing and groaning and, in fact, the day's run was no less than 181½ miles. In the afternoon I suddenly tumbled to why I was feeling so ill; I suddenly realised that I had felt off colour, or, as I thought, seasick, every time I had drunk some of the Australian champagne. The night before I had had a half bottle of it, and no other drinks. Half a bottle is, after all, only two glasses of champagne, but I felt really ill, as if I had been badly poisoned. I think that the sea movement must have turned the champagne into acid. Throughout April 30 I still felt ghastly, with my ears humming, and a sensation as if I could float off into the air. I drank water with a teaspoonful of bicarbonate of soda which, I hoped, would relieve my misery. May Day was not much better; it was one of those days when everything seemed to go wrong, or be awkward. My flying fish for breakfast were burnt, uncooked inside, and greasy—all at the same time. My big loaf was uncooked inside like my previous baking, though I had left it in the oven for 1½ hours. I seemed to bump my elbow everywhere, particularly on the companion steps, when I drew up the pump handles for sea water, the fresh water, and the galley sink; also I caught it every time on the sharp edge of the cockpit winches. I was a fool to struggle with the main boom reefing handle; the reefing gear had jammed and I was using brute force to turn the handle, when it slipped and I gave my elbow a frightful dint. This made me feel angry with myself, and I wrote in the log: "How damned ungrateful I am! I am lucky to be able to draw those pumps and work the winches. Thank God I can use my elbow and am well enough to eat a breakfast."

Navigation was intriguing. Where I was on May 1 the sun passed nearly overhead, within 30′ of angle from the boat, equivalent to 30 miles on the earth's surface. In a few minutes the sun swung from nearly due east to nearly west. I got five sun sights within sixteen minutes of time, and the noon position point was within a mile of four of these sights. It was a good day's run—171 miles, making 678 for four days, an average of a shade over 7 knots.

The poisoning (or whatever it was) had taken the stuffing out of me, and I spent much of May 2 lying down and trying to sleep. I felt better for the rest, and needed to, for in the evening there was a bite in the wind, and the going was getting fairly rough. I got into trousers and jersey again, feeling sad at the ending of that lovely heat. I had to hunt for some pyjamas, and more bedding. I rigged the Chinese lantern again, with sundry curses at being thrown about. That lantern was a magic job; it flickered wildly, frantically, but stayed alight, no matter how hard the wind blew or what the boat did. It not only stayed alight, but I had trouble putting it out in the morning! I saw a flying fish fly past in the dusk six feet away, like a bird. Three others rose just ahead of the stem, and turned sharply round in formation to avoid the boat and shoot off downwind. A pretty clever design of hull and rig is a flying fish.

Gipsy Moth was sailing fast through the North-East Trade Wind belt. It was rough going, with the wind at 30 knots a lot of the time. The boat was heeled over to port the whole time, up to 55° of heel, with an average of, I would say, 35°. The discomfort below, living 24 hours a day at this heel, with rough going, was extreme, but I was determined to sail *Gipsy Moth* at her maximum speed to find out what she could do.* She could only sail at maximum speed on the wind if heeled to between 20 and 45°. Down in the big Southern Ocean seas I dared not sail her at full speed at this initial heel, because a big wave would capsize her. But up here in the Trade Wind zone I did not fear any waves bigger than the ordinary run of sea. On May 2 the run was 170 miles, and on May 3, 188.

Gipsy Moth was making heavy weather of it, plunging and lurching into the waves. It took me rather long to change down the 300-foot jib to the 200-foot jib because of my painful arm. It is

---

* If you tilt your chair at an angle of 35° and imagine living for nine days with your kitchen, dining room and bedroom tilted at that angle, and then suppose that it is all being bumped about like an iron-wheeled cart pulled over boulders, you will get a fair idea how uncomfortable life was in *Gipsy Moth*.

surprising how many parts of the job have always been done by that arm only, in spite of the fact that I am pretty well ambidextrous. However little I used the arm, it was too much for it; it was swollen below the elbow, a longish lump about 4 inches long by 2 wide, hot to touch and very tender.* At noon on May 3 I discovered that I needed only another run of 164 miles to make good 1,200 miles for the week, and I went against my true judgement, and hoisted the trysail. After that *Gipsy Moth* certainly was cracking along. I logged: "We shall get the lee deck thoroughly submerged with this sail up."

My elbow was very painful next morning, but I managed to hoist the mainsail after dropping the trysail. I left the bandage on my arm because it seemed to help, and it protected the place from knocks to a certain extent. At noon I could log triumphantly: "Well! We've done it. A run of 179 miles today makes a total for the week of 1,215."

That called for a celebration, and Father Neptune and I got at the keg again. Father Nep deserved a toast, because it needed an extraordinary, once-in-a-lifetime set of conditions for a single-handed boat to do so well. There was enough wind without the usual bad sea that goes with it, the wind from the right direction, and also the fair certainty that neither the wind nor the sea would suddenly increase to knock the boat down. So I drew a glass for Neptune as well as for myself, and tossed his into the ocean for him. (I shouldn't be surprised if he becomes a regular customer of Whit-breads after this voyage.)

I was sailing almost exactly along the old clipper way for April. The sea was a darker blue, and on May 5 *Gipsy Moth* began passing through lanes of sargasso weed, yellowy brown rows of it, trailing downwind. There was still a fresh breeze from NE by ½ N. I had reached the edge of the North-East Trade Wind belt. (Isn't the French word for it, *Alizé*, much nicer and more expressive?) And I was enjoying what I assumed to be a last gallop through it. Noon brought another big run of 180 miles. A hunk of sargasso weed caught astride the self-steering oar, and I could not see how it would become dislodged. There was too much pressure of water for me to pole it off, but I decided to have a go if it was still there later on.

---

* In fact I had bursitis as well as two small chips of bone off the elbow.

Gipsy Moth was back at her bloody pet trick of either sliding off to leeward, or coming up into the wind and stopping dead. At 21.00 I logged:

. . .

"Hell! I have been at that trimming off and on since about 16.00. This afternoon I wanted a sleep after lunch. The boat had been going perfectly well till then, but *five times*, as soon as I got into my bunk and was dropping off to sleep, she came up into the wind, and would have got into irons if I had not dealt with her. With all the hauling of sheets etc., my elbow is now very painful."

. . .

During the night I had to get up and hunt out some codeine as my arm was too painful to let me sleep. I read a chapter of *Tarka the Otter* by my old friend, Henry Williamson. It was an account of Tarka's being hunted and I found it just as excellent today as when it was first written.

The run at noon on May 6 was 175 miles. That afternoon I sailed out of the Trade Wind belt. It had lasted longer than I had expected, and as a result I was now 200 miles west of the April Clipper Way. I suppose the clippers waited until the North-East Trades petered out before turning north. In the last 8 days *Gipsy Moth* had reeled off 1,416½ miles practically in a straight line. This was an average speed of 177 miles per day or 7⅜ knots.* I think this was the easiest sail I had on the voyage, and in the most pleasant weather.

---

* For comparison, the fastest boat in the Fastnet Race for 1967, *Pen Duick III*, skippered by my old rival and friend, Eric Tabarly, averaged 166 miles per day, but of course she had to sail through variable winds.

SEVENTEEN

A PLEASANT SAIL AT LAST!

NOW IN near-calm conditions began the endless wearing ship, resetting sails and retrimming the self-steering gear to coax it to take charge after the yacht had tacked herself time after time with all sails aback. It was tedious work but the weather was lovely. I sat in the cockpit watching the sun go down beyond a gently heaving sea with a glassy surface. Anything more lovely I could not wish for as I sat listening to Ravel and Gershwin played on my recorder.

On May 7 I was hailed by the *Esso Winchester*, the first ship I had seen since Cape Horn. To my disgust I found that this first contact with people was making me tremble, but it reminded me that three months' solitude is strong medicine. One may behave as usual, but for a while one's feelings are changed. The beauty and magic of nature is as if seen under a magnifying glass, and life seems lived to the full. Anyway, to live life to the full is to do something which depends both on physical action and on the senses and also, at the same time, on the man-developed part of the brain.

I was becalmed or ghosting along at 2 knots or less, but I didn't much mind. I felt that in some ways I should be sorry when the voyage came to an end. I ghosted on through patches of yellow-brown sargasso weed, which wrapped itself round the self-steering oar and put the boat off course. That weed was a nuisance. I had managed to clear the oar of the big chunk which had fouled it earlier, but more weed came. And as fast as I could clear it from the oar, still more weed collected there. It slowed down the boat, and upset the steering.

On May 10 I decided to try to fit the new wind vane that I carried as a spare in the forepeak. It seemed that the great amount of play in the holes holding the bolts through the shaft must be causing much of the trouble with the self-steering gear. I worked at this all morning, and it was a tricky job, for those big vanes were the most awkward things to handle at sea: a puff of wind would whip them out of your hands in a moment. But luck was with me; I had a calm sea, little breeze and no accidents. By noon I had the new vane rigged and fitted, and it seemed to be working well.

That afternoon I saw another steamer, away astern, headed, I guessed, about east by north, and I logged: "Really, this is getting like Piccadilly for traffic!" In the evening I wrote:

• • •

"Well, I have had peace from the self-steering gear since I fitted the new vane; no trouble at all, though several times quite becalmed. I think the other one was too heavy with the counterpoise and the extra wood used to repair it in Sydney. Also, owing to the holes in the wood being so greatly damaged, and enlarged by the shaft pins, the vane had to move through quite an angle before it acted at all. The bolt through the shaft was chewed to the thickness of a matchstick by the shaft, and actually snapped when I tried to withdraw it from the wooden frame. 2,164 miles to go to Plymouth. It is a pity that I bragged about my big 8-day run—any old sailor would say you can't do that sort of thing with Neptune and get away with it! Look at the result—only 310½ miles in the past four days, and not even in the right direction; becalmed for a lot of the time and no end to this in sight!"

• • •

May 11 brought no change in the weather. At dawn the sea was like the shiny oiled hide of a great beast, with life and movement rippling and heaving under the skin. Later in the morning I could see breeze on the water, and *Gipsy Moth* actually touched 5 knots for a bit. But the wind made a BF of me. I tacked to the east, and it chased round after me until I was headed south. I tacked back to the north, and the wind came back and pushed me off to the northwest.

My arm continued to give me much pain. I don't like taking drugs of any sort, but that night I gave in and took another codeine. The curious thing was that not only did it ease the pain of the elbow almost right away, but also the elbow seemed better in the morning because of it.

I made a later start because I had been up almost every hour to trim sails during the night, but then I got down to more major work on the self-steering gear. I fitted a new bush to the bigger of the two bearings of the horizontal fore and aft main shaft. To do this I had to dismantle the gear first, and the biggest job was getting the steering oar detached. My Aussie friends who reconditioned it had made it a very tight fit. The woodwork had swollen since, and I could not get it off until I had chiselled enough wood away. This was a difficult job with the thing outboard of the stern, and my having to work by feel without being able to see what I was doing. However, I got it off in the end, and the rest of the job went smoothly. But, heavens, that thing was heavy! It was a struggle for me to handle it. Luckily it fell calm, which helped. I overhauled the rest of the gear, and felt that it should function better after this.

That night I logged:

• • •

"The fickle moon is on his back again under Venus, which does not seem quite right.* A lovely night. The Pole Star climbs up the heavens from night to night. With music and the remains of a bottle of Bacardi, it builds up to the most pleasant part of the whole voyage."

• • •

My arm seemed to get worse, and by May 14 the lump at the point of my elbow had become red and shiny like a huge spot or boil. The lump was about three inches long by one and a half inches wide, and nearly as hard as bone. I put on arnica twice, but it seemed to enrage the place. But I managed to last out the night without any more pain killer. I got some relief by hanging the arm down over the side of my bunk. In the afternoon the M/S Missouri, of New York City, NY, turned to have a look at Gipsy Moth, and we exchanged toots. I was waiting to set the big genoa in a lull, and did so after she had gone.

That night I logged:

• • •

"Last week, my fifteenth week at sea, was the slowest of the whole voyage, only 509 miles. This was due to calms and light airs while crossing the Azores High, the permanent high pressure system of the North Atlantic. I suppose it is only fair, as the previous week, the fourteenth, was the fastest of the whole voyage, 1,244½ miles. It has turned quite cold. The sea water was pretty cool this afternoon and I think I must have switched into a branch of the Gulf Stream coming down from the north-west."

• • •

---

* When at sea, for some reason which I cannot explain, I always think of the moon as being male.

But the wind freed at last, and on May 15 *Gipsy Moth* was running before it with a jib poled out. I tried to remember when last I had a free wind, and believed it was at the Horn! I had certainly been on the wind for a good many thousands of miles, and a free wind made a very pleasant change.

I fell for some more codeine, not so much to relieve the pain in my arm itself, as to get some sleep, which the pain prevented. How I needed sleep! This extract from my log next morning (May 16) helps to explain why:

• • •

"08.25. Since 07.15 I have done the following deck work. Transferred fore and aft pole-guys from starboard to port pole. Poled out. Topped up pole as soon as winch free. Unhanked 300-ft jib from starboard topmast stay, and transferred it (later) to port side ditto. Outhauled the clew of 300-ft jib to the pole-end, after fitting sheet at right length. Hoisted sail. Trimmed topping lift, outhaul and guys till sail setting to satisfaction. Transferred big genny from port side topmast stay to starboard side ditto (after first dropping the sail!) then rehoisted."

• • •

Later that day there was a class I, 3-star shemozzle, due to an innocent-looking rain shower. It started with a deluge, and I piped up from the main boom to the big water tank. While I was below for a few moments, dealing with the pipery, the wind came in from the opposite direction, not very strong, thank Heaven, but a fresh breeze. I had 1,550 square feet of sail set (a single tennis court has an area of 2,106 square feet). The wind switch put all the sails aback. The poled-out jib was in the way, preventing me from wearing the ship round, so I had to drop the big genoa, or rather let the halliard go, because the wet sail, pressed hard against the forestays and shrouds, would not come down. I ended up with all three headsails down. After the deluge finished, I hoisted the genoa staysail and got sailing again, but immediately I went below the wind came in from the south, fresh. The sails were all aback again, and I could not release the mizzen sail because the boom vang was jammed tight in the jam cleat. At last I had the boat hove to in a new rain storm, while I waited for the wind to make up its mind. One good thing was that the rainwater whistled into the tank, and filled it up to its 40 gallons, enough to see me through handsomely to Plymouth (considering that I was down to my last bottle of gin to mix with it!). After the shemozzle, I enjoyed a hot rum and lime, which I reckoned it warranted.

Although crossing the Azores High made for the slowest week's sailing of the voyage, it was easily the most delightful part of it. I used to stand myself a pink gin in the cockpit at sundown, with soft music off scene. I collected some weird creatures in the sargasso weed. One horrible thing looked like a miniature dinosaur with six stumpy legs, each of which had a big sucker instead of a foot. It placed these stumps one at a time as it walked over the weed. I put two Portuguese men-of-war in a bucket. Their mauve-and-blue-tinted air bladders nosed their way round the bucket, and I was surprised to see how they shot out their long dangling tendrils like a flash. But I did not see any of these strange creatures, or any of the crabs, eat each other, or even attack each other.

On May 17 a school of black fish (pilot whales), surfacing lazily, went past astern. I next saw them a mile to the north. It was hot and I felt languid and tired, and off colour. The radio telephone worried me—I wanted to be free of everything but the job of sailing. My arm, which was still more painful that day, was also having a bad effect. Unfortunately, it had had two nasty jabs the day before while handling the pole in the shemozzle.

In the small hours of next morning I saw a motor vessel, bearing 255°, overtaking me. I had had a good sleep, and my arm seemed slightly better, though the pain had extended in a line up to the armpit, which I supposed was the poison reaching the gland there. The motor vessel was the *Sea Huntress*, which the *Sunday Times* hired to hunt for me. I wished that I could be left alone to get on with my job.

The *Sea Huntress* came alongside at 08.10 and someone offered me some gin, but I declined it. I wished she would go away so that I could gybe. She had already been a nuisance through the night, because I had had to keep an eye on her during the darkness, in case she was a tunny fisherman, which would have had right of way. While the *Sea Huntress* was close in daylight, taking photographs, I had to delay my day's routine, such as getting breakfast, until she had left. I wanted to gybe, which involved dropping the pole boomed out to port and, after the gybe, booming out the other pole on the opposite side, but I did not want to do this while being watched from close to, because I was well aware how clumsy and unseamanlike I would appear to be with my painful elbow.

After she had gone and I had finished my work on deck, I wrote up my log, recording:

• • •

"Yesterday I crossed the 1960 track of *Gipsy Moth III*, when Sheila and I sailed back in her from New York after the first Transatlantic Solo Race and we called in at delightful Fayal. I felt quite nostalgic about it. Even the lonely sea and the sky looked the same. I used to have a theory when I was flying alone over a lot of seas that, with experience, one would be able to fix a position roughly just by the look of the sea from the air."

• • •

Just before dusk I tried to photograph a dolphin scratching its back on the stem. A school of dolphins was playing a favourite game of dashing to and fro past the bow, to see which of them could touch it without being caught by the stem slicing through the water. I stepped quietly across the foredeck, but must have made a noise, because they all vanished, except one, which turned up again, and made agitated passes ahead of the stem, just like a child which has lost the rest of the party.

Throughout May 19 I did nothing all day, except navigate, feed and put hot packs on my elbow. This had started oozing, and I applied scalding hot packs, bandaging the elbow with some lint. On May 20 I was still 1,120 miles from Plymouth. As I had only once on the voyage made this distance in a week, I guessed that I could not be in in a week's time.

But I was picking up speed, with a run of 179 miles that day and 171 miles on May 21. There was quite a big sea running then, and I was kept busy sewing the genoa staysail, a job I disliked very much. It made my back ache, which I supposed must be due to boredom, because I don't sew with my back! That night it turned rough, with a 35-knot wind with a bite in it. It was difficult to stand in the cabin, and quite dangerous in the cockpit and on the deck. I started on the long and tedious job of setting storm headsails.

Daybreak at 03.30 brought a wild-looking sea and sky. *Gipsy Moth* had done 5.85 knots all night under the two small headsails, reaching. I wanted to add a reefed mizzen, but the wire splice of the mizzen halliard drew at the masthead, and the halliard came down inside the mast; the sail came down outside it. I needed that sail badly, but could not climb to the masthead to replace the halliard in the rough sea running. I decided that I could make do with the mizzen *staysail* halliard, which is on the forward side of the mast, if only I could get it over the crosstree. I tried to pull it over the crosstree with the boathook while standing on the mizzen boom, but the 8-foot long boathook is a piece of heavy, waterlogged mahogany and I could not hold it against the wind. Next I tried shinning up the mast, but got cramp in the instep of the leg I damaged before starting the voyage, and had to give that up.

Then at last my wits came to the surface. I made up a heaving line of a spare signal halliard, with a weight at the end, to throw over the crosstree, but the wind kept on carrying the heaving line away and twisting cordage round everywhere. At last, after many failures, I got my heaving line over and used it to pull the halliard through after it. The mizzen was then set again, to my delight, though I must admit that I had a very sore arm afterward.

During the following night (May 22–23) I slept soundly for over four hours, after doctoring my arm at 03.30 with scalding hot packs. I used a cloth with a picture of the House of Commons on it, which seemed to keep in the heat better than the others. When I awoke I thought the speedometer must have gone wrong because the needle was up against the stop at 10 knots almost continuously. Reluctantly I got up, and found that, according to the log, *Gipsy Moth* had sailed 41.9 miles in the past 4 hours 52 minutes, an average speed of 8.6 knots. When I got on deck to reduce sail the lee deck was boiling along under water, with half the main boom in the sea at times. It was highly exhilarating, but I didn't want trouble at that stage of the voyage. I looked aloft, and all the gear seemed all right, but I hurriedly dropped the mainsail, followed by the mizzen, followed by the working jib, leaving only the storm staysail. With this small sail *Gipsy Moth* still did 5½ knots. There were some big rough seas running, and the wind was up to 40 knots.

Throughout that day *Gipsy Moth* slid along well—I felt that she wanted to be tugging at her mooring in Plymouth Sound! In the past 5 days she had knocked off 810 miles, an average speed of 162 miles per day. That evening I serviced and rigged the "Not-Under-Control" lights, and to my amazement they worked. These two red lights, one above the other in the stem, indicate that *Gipsy Moth* is not under control, and I light them if I am asleep while sailing in a shipping lane at night. A sailing vessel is supposed to have right of way over everything except fishing boats, and with luck those might move out of the way if they saw red "Not-Under-Control" lights coming. With those two reds, and the navigation lights, and the hurricane lamp, and an inspection lamp in the cockpit, *Gipsy Moth* must have looked rather like a Christmas tree! Having right of way is not of much value at times with big steamers. They are not expecting a small boat in deep waters, and some appear not to be keeping a watch.

My fuel oil gauge was down to 2 gallons, so I hooked out a Shell plastic container holding 2 gallons, and emptied that into the tank. I did not want to risk running the tank dry, in case I got an air lock in the fuel system, just when I most needed the motor for charging the batteries. I now had nearly 4 gallons in the tank and 2 gallons in reserve. It was a big relief to have that much, because I should need a lot of lights in the western approaches to the Channel.

A big event on May 25, at 02.30 in the morning after I had been up to tack ship and was rooting about in one of the lockers when I got below, was finding a fresh lemon. I had a delicious hot honey and lemon. That must have helped me to get to sleep, for I was asleep at 08.30 when two RAF Shackletons buzzed me. I was deep in dreamland, and cursed them, lying doggo. Then I thought this was mean, considering all the trouble they must have taken to find me, so I turned out. I hoisted the Royal Yacht Squadron burgee and the White Ensign for the first time since leaving Australia.

With sunshine and a sparkling blue sea, *Gipsy Moth* was running fast for the Channel, rolling and cavorting as if enjoying herself. What a difference the sun makes! I felt the thrill of fast passage-making in a small boat, with the hope of crossing my starting line in 50 or 60 hours' time. I hoped then to cross it at 11.00 on Sunday morning, May 28, which would make the passage 119 days, or 17 weeks. That was a lot slower than I had hoped for. I had had sailing troubles, but one must expect those. This wonderful sailing in the Atlantic seemed so enjoyable, and somehow not fearsome as in the Southern Ocean. One soon forgets that there is not only the boat to worry about on this sort of long adventure; there are attitudes of mind, which one wishes to suppress by trying not to think of them, an obvious one being fear. At times one is attacked by the futility of making an effort incessantly, day and night for four months. It is difficult to keep up an effort incessantly by day and night.

Usually after a solo voyage I dread fresh contact with the land, but this time I felt more relaxed, and resigned to whatever might turn up. Perhaps my previous voyages were not long enough. What effect had four months of solitude had on me? What habits had I developed? One unsociable habit, which had become strong by then, was that of dropping asleep at any time of day. I never had enough sleep. I was usually up half a dozen times in the night—last night, which I reckoned trouble free, and when I should have been sleeping deeper than usual because of taking some more pain killer for my arm, I was up four times. I would eat huge breakfasts, and often have to stop in the middle of breakfast and sleep before the end of it. I reflected: "If I am dining out in London in a few days' time, what will my hostess think if at the end of the soup I say I must sleep for ten minutes before the next course?"

Then there was talking to oneself, always thought to be a sign of going barmy—because mad people do it, I suppose.

• • •

"I have spells of this and have now almost given up trying to suppress it. It usually starts with a difficult problem or an awkward situation. And I think it helps; when working a sun observation, for instance, it cuts down the blunders to say the figures aloud. When caught out badly, with everything going wrong in a squall, or with the boat out of control, it is much easier if I say aloud to myself what is the next thing to be done. It stops the panic due to the brain juggling with several things all needing to be done at once."

• • •

I dug out my charts for the western approaches to the Channel. That night I moved on to the big-scaled chart, No. 1598, crossing the Continental Shelf into soundings, sailing in a few miles from a depth of over 2,000 fathoms to one of less than 100. I remembered that I usually seemed to run into a tunny fishing fleet thereabouts, so took care to service and rig my "Not-Under-Control" lights again.

There had been a big sea running for several days, spectacular enough for me to try for some photographs of it. (By the way, trying to photograph a big sea is the surest way of quietening it.) I waited for an hour, very uncomfortable, and nothing worthwhile came along. Then, as soon as I got below and my oilskins off, *wham, wham, wham,* three seas in succession bowled down *Gipsy Moth* and gave the deck a proper sluicing. They would have made a wonderful photograph! However, those seas seemed quite friendly, and I had had no fears of a 60-footer prowling in the background waiting to pounce.

Two Shackletons came and woke me again next morning about 06.00, when I lay doggo. I thought that they were practising their anti-submarine attacks, for which I cursed them. At noon, a BBC television launch turned up, and the wind died away. I tried to mend my starboard navigation light, but failed—of all the miserable designs that I have come across that thing took the prize! *Gipsy Moth* was nearly becalmed, with 210 miles to go. By 19.30 an Independent Television vessel, and another one, had joined the cavalcade. They seemed very much on their best manners; none spoke to me, and all left me alone. This was just as well, as there was plenty to do. An hour after midnight that night I logged: "Blast it, the wind has backed to the east, and, of course, is heading me."

About 21.25 on May 27 an extraordinary event occurred. The wind was steadily backing while I was speaking on the R/T to a naval escort vessel which had turned up. I noticed that the heading had reached NNE, so I said I must sign off so that I could go and trim the sails. As I moved out of the cabin the yacht went aback. Then, for perhaps 20 minutes, she must have looked as if she had been stung by a wasp. As fast as I wore her round, or tacked her, or brought her to the wind, or paid off downwind, the wind changed completely. The sea looked odd, with waves leaping straight up into the air, like tongues. I think I must have been at the centre of an eddy of air being sucked up into an enormous black cloud, just like the start of a waterspout or whirlwind. Several times *Gipsy Moth* was bowled well over; then complete calms intervened. Some birds, which I took to be swallows (they had swallow tails but their necks were a burnished bronzy colour) got very agitated, and several flew right into the cabin. One perched on an electrical lead above the chart table, and had a snooze with his head under one wing. He stayed there all night and left some time in the morning after dropping his visiting card on the chart. During the night I might have sailed bang into a fishing boat which was stationary directly ahead. I just chanced to go up into the cockpit for a look round, and there it was.

On Sunday morning, May 28, I logged:

• • •

"Thunder showers. Too much trimming for too little distance. *Wind wind wind, where art thou?* This business is quite a strain. I wish I could get into port. It looks as if there is no chance today."

• • •

At noon I counted thirteen ships around, including five naval vessels escorting me. I was in a quandary, with the light breeze blowing, interspersed with calms; I could improve the speed by poling out a big sail and it seemed that this would enable me to reach Plymouth before dark, but it would be at the price of considerable extra effort, and would result in my arriving even more tired than I was, with the likelihood of a terrific strain ahead of me. On the other hand, if I did not speed up, I was likely to be out at sea for another night, and that would be a great strain too, with all the ships and boats around me.

At 15.20 the huge aircraft carrier HMS *Eagle* passed close by, with her crew lining the deck and giving *Gipsy Moth* three cheers. I dipped my ensign in salute. This was a great honour, which I found most moving. It must surely be unique in the history of the British Navy for a warship with a complement as big as the population of a small town to salute so ceremoniously a ship with a crew of one!

Presently, when a minesweeper followed suit, I got a little nervous—I could picture myself dashing out to the stern and dipping the ensign, which is hoisted to the top of the mizzen mast, at frequent intervals for the rest of the day!

Late in the afternoon the breeze quickened a little, and at 16.40 by my ship's time I was 13 miles off Plymouth Breakwater, and knew that I *would* get in that night.

At 20.56 I passed the breakwater, and Colonel Jack Odling Smee, the Rear-Commodore of the Royal Western Yacht Club, fired a finishing gun from his yacht anchored off the breakwater, a sign for a beacon to be lit on Drake's Island.

Gipsy Moth had completed her passage home of 15,517 miles in 119 days, an average speed of 130 miles per day. The whole voyage of 29,630 miles had taken just 9 months and 1 day from Plymouth to Plymouth of which the sailing time was 226 days. Perhaps I might add that, with eight log books filled up, I had also written more than 200,000 words.

AN EPILOGUE

By J. R. L. ANDERSON

FOR TWO days—Saturday and Sunday, May 27–28, 1967—people in thousands congregated on the grass and ramparts of Plymouth Hoe to greet Sir Francis Chichester on his return from Australia. Millions more sat watching television screens, expectant, and at last wildly excited to see a slight figure step into a tender to go ashore as light was fading, leaving his *Gipsy Moth IV* to other hands after nursing her alone from Plymouth to Plymouth round the world. It was a monarch's welcome. Why?

Other men have sailed round the world in small boats, some much smaller than *Gipsy Moth IV*; other men have sailed alone; other men have gone on sailing far beyond Sir Francis's 65 years. But few men in any walk or run of life have touched the world's imagination as Chichester has. Lindbergh, perhaps; Hillary and Tensing—but such comparisons are meaningless. At these rare heights of human achievement each man stands alone, without peers. The salute for Chichester is for achievement, yes, for tenacity, courage, self-dedication, all that. But there is something more.

First, the achievement: what did Chichester achieve between August 27, 1966, when he sailed from Plymouth, and May 28, 1967, when he returned after circumnavigating the world, out by way of the Cape of Good Hope, back by way of the Horn? I asked him to set out what he himself felt that he had achieved, and here is his own assessment:

1. Fastest voyage round the world by any small vessel. (Approximately twice as fast.)
2. Longest passage that has been made by a small sailing vessel without a port of call (15,500 miles).
3. More than twice the distance of the previous longest passage by a singlehander (15,500 compared with 7,400).

4. Twice broke the record for a singlehander's week's run by more than 100 miles.
5. Established a record for singlehanded speed by sailing 1,400 miles from point to point in 8 days.
6. Twice exceeded the singlehanded speed record for a long passage, Nance's 122½ miles per day for 53 days (this however was an extraordinarily fast passage for such a small boat). *Gipsy Moth*'s speeds were 131¾ miles per day for 107 days, and 130¼ miles per day for 119 days.
7. Third true circumnavigation of the world rounding the Horn by a small vessel where the track passed over 2 points antipodean to each other.*

The interesting thing about this list is that it is wholly technical. The longest singlehanded passage, the fastest runs, the true antipodean circumnavigation—these things will stand in any book of records, but they are not, I think, what brought the crowds to Plymouth Hoe. The *essential* Chichester achievement is something more deeply personal—and personal not alone to him, but embedded in the hearts of every one of us. He has succeeded in making dreams come true, his own private dreams, and the dreams that most men have from time to time as they fare on that "long fool's errand to the grave." For 99.999 (recurring) per cent of mankind, dreams remain locked up in the secret compartments of the soul. Not for Chichester. For him, to dream is to determine, and to determine, to achieve. People will say, "Oh yes, but he has been lucky. He has made money, he has found rich backers. He does not have to travel daily on the 8.15." But surely this is part of the achievement! No one *has* to travel daily on the 8.15. We get caught in the ruts of life because we let ourselves get caught. It may be a good thing for the social organisation of the world that we do—a community of Chichesters would be impossible. But the individual who refuses to accept those ruts is good for all of us. And Chichester is that individual carried to the *nth* degree. Not once, but several times in his life, he has set himself some task of incredible skill and endurance in the air and at sea, and then not rested until he has brought it off—or, as with the flying accident that ended his first attempt to circumnavigate the world, been brought to a halt by events that not even he can control. Even that flying accident, final as it would have been for most men, for him brought only temporary fail-

---

* The first two were by Conor O'Brien (3 years) and Marcel Bardiaux (7 years).

ure. He took out that dream thirty-five years later, adapted it to sailing instead of flying, and made it come true. This is the Chichester we salute. He has lived not alone his own dreams, but ours, too.

CHICHESTER LANDED at Plymouth late on Sunday evening, May 28, expecting to sail on to London in a day or two. After his great reception by the Lord Mayor and people of Plymouth, two other historic events awaited him in London—the accolade of knighthood to be conferred on him by Her Majesty the Queen with the very sword given by Queen Elizabeth I to Sir Francis Drake after that first circumnavigation of the world by sail close on four centuries ago, and a luncheon at the Mansion House given in his honour by the Lord Mayor of London. Provisional dates for these occasions were arranged while Chichester was still at sea; they were to take place early in June.

It needs little reading between the lines of Chichester's factual narrative to understand something of the physical ordeal he sustained on his voyage. With a courage and self-discipline that defy description he drove himself to the limits of human endurance. And he had to pay. A week after landing at Plymouth he collapsed with a duodenal ulcer, and he spent the next month in the Royal Naval Hospital there. Being Chichester, and with his voyage to his starting point on the Thames in London still unfinished, he was on his feet again quickly. At the beginning of July he sailed *Gipsy Moth IV* to London, accompanied by Sheila and Giles Chichester, and his friend Commander Erroll Bruce, RN.

On July 7, 1967, the Queen received Chichester at Greenwich, and knighted him with Drake's sword in public, in the Grand Quadrangle of the Royal Naval College. Near by, in her permanent berth at Greenwich, *Cutty Sark*, among the most famous of the clippers whose way Chichester had followed round the world, was dressed overall for the occasion.

After the Queen had visited *Gipsy Moth IV* at Greenwich, Chichester sailed on to Tower Pier, where he was met by the Lord Mayor and Lady Mayoress of London, Sir Robert and Lady Bellinger. Then followed a drive through the City to the Mansion House, a triumphal procession rather, in which the people of London took Chichester to their heart. He and his *Gipsy Moth IV* had done their job—the smallest wool clipper ever to leave Australia, sailed by the smallest crew, had faithfully delivered her token cargo of miniature bales of wool across the world.

Chichester cannot write this epilogue, because he could not see himself as the crowd of cheering Londoners saw him. I did. Slight (until you caught a glimpse of the muscle in wrist and forearm), weatherbeaten, wearing thick glasses, Chichester gave himself no airs, and when he acknowledged the Lord Mayor's address of welcome, the crowd's cheers, he spoke more of Sheila his wife and Giles his son than of himself. He was the nation's hero, but to me he seemed to epitomise not scarlet and lace, but that incredible endurance that the people of England have shown when it was needed of them, the endurance of the men who sailed with Drake, Anson, Cook and Nelson, for England. And that, I think, is what everybody felt. And that is why we cheered.

A WIFE'S PART IN HIGH ADVENTURE
By SHEILA CHICHESTER

WHY WEREN'T you worried?"

Over and over again, all round the world, I was asked this question, by individuals, press and television. I find it hard to answer. To attempt an answer now I must go back a bit in time.

In 1960, during the first solo Transatlantic race, I prayed daily for the five yachtsmen who took part. I had some cards sent to me by an unknown man in Scotland, who said he always prayed for yachtsmen at sea. When I arrived in America on that occasion, I found other people interested in this form of prayer. Always I have believed firmly in the power of prayer; it is a great output of strength, and few people realise that they have got such strength. It takes time to learn how to control the power of prayer, but once you have faith the power is there. Think of turning on an electric light—you may not know where the power comes from, but the light comes. In America, I made friends with people who had similar beliefs, and later they were to help me in the other ventures which Francis undertook.

In 1962 our new yacht *Gipsy Moth III* was dedicated by "Tubby" Clayton in a short service of blessing. At the same time, I got together a few personal prayer cards for Francis. On the back was the beautiful drawing of Ulbrecht Dürer's praying hands, and on the other side I had the prayer of Sir Francis Drake and a special grace which "Tubby" Clayton suggested for him. I should think that not more than ten people used this card every day on that occasion.

In 1964 I had a similar card. This again had Sir Francis Drake's prayer, but with a different passage from St Augustine. I gave these cards to friends of mine who were experienced in the power of prayer, and when Francis started on that new venture, I felt quite confident that he would make it. I am not trying to say that prayer alone helps you, but the spiritual side in any venture is of immense importance. In a way, it is far more so than the material side. But one must also make one's plans, and be properly prepared as well.

In 1966 we had the new yacht *Gipsy Moth IV*, which I launched in March. After agonising financial worries, frustrations, and many things going wrong, we managed to get her ready for sea, and brought her up to Tower Pier, London, where the voyage was to start from. "Tubby" Clayton again came on board, and we had a short service of dedication. The boat was not really ready, and I knew this. I also knew that she was badly balanced, and very uncomfortable to sail in, but I hoped, and prayed with faith, that divine providence would watch over Francis and that he himself, being very clever at these things, would be able to adjust her as she went along. So when I said goodbye to him at Plymouth I felt quite calm, although physically exhausted.

From then on, wherever I went, I was asked the same questions: "Why? Where? When?"

"Why does he do it?" To which I replied, "He likes doing it, and it's the sort of life that suits him."

"Where?" Well, this question was to be answered by the positions which gradually became famous as people took to looking for them in the newspapers which helped to sponsor the voyage, and as schools obtained maps and charts.

"When?" was always "When will he get there?" This was marked by certain big landmarks, such as passing the Cape of Good Hope, Cape Leeuwin, Bass Strait, and later the Horn.

Months before Francis left I had booked myself a passage to Australia on *Oriana*, which sailed at the end of October, 1966, and we made plans to speak to each other on the radio telephone, as we knew that we should pass within five hundred miles of each other, if everything went according to plan, and I had no reason to think it wouldn't. Perhaps I should add that, contrary to many people's idea, I did *not* often speak to Francis on the radio telephone—I think about twice after he left England during the first two or three days, once from *Oriana*, and a few times coming into Sydney, out of Sydney, and coming into Plymouth. For the rest, with other people, I depended on the newspapers which gave reports from Francis twice a week. These reports were always read over to me before they appeared. I did not want to speak to Francis myself, because I knew the immense amount of work it took to keep up batteries and to prepare his dispatches, and I did not want to distract him, or to remind him of any responsibilities at home.

At this time I had a big circle of prayer cards—that is to say, I gave about twenty-five cards to friends who asked for them, some in America and later some in Australia, and this "circle" must have grown in a fantastic manner, because by the time Francis came home to Plymouth, I think undoubtedly that there were millions of people praying for him. Many were children, and many more were in religious groups and communities. The rectors of our own church, St. James's, Piccadilly, and of the sister church, St. Anne's, Soho, who use the little chapel of the House of St Barnabas, prayed regularly for him at services.

I left for Australia in the *Oriana* at the end of October, and many of the passengers were anxious, and used to say to me, "Have you heard from him?" "How is he?" "Aren't you worried?" My reply was always, "No, I'm not worried about his safety," because I wasn't. I was just quietly confident that he would do it.

There were about three times during the whole circumnavigation when I was worried about the success of the voyage. Once was in *Oriana*. We were trying to make radio contact with Francis, and we heard him saying, "I'm going to Fremantle, I'm going to Fremantle." I had heard by a dispatch from London from *The Guardian* that his self-steering gear had broken.

When I had this message, the chief radio officer said to me, "Oh dear, I hope he won't go to Fremantle, it will spoil everything!" I said, "Well, we won't say anything about this, and tomorrow the situation may have changed." As we ourselves were close to Fremantle, it did pose a problem for me because naturally I wondered, "Shall I get off there?" But I decided that it was no good worrying. I went to bed and slept soundly (as is my custom), and next morning I received a message pushed under my door, saying, "It's all right, he's going on to Sydney." The next night (November 19) we talked to each other, 1,000 miles apart.

The only other times I was worried were by the frightful hunting for him as he got near Sydney, and later, near to Plymouth. I have known other yachtsmen to be damaged by enthusiastic press people in boats, and I thought how dreadful it would be if so near his goal anything should happen to him.

While we were in Sydney, getting him ready for the second leg of the journey, there was immense pressure from sponsors, press, friends, and so on, trying to persuade him not to go on. I paid not the slightest attention to this; it would have seemed unthinkable to me for Francis not to have gone on, and it never occurred to me that he might give up. While we were in Sydney I had hundreds of letters from all sorts of people, who told me that they had prayed for Francis, and watched his passage with the deepest interest. No one ever approached me and said, "Don't let him go!" This I found interesting; people may have thought that my opinion didn't count, or they just didn't dare suggest such a thing to me because I was so confident.

The radio communication with *Gipsy Moth IV* was something really marvellous, and the men who worked it were wonderful people. They always gave me immense confidence. These radio men, I think, also understood the mysterious link of prayer mixed up with this communication.

When Francis left Sydney, he says that he wondered if he would ever see me again. Personally, I was quite confident that all would be well, although I was sorry to see that wretched hurricane advancing on him. When he radioed Sydney that he had capsized, he asked them not to tell me until the morning, as he did not require assistance. My hostess, Bar Eaton, called me at seven o'clock, and I remember feeling worried at her being disturbed so early. Then I was given the message. I surprised myself how calmly I took it down. I'm afraid the first thing I thought was—Oh dear, all that wonderful stowage and that beautiful key plan, what a muddle it must be in now! Hugh Eaton said to me, "Do you think you should tell Sir Alan MacNichol [he is the commander-in-chief of the Australian Navy], and they could, perhaps, send out a helicopter?" I thought quietly, and said, "No, I don't think Francis would like that." He would not want to be worried, and with that wind I realised that he could quickly run back to Sydney if he wanted to, though I didn't think he would. I did, however, ring up the head man of the Sydney radio, asked him to repeat the message to me, and I said to him, "How did he sound?" "Oh," he said, "he sounded his usual cheerful self and he was quite adamant that he did not want assistance. I'm sure he'll be all right." The radio men had faith in him, as I had.

That night Francis came through to me on the telephone and asked me to take the story of the capsize, which I did. We talked for nearly an hour; he was in good heart, and I did my best to cheer him.

I left Sydney a week after Francis did, and stayed in Hong Kong. While I was there the P and O liner *Himalaya* came in, and I called on the Captain, because she had been struck on the same night as Francis by a giant wave in the Tasman Sea. The *Himalaya* had picked up Francis's radio message, and the Captain called his radio officer, who played me a tape of Francis's voice. They had taped the message because they heard the word "capsize," and they thought they might have been wanted. However, when they heard the words "no assistance," they decided, after a conference, to go on their way. I was fascinated to hear Francis's voice so loud and clear talking to Sydney radio, asking for weather reports, etc.

In Hong Kong I was asked the same old questions. "Why wasn't I worried?" "What was my secret?" I always found it difficult to reply, but I was determined not to let people get depressed or worried over Francis, because this is a negative force, and I believe in positive thinking.

When I arrived in London by air from Hong Kong, I found some of the press waiting to meet me, and they asked when did I think that Francis would pass the Horn? I predicted roughly about March 20 and again it turned out in the end that I was right. This was not hit and miss—it was the result of careful thought and checking, and also of feeling very closely in touch with Francis. I can truly say that I sailed with him in spirit throughout the voyage.

When I got home a remarkable man called Brother Mandus got in touch with me, and came to see me. He has an enormous global prayer group for sick people and others in a World Healing Crusade, and with his people he had been praying daily for Francis. We both agreed that prayer is a thing which multiplies and multiplies in the most extraordinary fashion. I gave him a recording to help his sick people all over the world.

It may sound inhuman, but I never really had a sleepless night. I think this is because I am such a believer in the great spiritual forces. I should like to quote here from a letter which Claude Muncaster, the artist, sent to me. After speaking of the significance of the venture for this nation, and for young people, he added: "Besides this, there is an even greater significance. This is a significant illustration of the power of thought coming from thousands and thousands of people, not just well wishing. That happens anyway. This is another, greater, power—the power of prayer, if you like, although people don't know about it as such, has gone out as a sort of protection. He has been surrounded by a protective envelope of power."

This puts my feeling into words far better than I can express them.

My faith was also backed by knowing what ocean sailing is like. Of course, I had never been in the Roaring Forties, but I had twice crossed the Atlantic with Francis. I knew his abilities, knew that we had prepared as well as we possibly could, and there was no point in worrying. I felt all the time almost as if something outside myself was controlling me. I was very intrigued by one particularly happy incident. Francis completed his circumnavigation of the world on April 11—my birthday. To me, this was more than a coincidence.

MY THANKS TO MY SUPPORTERS

THIS SOLO circumnavigation was, apart from the actual sailing, a surprisingly intensive joint effort put up by many friends and supporters. I find it difficult to thank everyone who helped me, but I would like to name a few who, as the venture progressed, so willingly gave their assistance.

In England before the start: Paul Hodder-Williams and George Greenfield who both backed the idea from the moment it was mooted; Harold Evans of *The Sunday Times* and Alastair Hetherington of *The Guardian* who believed the project sound enough to buy the radio despatches. I have written of several supporters and helpers in the book: Colonel Whitbread, Lord Dulverton, architects Warwick Hood and Alan Payne, their Excellencies the Governor-General and Lady Casey, Captain Max Hinchliffe, RAN, Jim Mason, George Gardiner and John Pleasants; the four apprentices of Kelvin and Hughes; John Fairhall, Murray Sayle and Nigel Forbes.

Other helpers who were not written about in the book include: Monica Cooper and the staff of Francis Chichester Ltd, George West, Supervisor of the GPO Marine Radio Section at Brent, Ernest Rayment of Kelvin and Hughes who helped me collect my library of charts.

In Sydney many people made us feel at home as well as helping us in every possible way: the Lord Chief Justice and Lady Barwick; His Excellency the British High Commissioner and Lady Johnston; Hugh and Bar Eaton; Commander Wood, RN, of Canberra; the Flag Officer and staff of the RSYS; the Commodore and Secretary of the CCA; President Nancy Leebold and the officers of the Australian Institute of Navigation; William Vines, Managing Director of the IWS; Jim Sare and Darli McCourt of Hodder and Stoughton, Sydney, who dealt with thousands of letters, mostly from young people; Terry O'Keefe and Pat McCarthy of IWS; Colin, Lorna and Robert Anderson; Peter Green; Captain James Dunkley of *Oriana* who looked after Sheila so well, and took home my charts used on the passage Plymouth to Sydney.

On return to England: the Commander-in-Chief, Plymouth, and Lady Talbot; the Lord Mayor, Lady Mayoress and the Corporation of

Plymouth; Mr Lloyd-Jones, the Town Clerk and Mr Bottom, the Public Relations Officer; the Vice-Commodore, flag officers, and Captain and Mrs Terence Shaw of the Royal Western YC of England; Surgeon Rear-Admiral Stanley Miles and the staff of the RN Hospital, Plymouth; Dr Gordon Latto; Frank Carr, who collated for me all the historical details of Sir Francis Drake's knighting at Greenhithe by Elizabeth I; Erroll Bruce, our delightful sailing and naval etiquette master on the sail up from Plymouth to London; Lord Simon, Chairman, Commander Gilbert Parmiter, harbour master, and the staff of the Port of London Authority; Chief Superintendent D. Davies of the Thames Division Metropolitan Police and his staff; Captain and Mrs Arples and the staff of the Training ship *Worcester*; Sir Richard Colville, press officer to HM The Queen.

At Greenwich: Admiral-President Sir Horace Lyddon and Captain M. A. J. Hennell of the Royal Naval College, Greenwich; the Lord Mayor of London and Lady Bellinger; the Corporation of the City of London; the Remembrancer Sir Paul Davie and Colonel Britton.

I would like to thank, too, Raymond Seymour, our guiding star in public relations, and John Fox of Whitbreads whose help was invaluable.

All these people did far more for me and the voyage than they need have done.

Finally, after the oceanic hurly-burly was done, John and Helen Anderson, who achieved the editing of about 400,000 words that I have written about this voyage, to bring it down to book size ready for printing in September 1967. If you like the book praise them; if you don't, blame me.

F. C.

September, 1967

Acknowledgement is due to *The Times* for permission to reproduce the extract by Murray Sayle which appeared in *The Times* on March 21, 1967; to *The Sun* for permission to quote the interview between John Seddon and Alan Villiers (January 12, 1967); to *The Guardian* for permission to quote from Alan Villiers' letter, published January 11, 1967; and to Rupert Hart-Davis, Ltd, for permission to quote from *A Gypsy of the Horn* by Rex Clements.

APPENDIX I

LOG BOOKS

THE NEXT six pages are reproductions from log books. The first page is from my log of October 14, 1966 and shows what a labour it is to take sun sights by the long old method. Only two sights are worked out on this page. Opposite is a page from my log of May 21, 1967 showing six sun sights produced by the short method. The next two pages cover ten hours of my log for Saturday, May 20. I filled six log books like this on the voyage besides radio log books. For comparison, the last two pages are from the log of the *Cutty Sark* on its record-breaking round trip in 1885. The whole log is contained in about forty pages like this. I had them with me on my voyage in facsimile form, kindly provided by the *Cutty Sark* Society by whose permission these two pages are reproduced here.

14 Oct Sight Reduction.   (8 mins late)

No 1. G.M.T 09 21 25   Hs 46 14½   Rough az 50°T.
GHA ☉ 0800 m   303°27.8' 1E   –4   Lat 37 08½ S
       01 21 25   2 21.3 Cr +12½   Long 00 22½ E
       ——————   ———————   ——   Dec 08 02 S
   Long E +   3 23 49 Ho 46 23
       ————   22.5½ ——————
     LHA   324.11½,
              35 48½   A z
Log hav 35 48½ 8.97548   L.Sin LHA 3548½ 9.76716
Log Cos 37 08½ 9.90154   L.Cos dec   9.99572
Log cos 08 02   9.99572   L.cosec z.d. 4334 10.16.166
                ————————   ——————————
                8.87274   9.92454
hav d lat 29 06½   .07459
                   .06315   Az 57°
        4334 = z.d. = .13774
I tc = 46 26
– Ho 46 23 = 3' away

No 2. G.m.T 11 56 48   Hs 60 36   Lat as above.
GHA ☉ 10 00 00   333°28.1'.4 – IE   Long as above.
       01 56 48   29 12.0 13+Cr²   Dec 08 05 S.
   Long E +   00 22.5 Ho 60 45
                ——————————
                36,302.6
                           A z
Log hav 03°02.6' 6.84663   L.Sin 03°02.6' 8.72360
Log Cos 37 08½ 9.90154   L.Cos dec   9.99566
Log cos 08 05   9.995**   L.cosec z.d. 29°11½ 10.31193
               ————————   ——————————
               6.74383   360° 9.03119
hav d lat 29 03½   .00056   Az 6°.
       29°11½'> z.d. = .06350   = 354
· Hc = 60 48½
 – Ho 60 45 = away 3½'

May 21 the S/k Sun Obs — Page 124.

Wth 12 11 22   43 N 28 W   Ho 60 50 124
Cor   02 30½ +   Cor   13 +
Z   12 13 52   E   1 +
GHA 12 00 00   ooo 53.1 61 02 +50 +7 36   Ho 61 04
         13 52   3 28   51
       Long W 364 21 Hc 61 07   Dec 20 06 N
              25 21 Ho 61 04 = away 3'
              339

No 2 Page 126   Ho   66 38
 W = 13 36 14   14 +
Cor   02 32   Ho 66 52
     13 38 46   Z3   23 08
GHA 12 00 00   ooo 53.1 66 59 +60 182 R
     01 38 46   24 41.5   7
       Long W. 25 35 + Hc 67 06   Dec 20 07 N
       Try it 25 35 Ho 66 52 = away 14   Lat 43 15
              24 35
              01.0

May 22. Pge 128 ho 1 Monday   45 N 22 W   Ho 59 58
wth 11 58 09   13 +
Cor   02 49 +   1 +
GHA 12 00 58   Az.   Ho 60 12
     12 00 00   ooo 52.2 59 34 51 138
        58   14.5   15 +
    Long W —   36 1 02 Hc 59 49
              22 07 Ho 60 12 = Towards 23'   Dec 20 18 N
              339

No 2 W = 13 36 56   Ho 65 24
Cor   02 50 +   14 +
     13 39 46   Ho 65 38
GHA 12 00 00   ooo 52.2 64 53 59 - 360
     01 39 46   24 56.5   19 +   173
       Long W. 25 49 Hc 65 12   A3 187
              22 49 Ho 65 38 = Towards 26' Dec 20 19 N
              31

24 May ho 1. P.134   47 N 16 W.   Ho 32 10 +
 W = 08 44 20   Cor   12 +
Cor   20 +   Az.   1 +
mT 08 44 40   95   Ho 32 23
HA 08 00 00   30 0 50 1 Hc 32 05. 41
        44 40   11 10   22 +
    Long w — 31 2 00 Ho 32 23 = away 9   Dec 20 40 N
              16 00
              296

No 2 P.136 . W = 12 06 24.   Ho 61 23
mT 12 06 46   Az   Ho 14 +
HA 12 00 00   ooo 49.9 60 41 57 152   Ho 61 37
        06 46   1 41.5   39 +
    Long w   362 31 Hc 61 20½   Dec 20 41½ N
             16 31 Ho 61 37 = Towards 16½
             346

Sat 20 May.

77½/38.3
+ 0347. 80 4·4·6 7·8k(l) 160 ^{S} 16 ^{K}/p
15·25K.

75/X/7.8 Dropped mainsail.
Baro 1030 down 3 mi night.
+ 0555 70 462·4 8·1 k(l) 130 ^{S}·20 ^{K}

80/18.9
+ 0815 90 481·3 8·1 k(l) 140 ^{S}·20 ^{K}

72½/6.6
+ 0904½ Sun sight. 487·9 Transfer 23K at 089 - 18½N = 70½
Prr 115

4 0913 95 489·0 8·0 k(l)

1115 Zugld 0) 13 ð 1 chron hour moon
ch ⊙ of Z 0 5 22½ 27½° = 1150
w ⊙ of Z c2 09½ 28·34 - 54 = 2745=

90/15.6
+ 1104 Sun sight. 503·5 Transfer 8¾ 7·4K at 87½ 18½ =
S.T. Prr 115 69T

1108 85 504·0 8·1k(l)

1142 Baro 10·27 down 3 mi. 8 hr

87¼/7.9 1154½ Sun sight. Prr 115
γ7 = 76·8K/75°c 18·5w = 566 65·7K at 83°c 64½/45 9 at 79 c 60½

20May NOON 90 510·9
Abs ½ ht 3 pt l sun fix Best chunk 60 + 18½ N = 78½
42·29½N Dist to 45 = 380. M.
28·40W 48 to fix 696
Run 179. Lis TO Plym .44 11.20
130 11

95/11.4 1326½ 100 522·3
115
117½/3.5 award from 275°c
+ 1353½ 120 525·8
: (GOING) Snug to drift hole and gybe.

Sat 20 May   123

3.45 That nasty feeling of the boat only just under control with the R aerial up to 25 knots. The Hammer was at the end of the scale 10 k for quite long periods making the time went 35 h. Anyway ? reluctantly re bandaged my arm to keep the open place away from clothes and things. First I slacked off and opened off the main and mizzen booms. I decided that dropping the main was the best thing to do because if the boom did come across it could soon have: also it has a strong moment to turn the boat to wind. I hesitated quite a time because it is not often one gets the chance of a 10 knot sail but the thought of sorting out a schemozzle with my arm as it is decided me. We are still going up to 10 k without the main but not for such long periods. The next thing to come in will be that spoiled sail jib which I am not quite happy about.

4.13 Daybreak. Turned off P+S running lights and all cockpit light. Left masthead on

4.25 Drowned hurricane lamp too.

5.30 Dropped the spoiled sail jib also brought in the pole. Gybed. Hoisted main. Dropped genny staysail for repairs to a seam which has given way. The wind has veered and is

Ship "Cutty Sark" from Sydney
Nov. 12th 1885. AM Strong N'atterly wind & rain and
nasty confused sea. 4 AM. wind shifted to the N. W.
hard gale and nasty sea. Noon do w'r & sea
4 PM. do wind & sea Midnight do wind W. N. W.
Lat 48.20 S Long 39.10 W Course N 65 E. Dist 219 miles

13th AM. Strong W'. N. W'. wind & high sea. ship
constantly filling the decks fore & aft. 4 AM. Do N S
Noon strong breeze & clear Sky. 4 PM. Do W'm.
8 PM. decreasing breeze wind hauling to the N W. & cloudy
Midnight
Lat 45.06 S Long 34.15 W C½ N 50 E Dist 502 miles

14th AM. Moderate S. W. breeze. and fine clear weather
Noon Light S. S. W breeze and very fine clear weather
4 PM. do 8 PM. do Midnight
Lat 41.43 S Long 32.05 W C½ N 25 E. Dist 224 miles

15th AM. Light southerly breeze & fine clear weather
5 AM gentle breeze & clear W'm. Noon moderate East
breeze and fine clear W'm. 8 PM. moderate breeze & fine
clear W'm. Midnight fresh breeze & cloudy W'm.
Lat 39.29 S Long 31.53 W C N 4 E. Dist 154 miles

N. S. W.   Towards London.

No. 16th A.M. Strong Easterly wind & rain, 8 A.M. strong winds & squally, reeft the Mainsail. 9 A.M. Decreasing breeze noon almost calm, 4 P.M. Northly breeze, Midnight light north breeze and fine clear wr.
Lat 35.13 S Long 31.52 W in North 256 miles

17th A.M. Light Northerly breeze and fine clear wr. 8 A.M. Light passing showers of rain, noon moderate breeze & clear, 4 P.M. Fresh N N W breeze & cloudy wr. 8 P.M. N.W. breeze Midnight do wr.
Lat 34.45 S Long 31.28 W Course N 48 E Dist 28 miles

18th A.M. Moderate breeze and fine clear weather, 4 P.M. do wr. wind N.W. noon moderate breeze & fine clear wr. 8 P.M. do 8 P.M. Decreasing N.N.W. breeze & fine wr. Midnight.
Lat 31.45 S Long 29.24 W in N 50 W Dist 208 miles

19th A.M. Light Southerly breeze and fine wr. noon moderate S.E. breeze, 8 P.M. moderate Easterly breeze and fine clear weather, Midnight do wr.
Lat 29.81 S Long 29.37 W C. N 5 W Dist 188 miles

Appendix II

STORES AND STOWAGE

A Note on Stores by Sheila Chichester

Doing the stores has always been my job, and I find it an exacting one. In the summer of 1965 we all three lived on board *Gipsy Moth III*, and for a month Francis recorded *everything* that we ate. From this he was able to work out the quantities of stores for one person for 120 days, and it was on this that I based my planning.

Having worked out the quantities I needed, I then had a conference with the manager of the London Health Food Store because a lot of the things Francis took were vegetarian, and this is the best place to get them. We also ordered some free range eggs. I then had another comprehensive list for a big store, and asked them to pack everything in small amounts for easy stowing, and to number every package.

These things were all delivered to 9 St James's Place, and we put aside a room and packed solidly. At this point I handed over to the office staff. The only things that went wrong in this operation were the eggs, which unfortunately went bad, so that Francis had to throw away fourteen dozen. On the advice of a friend he wanted them coated with beeswax. Previously, we had always treated eggs with Oteg, but, of course, eggs did not have to last so long on a Transatlantic voyage of thirty days or so. The weather was hot when the time came for egg painting, and nobody seemed very keen to do them. However, they were done, but obviously not properly. Also I think the eggs came too soon—it would have been better if we could have put them on at Plymouth, but it is easy to be wise after the event.

We obtained a lot of Tupperware boxes, into which products were stored, numbered and listed. We had two lists, one alphabetical, and one of the Tuppers, showing what each contained, and also a key plan, for finding them after they had been stowed on the yacht.

It was a terribly hot time at Tower Pier, and unhappily the eggs were put too close to the engine. As we were going down the Thames I suddenly discovered this, and so I think they were stale, not properly coated, and possibly half-cooked before he ever left! This was a bad business, because those eggs represented protein, and as Francis doesn't have meat I was greatly worried when I heard they had all gone bad. I much regretted that I had not coated them myself, but I had so many other things to do.

During the summer before Francis sailed he practised baking his own bread, and had a small oven fitted on top of the Primus in the galley. This wholemeal bread was a great mainstay for him. He also took mustard and cress seeds to plant on flannel for vitamin C.

At his own request, Francis did not take much tinned fish on the passage to Australia, and I think he did not have enough. I saw that he had 100 tins on the return passage. He took quantities of natural foods, such as honey, raisins, nuts and Barmene which is a valuable source of vitamin B and yeast, and was a very good product to take. He also took a good supply of garlic.

Because of his very strenuous passage and his lack of time for cooking, substantial quantities of the food loaded in England were still uneaten when he arrived in Sydney. Everything was taken out and examined. The new stores taken on in Australia were all obtained by the firm of David Jones. I prepared my list, giving the exact quantities required, and I then had a meeting with the directors of the firm. After that I had no further worry. The things were marvellously packed, and were all delivered at the Royal Sydney Yacht Squadron, where the secretary kindly gave us a whole storeroom to ourselves, quite near the yacht. I have never been able to do stores so comfortably.

Even so it was a big chore, and I spent many hot days packing and checking. Giles helped me, but he had to go back to England before the work was done. However a very nice young man called Robert Anderson, and his mother, came in, and they were splendid.

On Sunday, a week before Francis left, we were packing in the yacht at a temperature of 100°, which was really trying. I went back to my hotel to have a rest, and I think it was because of exhaustion that I fell in my bedroom and tore three ligaments in my ankle. I had to keep my foot up for three days, and was heavily strapped and hobbled about for the rest of the time in Australia.

I think Francis's food was better on the return journey partly because of the fresh fruit which was beautifully packed for him, and also because he had plenty of potatoes. On the outward passage he did not have enough potatoes. The trouble then was that the shops in England had only new potatoes and it was feared that these would not keep. Undoubtedly he suffered from lack both of potatoes and eggs, though fortunately he had some dried eggs.

THESE LISTS of food and spare stores and stowage plans are not as complete as I would have liked, owing the inevitable shortage of time.

Stores Outward 1966

Alphabetical List and Stowage

Acid bulb tester	Middle settee-end port
Along the Clipper Way	Aft settee port locker
Australian flag	Forward port settee
Avon Redcrest 8 ft rubber dinghy	Afterpeak
Avon Redshanks 12 ft rubber dinghy, including sailing kit, mast, dagger board, rudder and sail	Dinghy well
Avon repair kit (leaks)	Main cabin port bunk
Barometer, Met	Middle port settee
Blocks—large quick release snap shackle (2)	Starboard forward drop
large ordinary (1)	Starboard forward drop
medium ordinary (1) (with shackle)	Starboard forward drop
small (3) (2 twisted) shackles	Starboard forward drop
Bolt cutters	Middle port drop locker
Bolts, tin of spare	Middle port drop locker
Boots	Locker under heads basin
Bosun's chair	Forepeak
Bosun's chair tackle	Forepeak
Bow fender	Afterpeak
Brace and bit	Middle port drop locker
Broom	Afterpeak
Buckets (3)	Afterpeak
Bulbs, e.l.	Middle settee-end port
Burgees (RYS)(2)	Forward port settee
Burgee(RCC)	Forward port settee
Brookes and Gatehouse spares	Port main shelf
	Middle port settee locker
	Forward starboard settee locker
Candles	After lower heads locker
	Middle settee-end port

CO_2 canisters (2)	Aft starboard drop locker
Cleats (flying) 6	Forward port drop locker
Collision mat	Forecabin port sailcot
Cordage including	
1 red light nylon line	
2 long light nylon lines	
String bag	Aft port drop locker
Deck inspection lights and cable (2)	Bottom forward chart locker
Dinghy oars	Forepeak
Dinghy air pump	Afterpeak
Distilled water	Starboard forward drop locker
Distilled water (1-gallon)	Starboard aft drop locker
Documents, plans and	
instructions	Top settee-end port
Downhaul tackle	Starboard forward drop
Drogues (3)	Forecabin port sailcot
Drogue warp 1,000 ft (green)	Forecabin port sailcot
EL bulbs	Port settee-end middle
Engine oil (Shell Rotella)	Dinghy well
Fender (bow)	Afterpeak
First Aid Manual (RCC)	Port aft settee locker
Flying cleat tackle	Starboard forward drop
Flying cleats	Port forward drop
Generating plant (petrol)	Forepeak
Grapnel (small)	Port middle drop
Grease (silicone)	Aft locker under chart table
Grease pump	Forward locker under chart table
Grease stern gland	Cockpit locker
Hacksaw	Port middle drop
Hammer	Port middle drop
Hengist and Horsa masthead	(Brooks and Gatehouse spares)
gear	Starboard forward settee
Hooks and coat hooks	Port aft settee
	Port main cabin shelf
Instructions, documents and plans	Port settee-end top
Jib bonnet	Forepeak
Kettle (spare)	Afterpeak
Lanyards and cords (thin)	Starboard middle drop
Log, rotating (spare)	Starboard middle drop
Log books	Port middle settee

Log leads and rotator	Port settee-end middle
Mallet, wooden	Port middle drop
Magazines	Port forward settee
Marconi spare parts	Afterpeak
Marconi transmission connection leads (various) including spare cable	Port forward drop
Meths—1-gal tin	Starboard middle drop
1-gal tin	Starboard forward drop
Empty 1-gal plastic container	Starboard forward settee
Mustard and cress seeds	Port aft settee
Nails	Chart locker bottom forward
Notices to mariners	Port middle settee
NUC pole	Forepeak
Nuts and bolts	Port middle drop
O_2 bracket	Port aft settee
Off-course alarm gear	Starboard aft drop
Oil—1 pint	Port forward drop
Padlocks and chain	Oddment bag port settee locker aft
Paraffin can 2-gal	Afterpeak
Perkins spare parts	Afterpeak and port middle drop
Perkins generator	Afterpeak
Petrol cans (2)—2-gallon	Heads locker
Pilots (12) vols. of sailing instructions	Port aft settee
Plastic bags	Forepeak
Rough weather table guards	Forepeak
Rubber dinghy air pump	Afterpeak
Rubber sheet	Port forward drop
Rucksack	Port forward settee
Reeds Nautical Almanac	Chart table shelf
Saw	Port middle drop
Saw (hack)	Port middle drop
Sextant	Port middle settee
Sextant, Flying Boat	Starboard middle drop
Sailbag (mainsail)	Forepeak
Sail repair kit	Forepeak
SS repair items in sail repair kit bag	
Self-steering oar, spare	Forepeak
Self-steering vane, canvas extension	Forepeak
Self-steering wind vane, spare	Forepeak

Screws and nuts (jar)	Port middle drop
Screw eyes	Port aft settee
Screws	Chart locker bottom forward
Screw oddments in bag	Port aft settee
Shackles	Port forward drop
	Chart locker bottom forward
Sheets (7)	Dinghy well
Shell Rotella engine oil	Dinghy well
Shock cord	Port aft settee locker
(bag of)	Starboard forward drop
Shoes	Locker under heads sink
Signal flags	Port forward settee
Steps	Afterpeak
Thermometer (sea)	Chart locker bottom forward
Tide tables (Australia)	Port aft settee locker
Torch spare part	Port settee-end middle locker
Trysail tackles in use	Dinghy well
Tubing (assorted)	Starboard forward drop
Uher tapes	Port middle settee
Underwater goggles	Port aft settee
Underwater wet suit	Forecabin starboard berth
Union Jack	Forward port settee
U2 battery spares	Port settee-end middle locker
Warps	Afterpeak
	Forepeak
Water can (plastic 5-gallon)	Afterpeak
(2-gallon)	Afterpeak
(1-gallon)	Dinghy well
Winch spare handles	
(4 mast)	Starboard forward drop
(1 main)	Starboard forward drop
(2 jib sheet)	Starboard forward drop
Wool (greased), for hull leaks	Starboard aft drop

Food and General Stowage

1 NUC pole
1 petrol generating plant
1 Bosun's chair
1 Bosun's chair tackle
Reel spare warp
1 sail repair kit
1 spare oar steering vane
Mainsail sailbag
1 canvas extension self-steering

for wind vane
Perspex rough weather table
fiddle (main table)
1 spare self-steering wind vane
1 pr dinghy oars
assorted plastic bags
1 jib bonnet
various unwanted sailbags

FORECABIN—STARBOARD

BUNK

1. Tupper	12 packets prunes
	2 packets currants (lb each)
2. Tupper	7 packets raisins
	3 packets sultanas (1 lb each)
	8 packets dried bananas (12-oz packets)
3. Tupper	9 packets dates (1 lb each)
	4 packets dried bananas (12-oz packets)
	2 packets hazel nuts (1 lb total)
	4 packets brazil nuts (2 lb total)
4. Tupper	2 packets walnuts (1 lb total)
	2 packets almonds (1 lb total)
	2 Christmas puddings (1 lb each Granose)
	1 Dundee cake
	10 packets brown sugar (1 lb each—soft)
5. Tupper	5 packets Italian brown rice (1 lb each)
	8 packets lentils
6. Tupper	5 packets wholewheat flour (100% self-raising) 3 lb each
	15 packets yeast
7. Tupper	3 packets wholewheat flour (100% self-raising) 3 lb each
	2 packets wholemeal flour (85% self-raising) 3 lb each
	15 packets yeast

8.	Tupper	2 packets wholemeal flour (85% self-raising) 3 lb each
		4 packets mashed potato
		5 packets Italian brown rice (1 lb each)
9.	Tupper	6 mushroom sauce mix
		6 onion sauce mix
		6 tomato sauce mix
		30 Surprise peas
10.	Tupper	15 vegetable curry with rice
		2 prawn curry with rice
		5 drums parmesan
11.	Tupper	13 prawn curry with rice
		11 drums parmesan
		1 packet mashed potato
		1 packet vegisalt
12.	Tupper	14 packets ginger nuts
13.	Tupper	4 packets cream crackers
		4 plain chocolate digestive biscuits
		8 bars wholenut chocolate (½-lb bar)
		1 drum white pepper (4 oz)
		1 drum bicarbonate soda
14.	Tupper	9 packets mashed potato
		5 packets raisins
		2 plain chocolate digestive biscuits
20.	Box	10 tins pears
		10 tins grapefruit
		10 tins pineapple
		15 tins sardines
		6 tins treacle pudding
		14 tins salmon
		1 jar blackcurrant jam
		2 tins golden syrup (1 lb each)
		3 Barmene (1 lb jars)
		1 tin olive oil (20 oz)
		2 tins maize oil (20 oz each)
		2 jars herbs (mixed)
		2 tins pioneer coffee (medium)
		3 tins drinking chocolate (1 lb each)
		4 packets raisins
		12 Jiffy lemons
21.	Box	5 jars coffee
		6 mango chutney
		1 blackcurrant jam
22.	Box	6 marmalade (3 West Indian, 3 Lime)
		3 redcurrant jelly
		3 black cherry jam
24.	Tupper	5 packets cube sugar
		6 bars mint cake
		16 bars raw sugar chocolate
		5 packets raisins

25. Tupper   6 packets of tea bags (36 bags each)
             1 packet ginger nut biscuits
    Poly. bag 5 long spaghetti

CUPBOARD (UPPER)

  3 tins drinking chocolate   24 tins minestrone soup
 16 tins green pea soup   6 tins peeled tomatoes
 20 tins tomato soup   1 doz packets minestrone

CUPBOARD (LOWER)

 24 tins butter   2 tins egg powder (4-lb tins)

CUPBOARD (MIDDLE)

 10 tins dried milk (3½-pt tins) 12 jars honey (6 thin, 6 thick)
 15 jars dried onions   1 box glucose tablets

AFT DROP LOCKER

 20 lb fresh onions   10 small loaves bread
  8 small loaves bread

HEADS—PORT

CUPBOARD

  8 oz cotton wool   2 Delsey
  1 bottle almond oil   1 household roll
  3 shaving sticks   6 Delsey
  6 corn plasters   5 Bronco
  3 tins Nivea   2 household rolls
  3 toothpaste   Dentisory
  6 pairs rubber gloves   Kleenex
  8 liquid detergent   Household rolls
  8 toilet soap   Kleenex
  1 Fairy soap

STARBOARD

LOCKER NO. 1 (TOP)

  7 towels   4 sheets
  5 face cloths   4 pillow cases
  5 tea towels

LOCKER NO. 2 (MIDDLE)

 13 dish cloths   2 dusters
  5 household rolls   Delsey for garden

LOCKER NO. 3 (BOTTOM)

 30 lb potatoes

LOWER LOCKER AFTER (UNDER SINK)

Drugs   Candles

Main Cabin—Port

BUNK

26. Tupper	2	packets tagliatelli
	3	packets capellini
	3	little cheeses
27. Tupper	4	lb wheat
	2	packets Fru-grains
	2	packets raisins
	2	little cheeses
28. Tupper		
Drum		milled nuts (mixed—no walnuts—7½ lb)
Tin	12	packets Golden Harvest digestive
	2	packets Golden Harvest ginger nuts
Tin	13	packets Golden Harvest ginger nuts
	2	packets Golden Harvest digestive
Tin	6	chocolate wheat digestive biscuits
	4	cream crackers
30. Box	6	lime juice
31. Box	24	tins saucelatas
32. Box	6	tomato ketchup
	5	mayonnaise
Box	24	tins Ryvita
Box	168	eggs
35. Tupper	6	tagliatelli
36. Tupper	6	capellini
37. Tupper		
Small	3	lb Gruyère and garlic

LOWER SETTEE-END LOCKER

2 whisky   2 wine
2 household matches   1 Bacardi

AFT SETTEE LOCKER

Underwater goggles   Mustard and cress seeds
RCC Journal (First Aid)   Bracket for O_2
Along the Clipper Way   Hooks, coat hooks, screw eyes,
12 pilots   shock chord: in box
Tide tables, Australia   *The Lonely Sea and the Sky*
Heron earphones   Bag of screw oddments

MIDDLE SETTEE LOCKER

Sextant   Uher tapes
Met barometer   Log books
Notice to mariners

FORWARD SETTEE LOCKER

Australian jack
2 spare RYS burgees
RCC burgee
Rubber sheet

2 spare belts (heel)
Magazines
Bag of signal flags

SIDEBOARD TOP DRAWER

Documents, plans and instructions

SIDEBOARD MIDDLE DRAWER

Brookes and Gatehouse spares
Bulbs, e.l. spares, e.l. bayonet
    plug
Candles, torch spare part

Log leads and rotator
U2 spares
Acid bulb tester

FORWARD DROP LOCKER

Spare shackles
6 running cleats
6 flying cleats
1 rucksack

1 pt oil
Various Marconi Kestrel
transmission connection leads
    including spare cable

MIDDLE DROP LOCKER

(Tools)
Perkins tool kit
Bolt cutters
Wooden mallet
Hammer
Brace and bit

Saw
Hack saw
Small grapnel
Jar screws and nuts
Tin bolts

AFT DROP LOCKER

Cordage
1 reel light nylon line

2 long light nylon lines
String bag

STARBOARD

FORWARD SETTEE LOCKER

31 grapefruit
24 lemons
All fruit

20 oranges ⎫
30 apples ⎬ in nylon nets
           ⎭

LOWER LOCKER

1 whisky
6 brandy

2½-bottles lime
3 wine

FORWARD DROP LOCKER

Distilled water
Flying cleat tackle

1 medium ordinary block with
    shackle

FORWARD DROP LOCKER (CONT'D)

1 tin meths, 1 gallon
4 mast winch handles
1 main winch handle
2 jib sheet winch handles
2 large quick release snap
  shackle blocks
1 large ordinary block

3 small blocks with shackle
  (2 twisted)
1 downhaul tackle
2 shockcord tackles
1 bag shockcord
Assorted tubing

MIDDLE DROP LOCKER

Assorted thin lanyards and cords
Sextant

Log (Walkers)
1 gallon meths

AFT DROP LOCKER

CO_2 canisters, Avon Redshank
1 gallon distilled water

1 packet greased wool
1 off-course alarm gear

FORWARD SETTEE LOCKER

Hengist and Horsa masthead
  gear

1 empty 1-gallon meths container
  (plastic)
Fruit

GALLEY SECTION

CUPBOARD OVER PRIMUS

6 household boxes matches

LEDGE UNDER GARDEN

Tupper: 5 lb carrots
       12 bulbs garlic

Moggie's cake

FORWARD LOCKER UNDER CHART TABLE

2 inspection deck lights and cable
Jars of shackles, nails and screws

1 thermometer (sea)

AFT LOCKER UNDER CHART TABLE

Silicone grease

AFTERPEAK

1 pr steps (gangway)
1 broom
1 plastic water can, 3-gallon
1 plastic water can, 2-gallon
1 paraffin can, 2-gallon
1 bow fender

1 large warp
2 small warps
Perkins spare parts and tool kit
  (Perkins tool kit in middle
  portside drop locker)
1 spare generator for Perkins

1 rubber dinghy air pump
3 assorted buckets
Avon redcrest including cover

Marconi spare parts
spare kettle

DINGHY WELL

2 petrol cans (2-gallon)
1 water tank, 1-gallon plastic
1 can Shell Rotella engine oil
1 trysail tackle

1 Avon Redshanks with sailing
   kit including mast, dagger
   board and sail
7 sheets

The Outward list of stores was compiled on board by the secretarial staff of Francis Chichester Ltd. The object was to enable me to find stores, replacements, etc., stowed away in the many lockers on the boat without having to turn out every locker hunting for these things. Important equipment in use is not listed, such as navigation instruments, fog-horn, loud hailer, Very pistol, torches, depth sounding lead, weights for the collision mat, frogman suit, etc. As these were always to hand, it was not necessary to list them.

For the Homeward stores (on following pages) Sheila was able to supervise the lists and stowage, assisted by Pat McCarthy and Norma Humphries.

F. C.

Stores Homeward 1967

Cheese
> Dutch Edam 6 × 2 lb   Tupper 19, cabin starboard pilot
> Cheddar 2 × 3 lb   Tupper 24, cabin starboard pilot
> Parmesan   Tuppers 14 and 8, cabin port pilot
> Gruyère   Cabin starboard settee locker aft

Chocolate
> Wholenut 2½ lb   Tupper 13, cabin port pilot
> Raw sugar 6 × 8 oz   Tupper 3, cabin port pilot
> Box Redtulip   Cabin starboard pilot

Chocolate Drink
> 12 × 16 oz packets   Tuppers 14 and 11, cabin port pilot

Chutney 4   Port main cabin forward settee locker

Coffee
> 6 × 6 oz jars   Cabin port forward settee locker
> 2 Continental   Tupper 22

Curry
> Vegetable 11   Tupper 7, cabin port pilot
> Prawn 10   Tupper 8, cabin port pilot

Eggs
> Fresh 16 dozen   Port cabin middle settee locker
> Dried 5 pkts × 12 oz   Starboard cabin middle settee locker

Fish (tinned)
> Salmon, 24 × 4 oz
> Tuna, 24 × 4 oz
> Sardines, 26 × 1¾ oz
> Shrimps, 10 × 4 oz   }   Starboard main cabin middle drop locker
> Herrings, 10 × 7 oz
> Roes, 10 × 3½ oz

Flannel   Tupper "B"—near garden

Flour   Tupper 20, cupboard opposite chair
> 12 × 2 lb 100% wholemeal   Tupper 9, cabin port pilot
> 1 × 3 lb compost-grown wholemeal   Round Tupper 20
> 14 lb   Tupper 21
> 10 lb   Tupper 22

Fruit
  Fresh
    Apples 9 lb (30) — Cabin starboard forward settee locker
    Grapefruit 50 — Cabin settee lockers port and
        starboard forward
    Lemons 50 — Cabin settee lockers starboard forward
    Oranges 36 — Cabin settee lockers starboard and
        port forward

  Jiffy Lemons 6 — Tupper 17, cabin starboard pilot

  Tinned
    Grapefruit 6 × 10 oz
        4 large
    Pears 12 × 8 oz   Starboard main cabin middle drop
    Pineapple 7 × 11 oz   locker
        5 small

  Dried
    Raisins 12 — Tuppers 1, 2, and 3, cabin port pilot
        Tupper "C" (little Tupper)
    Muscatels 16 × ½ lb — Tupper 23, cabin starboard pilot
    Prunes, 16 pkts (4 × 16 oz)
        and (12 × 8 oz) — Tupper 1, cabin port pilot
    Bananas 9 — Tupper 2, cabin port pilot
    Currants 1 pkt — Tupper 1, cabin port pilot
    Sultanas 1 pkt — Tupper 1, cabin port pilot

First Aid — Heads shelf (2 Tuppers)

Garlic 12 bulbs — Cabin starboard middle settee locker
        (little Tupper "G")
    Also in veg. locker and galley
        cupboard

Glucose Tablets — Tuppers 5 and 16; cabin port pilot

Honey
    Clear 12 × 16 oz and
        comb 3 × 32 oz — Forward port settee locker

Herbs
    1 mixed

Jam
    Black Cherry 1 — Forward port settee locker

Jelly
    Redcurrant 3 — Forward port settee locker
    Blackcurrant 2 — Forward port settee locker

Liquor and soft drinks

6 bottles lime	Forward port settee locker
24 bitter lemon	Starboard forward settee locker
6 gin	Port sideboard bilge locker
4 brandy	Port sideboard bilge locker
2 Grand Marnier	Starboard sideboard bilge locker
1 Benedictine	Starboard sideboard bilge locker
1 Drambuie	Port sideboard bilge locker
1 doz ½ French Champagne	6 bottles—Port sideboard bilge locker
1 doz ½ Austn Champagne	Starboard forward settee locker

Matches, 6 large	Tupper "Matches," Cabin pilot starboard
Marmalade, 10 lb	Forward port settee locker
Milk, dried, 7 tins	5 in port forward settee locker 1 in Tupper 15, Cabin port pilot
Mustard and Cress	Tupper "B," near garden

Nuts

Almonds, 1 pkt	Tupper 2, Cabin port pilot
Hazel nuts, 1 pkt	Tupper "C" (little Tupper)
Brazil, 1½ lb in shell	Tupper 2, cabin port pilot
Brazil, 1 lb pkt	Tupper "C" (little Tupper)
Milled, large pkt (7 lb)	Tupper 18 (round), cabin port pilot

Oil

Olive, 1	Galley
Corn oil, 2 × 20 oz tins	Port forward settee locker

Pastas

15 assorted, 16 oz packets	Tupper 10, cabin port pilot

Pepper

2 black, 2 white	Tupper 14, cabin port pilot

Puddings

Honey nut rolls, 4 × 16 oz; Date rolls, 2 × 16 oz Raisin rolls, 2 × 16 oz Chocolate sponge, 2 × 16 oz Marmalade sponge, 2 ×16 oz	} Port middle drop locker

Rice, 1 pkt	Tupper 16, cabin starboard pilot
Salad Cream, 4	Port settee locker
Salt, 1 Cerebos	Galley

Sauces
    Mushroom, 5 pkts
    Onion, 6 pkts   } Tupper 7, cabin port pilot
    Tomato, 6 pkts

Sausalatas   Box starboard cabin settee locker aft

Soda, Bicarb, 2   First aid Tupper and galley

Soup
    Minestrone, 12
    Green pea, 8   } Port middle drop locker
    Tomato

Spaghetti, 5 long Italian   Cabin starboard pilot

Sugar
    Barbados 15 lb   } Tuppers 3, 4 and 15
    Lump 4 lb

Syrup, Golden, 2 × 2 lb   Forward port settee locker

Tea
    China, 2 pkts (36 bags)   } Tupper 14, cabin port pilot
    China, 1 lb, tin

Tomato
    Ketchup, 10 bottles   Port forward settee locker
    Tins, 6   Port middle drop locker

Vegetables
  Fresh
    Onions, 30 lb   } Cabin port middle settee locker and
    Potatoes, 100 lb   Starboard middle settee locker

  Dried
    Onions, 6 pkts
    Lentils, 2 pkts   Tupper 17
    Peas, 18 pkts   Tupper 6, cabin port pilot
    Potatoes, 15 Pkts   Tuppers 6, 7 and 8

  Tinned
    12 small peas   Port middle drop locker

Wheat, 4 lb   Tupper 11, cabin port pilot
    Wheat kernels, 1½ lb   Tupper 14, cabin port pilot

Yeast, 26 pkts   Tupper "A" (small round Tupper)
                                    Cupboard opposite swinging chair

FIRST AID

Heads (Top) Tuppers 33, 34

4 Elastoplast strips
1 Elastoplast tin assorted
  bandages
2 crêpe bandages
1 triangular bandage
1 absorbent lint
1 absorbent gauze
1 cotton wool
1 pkt safety pins
1 Nomad tulle
1 lge surgical spirit
1 lge witch hazel
1 Dettol
1 Optrex
1 bicarbonate (for galley)
asstd scissors and tweezers
1 thermometer
1 Arnica ointment
1 Nivea
1 codeine
1 iodine, 1 butesin picrate
  (for burns)
6 pkts Elastoplast wound dressing
1 tin Elastoplast first aid dressings
1 pkt Elastoplast dressing—strip
  elastic
1 pkt boric lint
1 triangular bandage

3 pkts absorbent lint
1 pkt absorbent gauze
2 tins elastic adhesive bandage
2 tins plaster of Paris bandage
1 roll zinc oxide plaster
2 pkts safety pins
1 tube Savlon
2 tubes Asterol ointment
1 tube Hydroderm
1 bottle Friar's Balsam
1 bottle tincture of Arnica
1 bottle Optrex
1 cicatrin amino acid antibiotic
  powder
1 Dyspne inhal
1 pkt Entero-Vioform
1 bottle Dayamin vitamin tablets
3 pkts Wilkinson Sword Edge
  razor blades
1 Butesan picrat
1 Dettol
1 bicarbonate
A Traveller's Guide to Health
*St John's Ambulance Manual
  of First Aid*
Dr. Gordon Latto's letter
Alupent, asthma remedy is in
  heads cupboard

HOUSEHOLD

5 rubbers
7 dish cloths
2 gran cloths
3 face towels
7 towels
Nylon pillows

2 rugs
2 green wool blankets
2 sheets
dusters
3 sleeping bags (2 in forpeak)

TOILETRIES

5 Lux
2 Harpic
7 Delsey
6 Kleenex rolls
2 Bronco

8 Kleenex (small)
2 Kleenex (men's)
6 soap (small)
1 soap (large)
1 soap (Fairy)

LIST OF MEDICAL STORES

Paracetamol
Pethidine
soap
6 corn plasters
herbal tea
tetracycline
2 shaving sticks, Corvette
1 Savlon
Bepanthen
1 tin Elastoplast
2 Precortisyl

morphia
toothpaste
Brovon
Epsom salts
talc powder
bulb for spray
codeine
absorbent lint
2 Sleek
gloves
dental floss

Homeward 1967 (Last Minute)

General Stowage Plan

Forepeak
Spare wind vane
Pick-up boat hook staff
3 wool bales
Charging motor
Bag fishing gear

Harpoon and spear
SS topsail
Rainwater pipe
Spare SS oar
2 sleeping bags

Fore Cabin—Port
1 mattress

Sail Bin

Bolt cutters

3 small buckets
3 large buckets

Starboard

Upper Locker

Spare kettle

Box of oddments

Halfshelf

Bunk

Dinghy oars
Collision mat
NVC standard and lamps
Large plastic sheets and bags
Sail repair kit, cloth, shackles
　　and hanks
Bag of underclothes and shirts
Bag of flags
Pillows
Bedding

Spare Primus
Dinghy repair kit
2, forward hatch strongbacks

Winter clothes:
　　Bag No. 1
　　Bag No. 2
　　2 green blankets
Radar reflectors

SHELF OVER BUNK

LOCKERS

Forward	*Middle*
Sail repair kit No. 1	2 handy billys
SS spares	2 hurricane lamps
6 fan belts	
2 spare aerial leads	*Aft*
2 Perkins engine hoses	2 wooden cleats
Long green wire lead	Box Marconi spares
Needles and thread	Walker log
Walker log line and fin	Manuals and documents
Bag of corks	
Assorted pipes	
2 short pendants	
Shock cord	
Spare Walker log	
Rotator	
Bag of oddments	
Spare Primus can	

HEADS—PORT

MIRROR LOCKERS

After	*Forward*
1	1
Sailcloth gloves	Gloves
Tissues	
Delseys	
2	2
Lux	Dentistry
Soap	
SMC's tools	
3	3 F.C. personal

TABLE DRAWERS

1
SMC personal

2
Box chocolates
Anniversary bottle

3
Ship's Papers

CUPBOARD UNDER BASIN

Engine spares	Spare winch handles

STARBOARD

HANGING CUPBOARD

Clothes

ALCOVE UNDER CUPBOARD

2 bombs (stormoil)

UPPER SHELF

First aid
Tuppers 33, 34

LOCKERS

1
P and O pictures
Sheets
Towels

Face flannels
Dusters
Rubbers
1 yellow pillow case

2
Summer clothes

3
Summer clothes

MAIN CABIN—PORT

BUNK

Tuppers 1–15, 18

SHELF OVER BUNK

Biscuits (closed)

Hengist spare (open)

SIDEBOARD DRAWERS

1
Manuals and ship's papers

2
Electrical
Loud hailer batteries, clock
   batteries, spare spreader light

2 bags fuses
Spare dynalite reflector bulbs
Aladdin wicks
Hydrometer
Candles
3 boxes bulbs

BILGE LOCKER

4 gin, 4 Brandy, 1 Drambuie,
6 half French champagne

DROP LOCKER

Forward
Tools

Middle
Soups, baked beans, tomatoes,
   puddings, 12 cans peas

SETTEE LOCKERS

Forward
    Grapefruit
    Oranges
    Lemons
    12 × 1 lb pots honey
    6 bottles lime
    10 tomato ketchup
    3 mayonnaise
    3 × 2 lb honey with comb
    9 lb marmalade

    2 redcurrant jelly
    2 blackcurrant jelly
    1 black cherry jam
    2 golden syrup
    5 Marvel milk
    2 cans cooking oil
    4 chutney
    6 coffee

Middle
    Potatoes
    Onions
    Tin dried eggs

Aft
    5 Agfa films
    2 pkts Kodak Ektachrome
    1 pkt plus—X Panfilm
    1 transistor
    Light meter
    1 bulb lead
    1 hand bearing compass
    Hats

    Nikonos camera
    Adapter for recorder
    Binoculars, old
    Camera clamp
    Plastic camera lead and bulb
    Binoculars, new
    1 tape recorder

STARBOARD

BUNK

    Tuppers 16, 17, 19, "D," "E,"
      "F," 21, 22, 23, 24
    Thick paper bags

    4 glad wrap (presented by
      H.E. Lord Casey)
    Box of odd NAV papers
    1 painting of FCC

SHELF OVER BUNK

    Biscuits

SIDEBOARD

Wine Locker
    2 brandy
    1 Benedictine

    2 wine
    1 Grand Marnier

DROP LOCKERS

Forward
    Meths, 2½ galls
    Distilled water
    Bag blocks

Middle

24 × 4 tinned salmon	10 × 4 shrimps
24 × 4 tinned tuna	10 × 7 herrings
26 × 1¾ sardines	10 × 3½ roes

Aft

Compass (off-course alarm)

SETTEE LOCKERS

Forward

Champagne	Lemons
Tinned butter	Colin's claret
Tin Bulgarian Gouvetch	
Bitter lemons	*Middle*
3 Osborne honey	Potatoes
Grapefruit	Onions
Apples	Dried eggs

Aft

Sausalatas, 3 doz	15 doz. eggs
7 large bread	6 × ½ lb pkts butter
2 Vogest bread	Gruyère cheese

GALLEY SECTION—PORT

CHART TABLE DRAWERS

Aft	*Middle*	*Forward*
1 Navigation instruments	1 Navigation instruments	1 Watches, etc.
2 Tools	2 Oddments	2 Navigational oddments

CHART TABLE LOCKERS

Aft	*Forward*
Spare counterpoise weight for SS	

CUPBOARD ABOVE GALLEY

Butter
Eggs
Bread

DRAWERS UNDER GALLEY	LOCKERS UNDER GALLEY
1 Cutlery	1 Saucepans, frying pans
2 Cutlery	2 Gash bucket
3 Tin openers, etc.	3 Spare receptacles and cleaning material

PIGEON HOLE

Very pistol and cartridges

Sundry bosun's stores

STARBOARD

GARDEN SECTION

Upper shelf
Mustard and cress

Lower shelf
Assorted books

CUPBOARD OPPOSITE CHAIR

Cake (Lorna's)

3 Ryvitas
Neon lights (spare tubes)

Tupper ("B"), mustard and
cress, flannel

Tupper 20—candlestick,
compost flour, shovel, yeast

CUPBOARD OVER PRIMUS
Spare Tuppers and spare cups

LOCKER UNDER PRIMUS

Tap for beer

Squire's gin, 1 bottle

AFTER HEADS—PORT
Oilskins

AFTER PEAK
2 drinking water ⎫
2 empty   ⎪
1 Rotella   ⎬ 2-gallon bombs
2 Diesoline   ⎭

DINGHY WELL
Solar still dinghy mainsail bag

Appendix III

SAIL PLAN

Key

1. Big genoa 600 sq ft staysail
2. Light working jib 300 sq ft
3. Working jib 187 sq ft
4. Storm jib 107 sq ft
5. Genoa staysail 188 sq ft
6. Storm staysail 95 sq ft
7. Main sail 289 sq ft
8. Trysail 144 sq ft
9. Mizzen staysail 350 sq ft
10. Mizzen 143 sq ft

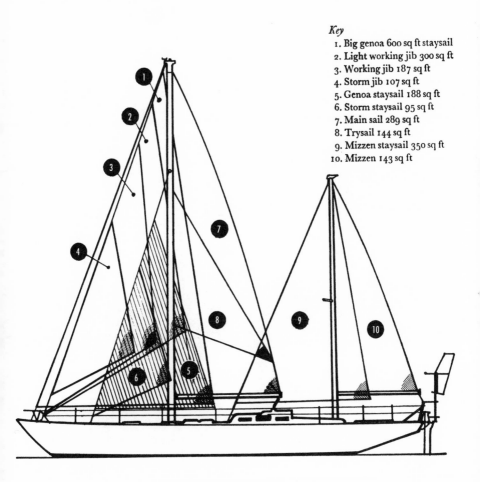

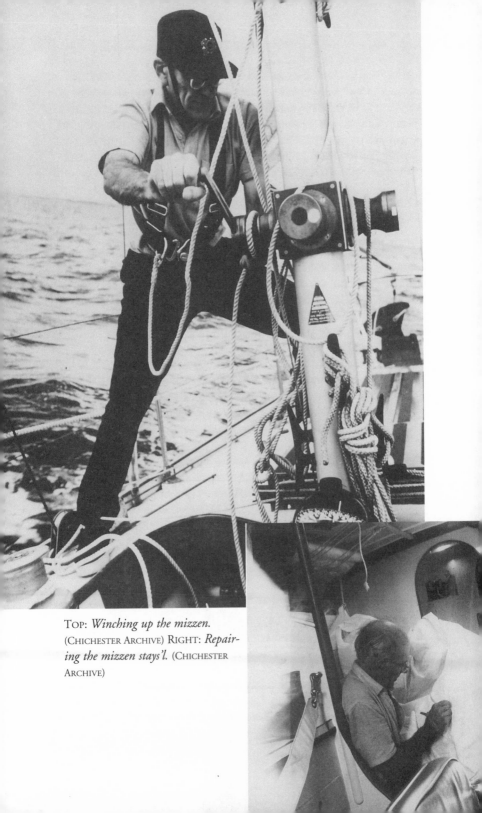

TOP: *Winching up the mizzen.*
(CHICHESTER ARCHIVE) RIGHT: *Repair-
ing the mizzen stays'l.* (CHICHESTER
ARCHIVE)

Top: *Francis Chichester and* Gipsy Moth IV *returning to Plymouth at the end of their solo around the world.*
(Chichester Archive)
Left: *H.M. the Queen after the knighthood ceremony at Greenwich.*
(*Press Association Photos*/
Chichester Archive)

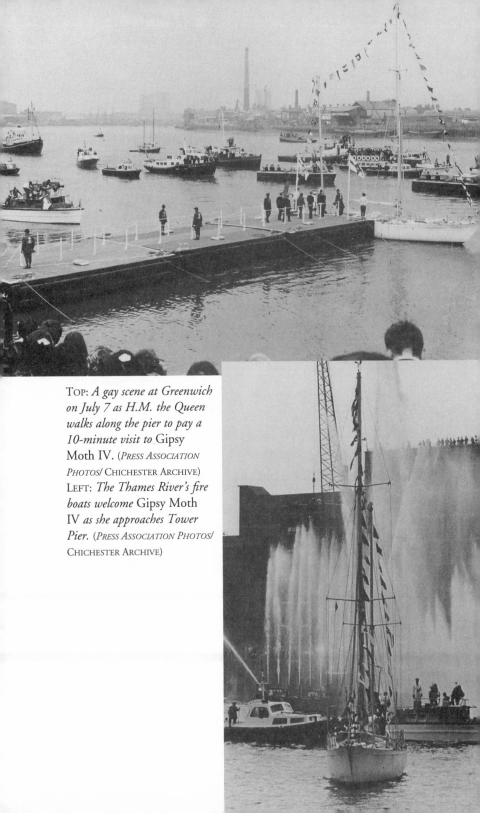

TOP: *A gay scene at Greenwich on July 7 as H.M. the Queen walks along the pier to pay a 10-minute visit to* Gipsy Moth IV. (PRESS ASSOCIATION PHOTOS/ CHICHESTER ARCHIVE)

LEFT: *The Thames River's fire boats welcome* Gipsy Moth IV *as she approaches Tower Pier.* (PRESS ASSOCIATION PHOTOS/ CHICHESTER ARCHIVE)

A wonderful welcome from the City before the luncheon at the Mansion House. (Press Association Photos/Chichester Archive)

Sir Francis Chichester (Eileen Ramsey/Chichester Archive)